Walking the Wheel of the Year

Emma-Jane Cross

GREEN MAGIC

Walking The Wheel of The Year.
© 2020 by Emma-Jane Cross.

All rights reserved. No part of this book may be used or
reproduced in any form without written permission of the author,
except in the case of quotations in articles and reviews.

Green Magic
53 Brooks Road
Street
Somerset
BA16 0PP
England

www.greenmagicpublishing.com

Designed & typeset by K.DESIGN
Winscombe, Somerset

ISBN 9781916014039

GREEN MAGIC

To the North, the East, the South and the West, the old ones and the new ones, Aho

* * *

To my Avebury Tribe, Teachers and Ladies who inspired me in the first place.

* * *

To Jacob and Nusse for wading through endless pages.

* * *

And to my Troels for believing in me, not letting me give up and for being my light, always.

* * *

Without them this book would not be in your hands.

* * *

I am and will forever be, eternally grateful…

Contents

Introduction	9
Chapter 1 – What is the Wheel of the Year	11
Chapter 2 – How to use this book	17
Chapter 3 – Creating Ceremony	20
Chapter 4 – Visualisation and Journeying	24
Chapter 5 – Samhain	27
Chapter 6 – Yule and the Winter Solstice	42
Chapter 7 – Imbolc	61
Chapter 8 – Ostara and the Spring equinox	77
Chapter 9 – Beltane	99
Chapter 10 – Litha and the Summer solstice	120
Chapter 11 – Lammas	141
Chapter 12 – Mabon and the Autumn Equinox	161
Chapter 13 – Samhain the Ending and the Beginning	180
Chapter 14 – Walking Your Wheel of the Year	188
Recommended Reading	190
Bibliography	192

Walking the Wheel of the Year

*Re-root in nature, reconnect your soul and
Re-route your life, as the Wheel turns…*

'The rain falls gracefully through the leaves. Each life-giving drop bringing nourishment to the earth. Soft rain. Nature's lullaby. Listening to it drip through the leaves, it brings me a moment of calm in this hectic, noisy city. In the centre of a park the giant oak tree stands gloriously before me. Respectfully I ask for permission to connect with its energy. The ancient soul agrees and gently I reach out to its majestic energy. Acknowledging at this time and place that we are both part of the natural cycle of life. A part of the universe. Dog walkers stare as they pass by, I disregard them. This is my time, my bubble of peace. Within the hustle and bustle of everyday life, this five minutes of peace and rejuvenation connecting to life force recharges my soul, reminding me that I am a unique part of life in this amazing universe. Refreshed, I walk away with strength and purpose…'

(A MOMENT FROM MY LIFE)

Introduction

Nature is a constant in our lives. Its cycles move around us, ever growing and changing within its own rhythm. In bygone times, our lives were deeply connected to and dependant on this cycle. We moved with the rhythms and respected the patterns of natural life. In modern society we are more disconnected from nature than we have ever been. We run life to our own rhythm. Often trying to dominate our desires upon Mother Earth, rather than working with the natural flow of life. It is no wonder with these conflicting rhythms that stress and depression are on the rise. Our discordant lifestyle takes us further and further away from nature that sustains us. Further from the source of life, starving our souls.

From the earth, and sky, we can learn more than we ever could in a classroom. When we take the time to stop and connect with the natural world, we find peace, understand our place in life and the universe and over time begin, to follow the natural rhythm our bodies are created to be part of. To connect with nature you do not need to have a specific religion or culture, you simply need the desire to reconnect with the world around you, and the openness to learn from that world. The goal is not to disconnect from your daily life but to integrate nature's rhythm into your everyday, to help you find balance and natural growth.

Our Celtic and Nordic ancestors understood the cycle of nature. For the ancient Celts and Scandinavians, seasonal changes were important both in agriculture and for survival. Today we follow a concept of linear time. However, when we lived closely with nature and depended on her for survival, time was considered a cyclical journey. The Wheel of the Year is a calendar focused on this cyclical journey of the seasons.

For the communities who depended on it, the festivals celebrated during the Wheel of the Year were used both religiously and practically. Dictating when to plough, sow and harvest.[1] The turning of the Wheel represents the continuing birth, death and rebirth of nature.

This rhythm is still relevant to us today. Because despite our technological advances we are, ultimately, still part of the natural world. On a biological level, we know this. Our DNA remembers it. And when we reconnect with nature, we not only find a form of peace but our health benefits and our stress drops. Research shows that children are healthier, happier and perhaps even smarter and

---

1   Edain McCoy The Sabbats a New Approach to Living the Old Ways pg 3

more creative when they have a connection to nature. Studies at the University of Michigan proved that people who spent one hour in nature experienced a 20 percent boost in memory and attention span[2]. Doctors in the Shetlands can now prescribe time in nature seeking to reduce blood pressure, anxiety, and increase happiness for those with diabetes, mental illness, stress, heart disease and more[3]. It's official. Connecting with nature is good for us.

However, this book is not just about rekindling a connection with nature. It is also about personal development moving in correspondence with the Wheel of the Year. The Wheel of the Year as we know it today combines both Celtic, Nordic and neolithic cultures. The original Celtic Wheel celebrated four fire festivals, evenly spaced throughout the year[4], celebrating the transition of the Sun throughout the seasons. Today, these are combined with Nordic and neolithic celebrations of the Solstices and Equinoxes.

For 22 years I have worked with the Wheel of the Year as both a tool to connect with nature but also as the foundation for my own personal growth. Instead of moving against the natural tides of life, I have embraced them. Reflecting the turning of the seasons outside in my internal personal development. By observing nature and combining these observances to highlight and empower my journey, I have found a foundation of peace that allows me to evolve, weather the storms and, ultimately, bloom into my fullest potential, understanding the rhythm of my own life.

And I want to share this journey with you. I came to working with the Wheel of the Year through Paganism and spent four years of my life at Avebury Stone Circle working with witches, Druids, shamans, Asatru, Pagans, as well as archaeologists, farmers and more. However, I don't believe that the cycle of nature has to have anything to do with religious dogma. Therefore, in this book, religious dogma finds no place. For me, there is no right way or wrong way to connect with nature and drive your own personal growth. In nature, there is nothing right or wrong, nature just is. Your life is your journey and it is up to you to find what works for you.

---

2   The Cognitive Benefits of Interacting with Nature, Marc G. Berman, John Jonides, Stephen Kaplan pp 1207–1212
3   'Doctors can now prescribe 'nature' as a therapy' Shetland News
4   Wheel of the Year Áine Stone.The Celtic Journey

CHAPTER 1

What is the Wheel of the Year?

The Wheel of the Year is quite simply a calendar of eight festivals that mark seasonal turning points. Initially it can seem like a lot of dates to take in and remember. But the dates are just markers. It is the energetic changes in nature that happens around these dates which is the important thing, not the dates themselves. Just like the infamous pirate code, the dates are guidelines, a living framework which ebbs and flows with the seasons. As you work with the Wheel and fall into nature's rhythm, you will begin to notice and feel these seasonal shifts and interpret them in the right way for where you are inside and where you are physically in the world.

SAMHAIN (October 31) (Fire Festival)

Samhain represents the final harvest before the long winter. In ancient times, this was the time of slaughtering the animals for the winter. It is a celebration of death. Not in a macabre way, but honouring. An acceptance that all life must die so that life can be created once more. It's a time to honour our ancestors and embrace the darker half of the year. This also marks the beginning of the Celtic New Year where the seasons die to be reborn again.

Walking the Wheel of the Year Themes:
Here we celebrate where we have come from, the gifts of our ancestors in our blood, skin and bone. We celebrate the final harvest of the year and look at the things we must cast away that have not served us. In this work, we recognise our own death and rebirth as part of our pattern of evolving and growing. At Samhain, we prepare ourselves for the darker half of the year.

YULE / MIDWINTER SOLSTICE (December 20–23)

Yule marks the winter solstice, the longest night and the shortest day of the year. It was a time of celebration of surviving the cold dark times, storytelling through the darkest night. In the Nordic culture this was a time of making boasts and oaths. From now on, the days become longer and we celebrate the rebirth of the Sun back to the Earth.

Walking the Wheel of the Year Themes:
Here we celebrate where we are now. The gifts we gain from those closest to us and the gifts we give to them. We investigate stories and teachings we have collected along our journey in life. Learning the wisdom anew. Yule has a theme of the sacred child and here we take time to connect with our own inner child's joy and see the world through the eyes of a child once more.

IMBOLC (February 2) (Fire Festival)

Imbolc is a festival of fire and light, and in many traditions celebrates the Celtic hearth goddess, Brigid. It marks the time where the shoots are just starting to appear through the ground, the buds are just beginning to open. This is a festival of purification, a festival of light, inspiration, the fertility of the land and new beginnings. Imbolc is also called Candlemas and was the time where the old candles used in winter were melted down and new candles were made.

Walking the Wheel of the Year Themes:
At Imbolc, we connect with the fresh burst of life in a whirl of inspiration. We create a vision of the life we want to manifest for ourselves. We share the shoots of our hopes and dreams, supporting each other's growth.

OSTARA / SPRING EQUINOX (March 20–23)

Ostara is the celebration of the Spring equinox. A point of balance between the Sun and the M<oon. Day and night are equal. The world around us is full of new life. The animals are birthing their young and awakening from their winter sleep. Light is overtaking darkness. It is here that we move from the dark half of the year into the light.

Walking the Wheel of the Year Themes:
At Ostara, we celebrate the new beginnings in our own life. We look at how to birth our dreams and plant the seeds of manifestation. Equinoxes are a time of cleansing and balance, so we work with these themes. We also investigate our shadow self, honouring and accepting our dark before stepping into our lighter self.

BELTANE (May 1) (Fire Festival)

Beltane is a spring celebration that honours the fertility of the earth and man. A time of lust, love, passion, fire and abundance. In Britain, M<ay Queens are crown and the maypole danced. This is a time of fun, flirtation, laughter and

dance. At the Beltane fires, the cattle were cleansed by walking through the fire. Beltane is when we connect to the throbbing heartbeat of the earth.

Walking the Wheel of the Year Themes:
At Beltane, the central theme is self-love. Here we work on the most important of all relationships. Our relationship with ourselves. We learn how we can better love and honour ourselves. We celebrate our most beautiful self and are empowered to step into a place of self-love.

LITHA / MIDSUMMER SOLSTICE (June 20–23)

Litha is the time of the summer solstice, the longest day of the year and the shortest night. It's a celebration of light's triumph over darkness and of the bountiful beauty that light brings into our lives. It is the height of the Sun's power, from here on the days become shorter.

Walking the Wheel of the Year Themes:
As we connect with the power of the solstice sun, we celebrate and discover our own self power. We step into our most powerful self and learn how to connect with that self when we need to.

LAMMAS (August 1) (Fire Festival)

Lammas is the first harvest festival. When plants drop their seeds to ensure future crops. In the Celtic culture this is a celebration in honour of the Celtic god, Lugh. His sacrifice and transformation. For them, and many other cultures, Lammas is the time of celebrating the abundance of the first harvest.

Walking the Wheel of the Year Themes:
At Lammas we return to our seeds planted at Ostara. We celebrate the fruits of our labour. Let go of the seeds we can release to plant in the next Wheel. We work at Lammas with gratitude. Bringing in the harvest was a community task and at Lammas we look to how we can find support to manifest our goals.

MABON / AUTUMN EQUINOX (September 20–23)

Mabon is a time of thanksgiving that celebrates the second harvest, the berry harvest and the autumn equinox. Once again this is a time of balance. Days and night are again equal. It is a time of preparation for the winter where we gather the sweet things we need, to sustain us in the dark.

Walking the Wheel of the Year Themes:
At Mabon, we celebrate the sweetness and abundance we have manifested throughout the Wheel. Again, giving thanks for our harvest and rewarding

our work. As well, we refocus our goals and intentions to complete the most important work before the winter comes. Again, we work with the cleansing and balance equinox energy. We also investigate and honour our light self before stepping into our dark.

And the Wheel turns once more to Samhain, the cycle of life, ending and beginning, ever flowing around us and within us....

WHERE TO START?

It takes five simple steps to begin your journey to a life in natural flow with the Wheel of the Year:

Create a Sacred Space

Dedicate a place within your home to honour your journey with the Wheel. A table, a tree stump in the garden, a window sill or a shelf. Wherever you can find a place that you will see every day.

This is your place to honour yourself and the world around you. Your place to focus on your goals and your constant development. Here you can place things of importance to you, objects that represent you, your life, your dreams. This space is ever changing. You can decorate it to correspond to the seasons at the time. Make it as beautiful and as cosy as you desire your life to be.

Every day, take 5 minutes to sit here to think about your goals, to be grateful for your life and to ask (if needed) for strength or energy to refresh your life and follow your goals.

Find Space in Nature

Find a special space in nature. I recommend it is a place where you will not be disturbed of feel as though you may be interrupted. It can be difficult when you live in the city to find such a place. However, in most parks you can find places of stillness and contemplation. Your space might change depending on your lifestyle. A person who travels much may have sacred spaces all over the world. Or it could simply be within your own garden. It needs to be a place you can visit frequently. Wherever you find, spend time here as often as possible. Not only is this a place to connect with nature, this is also a place where you can recharge and meditate.

Get a Notebook

Throughout the year it is a good idea to note your observations, lessons and development. This book should be kept just for this task. It can have pressed flowers, feathers, drawings, or it can be a book you can write in as you travel to work on the train.

WHAT IS THE WHEEL OF THE YEAR?

THE TREE OF LIFE – THE GATEWAY TO CONNECTION

The Tree of Life is a powerful meditation to ground, balance and connect with yourself and nature. The meditation brings peace and heightens the senses. Rerooting us in our blood, skin and bone bringing us into contact with the earth. It takes five minutes and can be done anywhere, although of course works best outside. For me, this meditation is the gateway to connection with nature. You can use the Tree of Life as a daily meditation, or use it when you feel the need to reground or rebalance.

Stand with closed eyes, begin to breathe slowly and deeply.

From your feet, imagine a root growing deep within the earth. Feel the wet moist soil, smell the musky earth. Feel your roots grow and spread until you are fully anchored in the earth.

As your roots reach closer to the centre of the Earth you can see a bright ball of energy at the heart of the planet. Vibrant life energy. As your roots connect to this energy, begin to draw life energy up the roots, this can be whatever colour light you choose. Feel the energy nourishing your roots. See them glowing vibrantly.

Draw this energy up towards your feet. Until you can feel the roots from your feet connected to the earth and the vibrant energy pulsating beneath your feet.

With your next breath begin to draw the energy upwards. Feel the earth energy filling your body through your legs. And as the energy connects with your feet, your leg so you see them beginning to transform into the trunk of a tree.

Feel the energy rise to your hips, your stomach. Allow yourself to strengthen your trunk become stronger, wider. Deeply rooted in the earth and connected to the centre.

Allow the earth energy to rise to your heart. Allow it to spiral slowly, Refreshing you. Take a moment here to feel your strength your connection.

With your next breath, send the energy from your heart through your arms and head. From here, feel your branches begin to form, reaching for the sunlight above. Feel the sap rising up into your branches, revitalising and refreshing. Allow your branches to spread as wide as your roots. Connecting with the sky energy and drawing it in to your heart.

At your heart centre, the earth and the sky energy spiral together. You are balanced between earth and sky. Rooted in the earth. Reaching for the sky.

Slowly, leaves begin to grow from the branches. Unfurling, warming in the light.

Feel the warmth of the Sun as you stand there, a strong tree in the woods. Stand for a while, fully feeling the balance of your branches and your roots.

As you stand there, rooted in the earth, rain begins to fall. Running down your branches, bringing new life to your form.

The rain seeps into the earth, feeding your roots, giving a second surge of energy up into your roots, into your trunk and to your branches.

Now feel the wind gently whistling in your branches. The cold hits the air. Your leaves begin to change colour, bronze, gold, brown and red. With a breath, let them fall to the earth allow them to rot.

Stand in your winter tree form. Feel the sap retreating from your branches. Release your connection with the sky and draw your arms back in towards your heart. When you reach your heart, you stand once more as a human in your upper body, and a trunk below. You can still feel within yourself the balance of the earth and sky energy within your heart.

With your next breath, send the energy down your body to your stomach, your hips, your legs, your ankles. Until you are standing once more in your human form, yet still deeply connected to the earth by your roots.

As you stand here you can still feel the balance you had as a tree between earth and sky. Take a moment to feel that connection.

With your next breath releasing your connection with the earth's centre. Leaving with gratitude. Withdraw your roots back up to your feet. Until you are once again standing on the earth, no longer rooted, yet still feeling that deep connection. Still feeling the balance that you felt between the earth and sky, remembering the connection you felt as a tree.

Once you are entirely in your body, slowly begin to open your eyes and begin to breathe normally. If you are outside, look at nature around you. If indoors, then look out of the window.

If possible, it is great to take a walk after this meditation and to look for the signs of nature around you, appreciating it's beauty and meditating on your part within nature.

CHAPTER 2

How to use this Book

In this book, you will find many ideas I have collected and practiced over the last 22 years on how you can celebrate the Wheel of the Year, use tools for personal growth aligned with the seasons, information on traditions and inspiration for connecting with nature and suggestions for seasonal activities. as well as guided visualisations and ceremonies. You may, like me, want to incorporate all the ideas into your own life, or you may prefer certain ideas and practices and not others. Take what works for you and leave the rest behind. You can always come back another time to get inspired.

You can choose to follow this book with the seasons or read it all at once. Inspiring you to observe the patterns of nature and use these to reflect, analyse and grow within your own life. You will look at the macrocosm of nature's rhythms to develop the microcosm of your own life cycle, using the eight festivals throughout the year as a time to reconnect, resonate, set and achieve goals. The tools you gain within this book will be available to you for life. The starting point in a journey that will change gradually as each Wheel turns and passes. From here on in, as the wheel of your own life turns, you will you be able to connect and develop with nature, evolving naturally along your journey in life.

Every chapter is divided into sections to make it easy for you to find inspiration and connect with each point in the Wheel in a way that feels right to you. Each chapter includes the following sections:

THE HISTORY OF THE FESTIVAL

This explains the historical background of each festival and how it was celebrated in different parts of the world.

GROWING WITH THE SEASON

A collection of personal development tools and processes you can use to align your personal growth with the turning of the Wheel.

TRADITIONS

A collection of different traditions from all over the world relating to the seasonal festivals.

CONNECTING TO THE SEASON

Here are some ideas and examples of things you could do to connect with the energy and traditions of the season. The activities are inspired both by my own life, by seasonal customs and by the personal growth processes described in this book, to help you create your own approach to 21st century seasonal spirituality.

CRAFTS

For millennia, people have celebrated the turning of the Wheel with great feasts and by making seasonal crafts. I believe that crafting each season, we focus our activity to what is happening in nature and this focuses our intent. As you walk the Wheel you adopt certain traditions at each festival. Things you like to do that remind you of where you are on the Wheel. So, here are some of my favourite crafts for you to try. Maybe you can begin to make your own seasonal traditions using the inspiration found here.

JOURNEY

For each season, there is a visualisation journey for you to try. Travelling via the world tree, each journey connects your unconscious to the personal development themes. Deeping both your connection to the season's energies and your personal development and growth (you can find out more about journeying in Chapter 4).

CEREMONY

I believe that one of the most beautiful and powerful ways you can connect to the season's energy is through ceremony. However, I also strongly believe there is no right or wrong way of performing ceremony. I have included some of the ceremonies I use myself for the festivals to inspire you to create your own (to find out more about creating ceremony, read Chapter 3).

This book is not just for an inspiring read. It is also intended as a tool-book for you to find your way or spiritual path to reconnecting with nature's rhythm. I would recommend reading it all the way through but when you find something you would like to try, make notes in the book (yes, you can write in here!) or bookmark activities you would like to do. Then as the Wheel turns, you can play around and find what works for you.

Although the traditional ending and starting point of the Wheel is Samhain, that does not mean you have to wait until Samhain to begin connecting with the Wheel. Jump right in! If you are reading this at summer solstice, you can work on claiming your self-power, or bake some bread at Lammas and give thanks for the harvest.

Don't worry about doing it wrong or right. Just have a go and find out what works for you!

CHAPTER 3

Creating Ceremony

In every chapter a ceremony celebrating the season is always included. As much as it is important to develop and grow with each season, I believe it is equally important to celebrate and mark the change of the season. Life should also be joyful, often we don't take the time out to enjoy it. Ceremony creates opportunity to mark the point of turning of the Wheel, to make it special and for me, ultimately take time to consciously be grateful for the gift of my life.

I believe the best and most powerful ceremonies come from the heart. Therefore, in my opinion, you should never do something in ceremony that you feel is not right for you. Ceremony doesn't need to be complicated unless you wish it to be. Above all, it should mean something and make sense only to you (and of course the other people in the circle, if you are celebrating together).

The ceremonies in this book are the ceremonies I used and are influenced by my own beliefs, formed over many years on my spiritual path. My own tradition or path is as a Pagan. I do not align to one specific path or tradition. Instead, I have created my own rituals and ceremony from a combination of the teachings I have received from Wiccans, Druids, shamans, Asatru, historians and also from guidance of my own totems, guides and ancestors.

Therefore, your ceremonies do not have to be like mine. When it comes to ceremony, there is no wrong and no right, just what works for you.

You can, of course, use the ceremonies included. However, I encourage you to have a go at making your own too. A ceremony always works best if you plan it before you do it!

Ceremony can take many different forms, depending on your own beliefs and traditions. Yet, if you look at ceremonies across the world, there are certain elements that traditionally create a ceremony, such as a sacred space, a purpose, gratitude.

Here is a list of the common elements that I believe go into making ceremony in any tradition. These are just suggestions to help you create your own:

1. Clarity of intention. Know why you are doing what you are doing.

2. Creation of sacred space. Choose a place where you will not be disturbed for at least 30 minutes (in nature most things are cyclical. So, I often work within a circle shaped space. However, I have worked within triangles too. Find the

shape that you like best). You can create a sacred space by:

   a. Laying out the shape of your sacred space on the floor with candles, flowers, crystals or leaves.
   b. Imagining yourself surrounded by a ball or bubble of energy.
   c. Creating an altar as the focus of your ritual.
   d. Create a shelter in the woods, if outside.
   e. Cleansing the area with incense, sage, salt water or even, as the Vikings, did using mead.

3. If you wish, you can invite spirits/deities into your space. These could be ancestors, gods, prophets, spirit animals or elements. You can call upon whatever has meaning to you.

4. A plan and purpose! Different ceremonies have different order of business. You may want to meditate, do a Tree of Life visualisation, journey, dance, sing, drum, do a crafting to focus on your intentions for this season or draw. You can do anything you wish within a sacred space. I would recommend not doing ceremony for ceremonies sake. For me, ceremony is not about public demonstration, it is about conscious connection. So, plan your ceremony and the purpose for doing it.

5. Give thanks. It is good to take a moment to appreciate and be grateful for our lives and nature.

6. Feast and offering. Sharing alcohol and cake or bread is a traditional way of celebrating and giving thanks. If you choose, you can leave some of your feast in an outdoor place as an offering, however this again is entirely up to you (please make sure that your offering is natural and suitable for the area. For example, did you know some flowers can poison sheep? Personally, I like to use bird seed).

7. Closing the sacred space. If you have created an energetic boundary such as a creating a circle in your mind and called in guests, you will need to thank your guests and close the circle space. I think of it as leaving nothing more than a footprint and good memories.

THE FIVE ELEMENTS

In the Walking the Wheel of the Year ceremonies, I work with the five elements. Each has a corresponding direction:

>   North – Earth
>   East – Air
>   South – Fire
>   West – Water
>   Centre – Spirit/ancestors/yourself/guides/gods

In some traditions, the circle begins in the east, some others in the north. I prefer to travel from the Earth as it is where all life begins and ends. However, if you decide to invite the elements into you sacred space, you must begin within the direction that feels right for you.

Within the circle, many people like to invite the elements into the space by following the direction of the Sun's movements to open the ceremony. To close the ceremony, working in reverse moving against the direction of the Sun. So, in calling the elements and inviting them to join me, I begin N, E, S, W and C. In thanking and closing the circle, I begin in the C and thank in reverse W, S, E, N.

There are many ways in which to connect with the elements. For me, within the balance of the five elements is the essence of life. The five ingredients we all need to live. Working with the elements, physically and spiritually connecting with them, brings you closer to your natural, instinctive self. One of my favourite elemental ceremonies was where each person had a physical representation of each of the elements and we got to physically connect with them, which did of course end up with many of us making mud pies!

THE ELEMENTS AND THE DIRECTIONS WITHIN FOLK LORE

Some say that the directions and correspondences come from early Irish poetry from the Lebor Gabála Érenn[5]. In the writings of Fiona Macleod (William Sharp, 1855–1905) there is a model of four cities in several poems[6]. These are said to be the original dwellings of the Tuatha De Danann, listed in early Irish poetry.

There are four ancient cities associated with the Realms of Faery in Celtic lore. Each of these cities relate to the four directions, the four seasons, and the four basic elements.

These are *Gorias* that is in the east; and *Finias* that is in the south, and *Murias* that is in the west; and *Falias* that is in the north. The symbol of Falias is the stone of death, which is crowned with pale fire. The symbol of Gorias is the dividing sword. The symbol of Fineas is a spear. The symbol of Murias is a hollow that is filled with water and light.

ALTAR OR HEARTH FIRE

Some people like to include an altar or hearth fire within their ceremony. I use all different sorts of altars, sometimes in the north or the centre, sometimes a real fire and sometimes no altar at all. There is no definition of what should be on your altar (this is my opinion however some people may disagree with me). There is a lot of inspiration online, in books and in your own heart for your altar. I would just recommend making it personal to you.

---

5   Alexi Kondratiev Celtic Rituals An authentic guide to ancient Celtic Spirituality Pg 79
6   Steve Blarmires The Little Book of the Great Enchantment. Pg 103

SIMPLE CEREMONY

Personally, I love simple ceremony and often find this the most powerful. By keeping your mind clear and your heart in a grateful and sacred space, simply lighting a candle, meditating, mindfully walking, singing, watching a sunrise, pouring a glass of wine on the earth with a word of gratitude, praying and dancing are all beautiful acts of ceremony and ways of connecting with yourself and the earth.

Ceremony is a beautiful way to practise gratitude, set intention, send healing, honour our ancestors and gods or simply to mark and celebrate the turning of the Wheel. However you decide to make ceremony, make it from your heart. And remember, the ceremony is as powerful as you intend it to be. If you don't feel ceremony is right for you, don't do it. Just as there is no wrong or right way of working with the Wheel, there is no right or wrong way of doing ceremony.

CHAPTER 4

Visualisation and Journeying

Visualisation and journeying are important tools on the journey of self-discovery and connecting to the seasons during the Wheel of every year. It gives us the opportunity to look deep within and take time out during each shift of the seasons, to focus on our internal journey and development.

The difference between journeying and visualisation is that in a journey you are in a deeper state of consciousness. A visualisation is normally guided all the way through, whereas in a journey you can encounter unexpected visions. Some people believe that in journeying you are travelling within other worlds and realms, alternative realities that are parallel to our own. Some people believe that it is simply a journey within the unconscious parts of our own psyche. Connecting with our unconscious is a powerful tool in self-awareness and, for me, knowing myself, consciously internally and externally, leads to living a powerful life.

Whatever you believe the journey to be, it is happening inside your head, but that does not mean that what you see and hear is not real, or at least relevant to you and your journey.

Tips for visualisation and journeying:

- Make sure you are comfortable, you will be sitting or lying down for a long time.

- If you need it, record the journey guide or visualisation to play when you are practising, to assist you in focusing on your activity.

- Choose a place that is quiet or put on some music that will help you focus and drown out background noise.

- It can be nice to journey outside. However, wrap up warmly and put a blanket between you and the ground, morning dew and wet grass makes the joints stiff.

- Make sure you are connected to the here and now. This could be in the form of a stone in your hand, a staff or something that connects you to your life.

- Within a journey, do not eat or drink anything offered to you it makes it harder to come back.

- Afterwards, do not try and come back to yourself too quickly or immediately begin rushing around. You have been working your brain in a different way, take time to allow it to adjust to another rhythm.
- If you find it difficult to return to a normal state, eat chocolate, it helps.
- Drink a lot of water afterwards.
- Write down the events of your journey.
- Do something normal afterwards.

Sacred Space

It often helps to think of yourself within a sacred space detached from your everyday life. Some visualise this as a circle, or bubble of energy, that protects you from unwanted outside influences.

Practising Journey Techniques

In order to get the most out of journeying, it is important to practise the techniques involved. The Tree of Life in Chapter 1 is a great way to practice journeying technique. As are the seven stages of relaxation below. I recommend trying both of these exercises at least once a week until you feel confident that these skills are flowing naturally.

Seven stages of Relaxation

This is a great tool for honing your journeying skills (as well as getting you relaxed for a good night's sleep!).

Sitting comfortably in your sacred space, begin to breathe slowly and deeply.

In the darkness before you, see a black cinema screen.
On the dark screen, begin to see a clear red number one.
Once you can visualise this clearly, allow the number to fade.
On the dark screen, begin to see a clear orange number two
Once you can visualise this clearly, allow the number to fade.
On the dark screen, begin to see a clear yellow number three.
Once you can visualise this clearly, allow the number to fade.
On the dark screen begin, to see a clear green number four.
Once you can visualise this clearly, allow the number to fade.
On the dark screen, begin to see a clear blue number five.
Once you can visualise this clearly, allow the number to fade.
On the dark screen, begin to see a clear purple number six.
Once you can visualise this clearly, allow the number to fade.
On the dark screen, begin to see a clear white or white number seven.
Once you can visualise this clearly, allow the number to fade.

Notice the difference in your breathing, in your being. Sit for a moment in the darkness.

If you can, imagine yourself stepping out of your body and looking at yourself.

Then step into yourself once more.

Notice your reaction.

Now reverse the process.

Concentrate upon the dark screen once more.

On the dark screen, begin to see a clear white or white number seven. Once you can visualise this clearly, allow the number to fade.
On the dark screen, begin to see a clear purple number six.
Once you can visualise this clearly, allow the number to fade.
On the dark screen, begin to see a clear blue number five.
Once you can visualise this clearly, allow the number to fade.
On the dark screen, begin to see a clear green number four.
Once you can visualise this clearly, allow the number to fade.
On the dark screen, begin to see a clear yellow number three.
Once you can visualise this clearly, allow the number to fade.
On the dark screen, begin to see a clear orange number two.
Once you can visualise this clearly, allow the number to fade.
On the dark screen, begin to see a clear red number one.
Once you can visualise this clearly, allow the number to fade.
Slowly begin to move your fingers, feet and arms. When ready, open your eyes.

If you have visualised a sacred space remove this now.

Are you ready to begin your journey?
Then walk with me as the Wheel turns...

CHAPTER 5

Samhain – Honouring the cycle of death and rebirth

In October, death is all around us. The trees are losing their leaves, one finale beautiful burst of colour, whilst the sap retreats to the earth. As the animals make their last preparations before hibernating, we too feel the urge to stay indoors, to retreat under a blanket and remain where we are cosiest and warm. All of life is withdrawing into itself. This is a time of rest and rejuvenation. The work of the year is almost complete. The Wheel will soon turn. Samhain is both the ending and the beginning of the Wheel.

HISTORY OF SAMHAIN

The Celts regarded Samhain Eve like our New Year on 31st December[7]. At Samhain, nature is retreating, the world is preparing for winter. It is a time of death. The ending of a cycle. The trees shed their leaves and plant life dies back. At Samhain, nature shows us her beauty in her death. The Celts believed that on 31st October, at the moment of nature's death, the barriers between the worlds became thinner and the ancestors walked among us[8] (hence the connection with ghosts and spirits on today's Halloween). It was a time of honouring your ancestors, your lineage. This yearly ritual meant that, contra to our modern-day mindset, the Celts knew who they were, where they came from. The past was an integrated part of their present. A little similar to the ancestor veneration tradition in China.[9]

However, Samhain was not a time of morbidity or grief. In the Celtic world, the coming together of the dead and living in one place, was a cause for celebration and a strengthening of the ties of kinship. It included, of course, a feast. There are lots of different traditions surrounding the Samhain feasts. However, all have a few similar elements. Firstly, food was set aside for the dead as an offering and it was a form of sacrilege for the living to touch the food for the dead during Samhain. The next is entertainment, celebrations in the hall around the hearth, ritualised games often involving apples. As these are the last

---

7   Alexi Kondratirev Celtic Rituals. An authentic guide to Celtic Spirituality Pg 105
8   Alexi Kondratiev Celtic Rituals. An authentic guide to Celtic Spirituality Pg 107
9   Chinese Sage "Ancestor veneration in China"

of the crops harvested associated with death, hence the Welsh name for Samhain which is Afallon, apple tree. In almost every tradition included is an offering both to the ancestors but also to the land spirits as thanks for their cooperation during the harvest and to replenish the lands energy[10].

There was another very practical aspect of the death theme at Samhain, as this was the time of slaughtering the beasts that would not make it through the winter. A form of letting go in the human world, in harmony with nature's cycle.

Samhain has another aspect to it. However, this aspect we will look at in our final chapter as there is plenty to see, do and celebrate at this, your first Samhain celebration.

GROWING WITH THE SEASON

Letting Go

Letting go is a theme that we reflect on as a focus for our personal development theme at Samhain today. Just as the trees have to let go of their leaves to become mulch that will feed and sustain the new plants as they grow in the spring, protecting them from the winter's cold, we too have to look at what it is we will let go of from the past Wheel. The ashes of these things become the nutrients that will feed our growth in the spring. Allowing us to step into our winter hibernation unburned and ready for rest.

At Samhain we ask ourselves – what will we take with us into this new cycle? What do we choose to leave behind?

Samhain is the perfect point in the wheel to strip ourselves of habits, people, negative attitudes that hinder our growth. We can also take the time here to assess our fears and our negative self-image. Once relieved of these burdens, we can be reborn again with the birth of the new year.

As the trees shed their leaves, so must we shed the unwanted debris of our own life. So now it is time to assess yourself and your life through the past Wheel. Although it is possible to do this process internally, I find it healthier to create a visual representation to help with the analysis process. If you are a very creative person you can make a collage or drawing of yourself with both the negative and positive influences in your life. If you are more structured you can write a table or a list in your notebook so you can assess your development. Remember to include your achievements, both the big and small things that make you happier in your life. Equally those things that make you sad.

When you have made the representation of your life, have a look at it. Take a step back and ask yourself:

- What becomes immediately obvious?

- Can you see the positive and negative influences within your last year?

---

10   Jean Markale.The Pagan Mysteries of Halloween: Celebrating the Dark Half of the Year. Chapter 3

- Importantly, can you identify the parts of your life and beliefs that are holding you back?

Remember, only you can judge and assess your life. Only you are qualified to know what is best for your soul.

Contemplate the patterns presented and your observations. Now ask yourself:

- What will I take forward with me in the new Wheel?
- What will I leave behind and let go of?

It may not always be possible to leave behind all you wish to remove from your life immediately. There may be deep rooted issues that will take time to heal and reconcile with. Just as it can take time for the skin to heal when pricked by a thorn.

In order to physically remove something from your life, you will have to put in the effort. For example, if you want to give up smoking, you have to choose not to buy cigarettes. This too will take time.

You will not act upon removing emotional elements from your life. Once you have chosen, they will be energetically gone. By doing this process, you will become actively aware if they try to re-enter your life and will take necessary steps to remove them.

To affirm your desire to remove these negative influences from your life, write each one on a small piece of paper. It is best to choose the most important for the next Wheel. I strongly recommend not trying to let go of everything all at once. You have many more wheels ahead of you, so remove what is most relevant right now and return to this process again next Samhain.

Now in your sacred space and in a metal container (believe me, I made the mistake of not using one, the result is not pretty) light a small candle or charcoal block. Read each statement aloud and then say "I banish you from my life", then burn the paper. Do not do this too quickly, take time to watch the paper burn, think and meditate on what it is you wish to remove from your life. Thank it and let it go.

Acknowledge the lessons this negative thing taught you. As every experience in life can teach us something, be it a positive or a negative experience (if you like, you can keep these ashes for the transformation crafting below or you can release them to the wind).

Beginning Anew

Samhain is also a time of new beginnings. The ancient Celts believed that the day started with the setting of the Sun, not at sunrise. So, with the setting of the Sun the new year begins in the darkness[11].

At this time, it is potent to contemplate the new things you would like to invite into your life this coming wheel. Take a fresh sheet of paper and write upon it

---

11 Edain McCoy The Sabbats a New approach to living the old ways Pg 4

the things which you wish to take with you into the new Wheel, the new year. Place these in your sacred space and give thanks to the universe or your gods or yourself for the gifts these things bring.

Transformation Crafting

The new year represents new beginnings and transformation. By harnessing this energy, we can transform the things we are letting go of and allow them to feed positive growth. Just as the fall leaves mulch down and will transform into the nutrients supporting the new growth in the spring.

At Samhain, I like to use a very specific process to emphasise my letting go process and support the transformation of the ashes of the old into nourishment for my new growth.

This is gypsy craft for rebirth and transformation was taught to me by a wonderful woman in Avebury Stone Circle.

You will need:

- An apple
- Some string
- A candle
- The ashes from your letting go (see above)

How to make:

- Cut an apple horizontally, across the centre (you will see a star made of seeds in the middle of your apple)
- With a spoon, cut out the seed star of both halves of your apple and set the seeds to one side
- Fill the hole with ashes of your negative traits (from the letting go activity) and the seeds
- Seal the apple together with string. Bind it together tightly
- Using a candle, dribble wax on to the string to seal the apple completely. This can get messy!
- Plant your apple, if possible, on Samhain (31st October), or on the morning after. As close as you can is fine. As you plant, imagine the habits or the things you wish to let go of disappearing into the earth, rotting and becoming nutrients for new healthy growth.

Remember, you will not see the effects of this for a while, plant it and forget it and when you look back in a few years, you will see the transformation manifesting.

ANCESTORS – FINDING OUT WHERE YOU COME FROM?

In the passage of time, our lives are really but a moment. A brief dance in the rhythm of life and evolution. Have you ever thought that your life's dance here and now, is in fact the product of many people's dances and steps that have travelled around our world? Your life, in the fabric of your DNA, is woven by the lives of many others. Although you are unique and how you choose to shape your journey is unique to you, ultimately you are, in your original form, an accumulation of many lives. You descend from these people, without them there would simply be no you. As the Celts honoured their ancestors at Samhain, this is the perfect time to ask yourself, where do I come from? It is time to look at the roots you have grown from.

I do not expect, or ask you to suddenly trace back your ancestors to some obscure Inuit tribe, although you are most welcome to if you so wish. I found it very interesting when my wonderful cousin decided to trace my family history and we discovered we are not only related to some of the worst characters in British history, the royal families of both Britain and France, we are also supposedly descended from the water goddess Melusina. Your recent family. Your parents, aunts, uncles, grandparents and great grandparents those close to you that have passed on will all help you to understand your roots.

By looking at the lives and personalities of these deceased family members, you will discover patterns, both genetic and influences passed on, that are still very much here in you and your life today.

For example, the shared family traits that we all have in my family is that we have a tendency to talk too much (as I am sure you might have noticed!). Infertility unfortunately runs in our family, as does the sight. Understanding these traits will give you a deeper understanding of who you are and how you came to be in this world.

It is not always a good thing to spend too much time dwelling on the past, as the present is too beautiful and exciting to miss. However, at Samhain it is enriching to spend time learning about and honouring our ancestors, discovering our own personal roots. After all, knowing where we come from makes it so much easier to know where we are going.

This is the time of the year to visit the older members of our family. Spend some time with these wonderful individuals. They have a wealth of family stories and memories that nobody else can share with you and without the tales being told, the stories will die with them. Also, this is a great point of the year to pull out the old family photograph albums to reminisce and remind ourselves who helped create our lives.

Place some pictures in your sacred space of your deceased loved ones and take time to honour them and connect with them in a celebratory way. A great way to do this is to share the stories of their lives. In telling these stories, reflect upon what it is this person taught you. Ask yourself, which aspects of their personalities do you see in you? What lessons did they teach you that you can still feel influencing your life today? It is wonderful to do this in a circle talk, or with friends and family. My partner and I do this each Samhain and I feel it brings us closer each time.

Each Samhain, I choose one picture of a deceased friend or relative that has played an important part in my life. As well as sharing their story with others, I honour this person by writing them a letter of thanks to them. I sometimes also spend some time that day doing something that I loved to do with them, or they loved to do.

SAMHAIN TRADITIONS

Labyrinth

Labyrinths have long been a part of the human psyche. Both within prehistoric art and within mythology. Pliny the Elder's Natural History from 77 AD mentions four ancient labyrinths: the Cretan labyrinth, an Egyptian labyrinth, a Lemnian labyrinth and an Italian labyrinth in Book 36: Stone[12]. Alternative labyrinth images are found carved in stone, upon pottery and the Romans built mosaics shaped in the labyrinth pattern. The pattern was used up to the medieval times, built into the cathedral floors of Chartres, Reims and Amiens[13]. In Britain, the labyrinths were carved in stone in Cornwall and built into the landscape from turf, such as at Safron Waldon. At the same time, 500 non-ecclesiastic ones were constructed from stone or turf in Scandinavia, usually by the coastline[14]. Of course, there is also the famous Greek myth of Theseus and the Minotaur. Throughout history, labyrinths have been used for both ritual and meditation purposes[15].

Labyrinths within myths are often connected to entering the underworld. At Samhain, people often gather in Avebury to walk the labyrinth rebuilt anew every year within the stones. When walking a labyrinth, we take both a physical and mental journey. You might see images from your life or dreams. For me, the labyrinth is always a rebirthing process. A moving meditation. There is something that speaks to our primal nature as we meander. I have walked labyrinths at night through the fire, facing my deepest fears; through the dawn, pink lit, clear and beautiful, finding a spiral moving upwards at the centre; I have walked them alone and yet been surrounded by my ancestors and once ran through a labyrinth with my lover, a playful game of chase. Each time has been memorable and unique. Sometimes, I have gone looking for the answer to a question, other times just to feel the dance of life. Whatever your motive, walking a labyrinth is a beautiful way to connect and centre.

You can create your own labyrinth from tea lights, stones, sand, built with

---

12 The Curious History of Mazes: 4,000 Years of Fascinating Twists and Turns Dr Julie E. Bounford Pg 31
13 L'architecture du 5me au 17me siècle et les arts qui en dépendent ..., Jules Gailhabaud, Volume 2 Pp 193–198
14 Labyrinths and Ritual in Scandinavia Maria Kvilhaug
15 ibid.

earth or with rolled up fabric or flowers. You could build a spiral as a community or a family, adding characters who question the walker throughout the journey. There are many different patterns as can be seen below, from the traditional to the triple spiral. You may not have the space to create your own labyrinth, so another way of recreating this journey is to draw a labyrinth. Drawing a labyrinth is not the same as walking it, it brings up images in the mind in a different way. It is definitely a mindful experience, whereas walking is more of a meditative state.

Labyrinths can be drawn or walked at any time during the Wheel. However, it is most relevant at Samhain when death and life are so closely side by side. As each leaf begins to fall from the tree, new sustenance is given to the coming life under the rotting leaves of the previous year. Travelling the labyrinth gives us a chance to go deep within ourselves, under our own skin, find our centre and travel outwards and onwards more consciously into our lives.

THE DAY OF THE DEAD

In Mexico on November 2nd they celebrate 'el Día de los Muertos'. The Day of the Dead. Held to welcome the deceased back to their living families for feasting and celebration. The Day of the Dead has been called a Mexican Halloween, but its origins are steeped in history and can be traced back almost 3000 years[16]. Today the celebration includes feasting, eating pan de muerto, the traditional sweet baked bread of Day of the Dead and people drink spicy dark chocolate or a corn-based liquor called atole. People wear skeleton masks to honour Mictecacíhuatl, the Aztec goddess of the underworld[17]. Offerings are made to the deceased and music, dance and fiesta is central to the celebrations.

CONNECTING WITH THE SEASON

Take a Reflective Walk

As seasons change, it is important to connect into the shifts of the patterns of the land. As you work more deeply with the Wheel of the Year you will become more sensitive to seasonal changes, both externally observing the signs of a seasonal shift and internally as you begin to feel the energy change. At each point in the Wheel, I recommend taking a walk, connecting and observing the changes in nature and in yourself. We continuously unconsciously mirror nature in our life's journeys and one of the most powerful life enhancing things we can do is to make ourselves aware of how that works for us. So, take a walk. It doesn't have to be in the wild, a walk in a park or graveyard also works. Anywhere you can observe nature. I would recommend returning to the same place throughout the Wheel so you can really begin to observe the changes. Do the Tree of Life meditation to begin your connection then as you walk, observe nature, what is

---

16 Day of the Dead (Día de los Muertos) History.com Editors
17 ibid.

happening physically in the world around you right now? Ask yourself how does that mirror where you are in your own life, emotionally and physically?
After your walk record your observations in your journal.

Celebrate the People Who are No Longer Alive

On Samhain Eve, share the stories of the people who have passed on, either with friends or family. On Samhain night we light a candle by pictures of our dead family and friends that we have put around the house to honour them. Then we share the photo albums and tell stories. For me, this has been a great way to get to know my partner and his family better. Make this evening a celebration of their lives.

You could also take the time to visit an older member of the family and ask them to tell you stories of your family. These stories will tell you a lot about yourself, if you look, and give you a better sense of knowing where you come from.

Another wonderful way to celebrate these people is to do something that you enjoyed with a deceased family member to honour their memory. Sometimes do this alone or sometimes with someone. For me, living so far away from my family, holding a memory day like this helps me maintain my connection with them and gives my new family a glimpse into the world I come from too. This can also be true for grandchildren that never met their grandparents or even great grandparents. Passing on memories and traditions is a wonderful way to celebrate the people we have loved.

Connection with Ancient Sites

Of course, you may wish to go deeper into your past to connect with older souls, the path walkers that roamed and shaped our Earth. Within most European landscapes, burial mounds and stone temples can be found and easily accessed. Within other cultures there are sacred landscapes, places of burial or burial rites, or even castles and famous battlefields or villages. It is simply a question of researching these places. Samhain is the perfect point of the year to visit these places. However please follow these guidelines (based on the *The Aslan Sacred Sites Charter*[18]) when visiting a site of spiritual and archaeological interest:
Firstly, do not enter the site without asking permission. After all you, would not simply walk into another person's home without asking or being given permission, why do we then assume we can enter someone's burial chamber without being polite? If you have received permission, you will know, enter respectfully.

Secondly, make sure that your first and foremost mission is to give thanks to these ancient ones. You can also ask advice and, if it is Samhain Eve, you can invite the spirits to join the land of the living until sunrise (be very sure if you

---

18   Sacred Sites: an overview Anthony Thorley. Celia M Gunn. Pp.159 -160

decide to do the latter, it is not always a pleasant experience for everyone).

Lastly, although it's respectful and advisable to leave offerings as a way of giving thank, please make sure these offerings are suitable. In Avebury, we had an issue of people leaving flowers poisonous to the sheep that were tending to the levels of grass in the stones. And in West Kennet Long Barrow there was an issue of people lighting tea light candles in the nooks and crannies of the stones, which over time was cracking the stones and leaving charcoal residue which messed up the carbon dating. Basically, leave a place as untouched as possible. I usually leave handfuls of organic bird seed. However you honour the ancestors, do it respectfully, these ancient sites need to stand for generations to come to receive the knowledge and wisdom we ourselves seek.

SAMHAIN CRAFTS

Make an Ancestor Tree

This is a great way for you and your family to have a sense of where you have come from. A fun way of doing this is by making an ancestor tree. Find old photos of your ancestors (or failing that, find names) and tie these to the branch of a tree. Share stories about your family members on Samhain Eve, toast your ancestors with a glass of wine (or whatever is your tipple) or, if you know it, eat their favourite food. Making an ancestor tree is a great way to celebrate them. After all, without them there would be no us.

Make a Jack O'Lantern

Today, one of the most common images associated with Samhain (or Halloween) is the carved pumpkin lantern. However, originally it was a turnip! The practice of carving lanterns from turnips (and other root vegetables) was practiced in Scotland and Ireland. Some schools of thought suggest that this was an ancient practice where the lanterns were made to frighten away spirits following deceased loved ones in to the Land of the Dead[19]. Whereas the commonly acknowledged origin is thought to have come from an Irish folktale about a man named Jack O'Lantern who, after trying to trick the devil, was cursed to roam the Earth with only a burning coal held inside a hollowed-out turnip[20]. Ultimately, these lanterns are thought to be a symbol of protection. But I think it is probably because it is so much fun that the tradition survives today!

How to make a carved lantern (from either a pumpkin, or a turnip):

---

19 Edain McCoy The Sabbats a New Approach to Living the Old Ways pg 30
20 "Go back to Halloween's roots and carve a turnip, charity suggests" Ashia Gani

You will need:

A pumpkin or a turnip

- A sharp knife
- A bowl
- A tealight

How to make:

- Cut off the top leaves and stems
- If you are using a turnip cut a slice off the bottom. This provides a flat bottom, so it will not roll away on you
- With a sharp knife, slice off the top to make the lid
- Carve out the centre
- Use a small knife to cut out a face (supervise children when doing this)
- Light the lantern with a small tealight candle
- You can leave the top off, or put it on. If you put it on when the candle is lit, the lid will begin to cook, so be careful!
- Put the lantern outside your house to keep all those evil spirits away from your home and protect your house!

JOURNEYING

We know from evidence that shamans existed at least over 40 000 years ago[21], in almost every world culture from Asia to America to Africa and Europe. Journeying is the art of using spoken word, song or rhythm with the intention to enter an altered state of consciousness in order to connect with the spiritual dimension of reality. It is a way of accessing our unconscious and of reaching a deeper understanding or guidance.

As such, journeying takes us within the deepest part of our soul. It can help us connect not only with the world around us but with our very fabric and very essence of ourselves, almost down to our DNA. Journey gives us a chance to stop and reassess our lives. It may not always be clear at first what the messages we find within our journeys mean. However, they are special to your own life path and eventually, as you develop and become more in tune, their meaning will become clear.

Journeying is a very powerful way to connect with the turning of the Wheel. However, like most skills in life, it needs to be learnt. Before attempting the

---

[21] Spiritual Information: 100 Perspectives on Science and Religion Charles L. Harper Jr., John Templeton Pp 280 -281

Samhain journey, please turn to page 25 to read the advice, guidelines and tools I recommend to help you prepare properly.

In this book, the journeys take a form of guided meditation using the travel path of the Celtic world tree. These guided meditations will teach you how to begin journeying alone. The Celtic world tree, as I was taught it, contains three worlds

- the underworld (our cave)
- the middle world (our grove)
- the upper world (our celestial world)

You will notice that in each journey through the world tree, there is repetition in the way you are guided into the world and guided home again. This is to support you to safely enter a journey state and to guide you back to your body again. The familiarity of the repetition of the journey guiding gives you a strong tool to be able to bring yourself in and out of the other worlds and will support your journeying abilities to become stronger and make your journeys clearer. As with anything in life, practice makes you the master, you will find that journeying comes naturally and easily as you walk the Wheel.

In the darker part of the year we journey into our underworld.

Samhain Journey

At Samhain we journey into the dark, into the realm of death. Be very sure of what you search for here. It is obviously the best time to reconnect with those we have loved on the other side or to ask for some ancestral guidance. It is also a good idea to have an offering when you travel into the deep. An apple or a pomegranate are fitting.

Now where you go on your journey will very much depend on your beliefs. The Heathens that follow the Norse gods will either go to Asgard or to Hel depending on who it is they seek. The Celtic priests, and sometimes Druids will travel to Tir-na-nOg, the land of the ever young (for those not up on Celtic myth, this inspired the land where the elves went to in the Lord of the Rings). In Buddhism, death is not the end of life, it is merely the discontinuation with this body and they have 37 different versions of heaven[22]. In different beliefs, you will find different stories and places of death. Focus on the imagery you know as it will not help you to transplant and attempt to follow imagery from a different belief system. It will unbalance you and you might lose your way.

The following journey is accessible to all belief systems. It may help you to record this first and have it playing to you whilst you journey. It may also help you to light incense and candles. Whatever suits you best. It is a good idea when we journey to have something in our hand that connects us with the earth. A simple rock will suffice.

---

22 Buddhist View on Death and Rebirth Ven. Thich Nguyen Tang

WALK YOUR PATH

Now it is time to take your Samhain journey......at Samhain you are connecting with your ancestors.

Breathe deeply and slowly, sitting or lying in a comfortable position. Make sure you're warm enough and have a glass of water close by. As you breathe, feel your surroundings slip away. As you cocoon yourself in a safe protective circle.

In your mind, begin to see yourself standing high on a hill. The night is dark and only a few stars glint in the deep black sky. Before you there are blackened fields, and a landscape you can hardly make out in the moonless night.

As you walk higher up the hill, you become aware other people, other beings slowly promenading higher and higher up the hill. Some of them carry flaming torches. You feel the heat of the fire. Smell the winter coming on the cold wind.

High up on the hill a lone tree stands. An ancient oak. The wind bustles around it but the oak stands strong as you gather in a circle around the tree. With one breath, the torches are put out. A low song begins deep, primal humming with the wind.

At the bottom of the oak, almost hidden in the trunk, you can see a wooden door, half covered with ivy. Slowly you walk towards the door. It opens with a creak and you can make out a dimly lit set of stairs spiralling up into the tree and spiralling down. Tentatively, you begin to make your way down the stairs. To each side of you is earth and roots. You can smell the musty damp of decaying earth around you.

Further and further down you travel until, at the bottom of the stairs, you find another door, bigger than the last. Slowly you open this door. It opens to a high cave, well lit. There is a warm fire burning in the centre. And a stone altar beside the fire, you place your offering on the altar and sit beside the fire.

Sit here for a while contemplating the reason for your journey. See if any messages or spirit folk come to you. Receive their messages with gratitude and store them away for reflection. When the time is right, explore the cave further. You will find two more doors. One leads to a river where you can see a ferry man waiting to help you travel, the other leads to a dark wood. Now it is your choice, take the river or the woods. The choice is yours. Go where your instinct leads you and know you will be able to find your cave when the time is right.

* * *

It is time to return. Through the woods or over the river, you travel until you stand before the door to your cave. The fire is still burning, sit awhile and contemplate the journey you have taken. Give thanks for the new knowledge you have gained.

Now when the time is right for you, take one last look at your cave. This place is always here, you can always find it again. Open the door to the stairway spiralling up. The smell has changed to a fresher smell. The stairwell is brighter than before. When you open the doorway at the top of the stairs you can smell dew. You step out into a glorious sunrise. A new day has begun. You are alone and can see the landscape rolling away before you.

Slowly become aware of the place in which your body lies or sits and allow your spirit self to step into your body and become one again. Gently allow the circle to slip away and bring yourself back to consciousness.

Drink some water, record your journey and get some fresh air.

***** If you find it hard to come back into your body after journeying, eat something. Anything will do, however I have found that chocolate, especially dark chocolate; works particularly well. *****

With all journeys, it is a good idea to write down or draw what you saw, the reason for your journey and any understandings you have gained. It helps you to reflect and return to the journey when you need guidance and inspiration. Do not worry if you cannot remember the entire journey, not everything that happens in the spirit worlds can be discussed here. It may be that you find that you want or don't want to share your journey and either is fine, remember only you can say what is right or wrong for you. The journey is your gift.

CEREMONY AND CELEBRATION

As much as it is important to develop and grow with each season, it is equally important to celebrate the change of the season. Life should also be joyful, often we don't take the time out to enjoy it. Ceremony creates opportunity to mark, give thanks for and celebrate the point of turning of the Wheel.

Ceremony can take many different forms and it is, in my opinion, best to make your own. Chapter 3 Creating Ceremony (page 19) will guide you into creating your own ceremony. Here is a version of my Samhain ceremony that you can use to inspire your own, if you wish. I like to work with the five elements, my ancestors and my guides.

Samhain Ceremony

My altar or sacred space faces the north.
I walk the circle three times, imagining a boundary of pure energy around me.

"A time that is not a time, in a place that is not a place".
At the north point of the circle I invite the elements of earth to join me.
At the east point of the circle I invite the elements of air to join me.
At the south point of the circle I invite the elements of fire to join me.
At the west point of the circle I invite the elements of water to join me.

Within the centre, I invite spirit to join me.

Silently I invite my ancestors and guides to be with me.

"Samhain is here, and it is a time of transitions.

The winter approaches, and the summer dies.
This is the time of the dark,
a time of death and of dying.
This is the time of our ancestors
and of the Ancient Ones."

I use a bell to begin my ceremony.

"In my circle I come to honour my ancestors, to say farewell to those who have passed on and to celebrate the new birth that death brings"

I name my ancestors and those recently passed over. Sometimes sharing a memory or two out loud.

"I give thanks for you all, the memories you have given me, the lessons that have inspired me and the love and laughter we have shared."

I toast my ancestors.

"With death. there comes rebirth. I let go that which does not serve me. From the ashes new growth comes".

In my Samhain ceremony. I like to make my transformation apple. After my ceremony. I will plant it in a place that I feel is special.

Sometimes, if I am alone, then I will do a journey at this point in my ceremony. In a group, we often dance or sing to bring our energy up.

To close my ceremony alone, or in a group, I share cakes and wine or apple juice.

In reverse, I thank the elements, guides and my ancestors for joining me and walk the circle round in the opposite direction from, the start.

After ceremony, it can be good to take a walk or at least open the windows to let in the fresh air to clear your mind and the space afresh.

Now it's time to celebrate Samhain!

> *Samhain night is cold and dark,*
> *The land becoming bare and stark.*
> *Tonight we celebrate the end of the year,*
> *As winter's icy winds draw near.*
>
> *We honour those who've passed,*
> *Invite them in, to share our hearth.*
> *Ancestors of our blood, skin and bone,*
> *Who gave us more than we've ever known.*
>
> *We raise our glasses and toast them well,*
> *With laughter and tears their tales we tell.*
> *Although gone, they are still so dear,*
> *They live in our hearts and are always near.*

SAMHAIN – HONOURING THE CYCLE OF DEATH AND REBIRTH

And yet with the rising of the Sun,
The old Wheel ends and the night is done
With the subtle turning of the Earth,
Life carries on. The new year is birthed.

The Wheel turns …

CHAPTER 6

Yule and the Winter Solstice – Honouring the Gifts and Joy in Life

The winter solstice, also known as Yule, is a time of joy and celebration. The high point, in the middle of the winter darkness. As Samhain was about remembering our past, at Yule we celebrate the here and now, as well as the birth of new things to come. Winter is by no means over, but this point in the Wheel marks the beginning of the end. In days gone by winter solstice was the time to slaughter a beast, make a feast and celebrate the survival of those that remained and had survived through the winter so far. It was, and is, a time of honouring people in our lives. A time of telling stories, gathered around the fire. the teaching tales that stayed with us throughout our lives.

Winter solstice is very significant in the Wheel as it is the first of the four solar festivals. The time of the shortest day and the longest night. And from that darkness comes the birth of summer Sun. From this point, the days begin to get longer and life will eventually return to the land. Although we are no longer a culture that relies on the land the way we did in the past, this returning of the light is still as important to us, both mentally and physically.

HISTORY OF WINTER SOLSTICE

In the Northern Hemisphere, winter solstice, is around the 21st of December. For me, this is a magical time, the birth of the summer! From this point on, our days become longer and our nights shorter. Celebrations of the lighter days to come and nature's continuing cycle have been common throughout cultures and history with feasts, festivals and holidays around the December solstice.

The oldest known festivals to mark the return of the Sun at this time were made in Egypt and Mesopotamian 4,000 years ago.[23] Both cultures held a twelve day festival around the solstice. in Egypt to celebrate the rebirth of the sky god Horus, who they believed they saw daily as the Sun in the sky.[24] The

---
23   Yule: A Celebration of Light and Warmth (Holiday Series) Dorothy Morrisopp.4–5
24   ibid.

Mesopotamians celebrated Zagmuk, to help the god Marduk tame the monsters of chaos in a twelve day battle for one more year of peace.[25] And, although we do not have written records of the celebrations, it can be seen by the positioning of ancient Neolithic structures, aligned to the winter solstice sunrise, such as Maeshow on Orkney[26], Long Meg in Cumberland and Castlerigg in Cumbria; [27]it is apparent to people that the winter solstice was of great importance.

The winter solstice has long been connected to the birth of the sacred child or new sun throughout human history. In pre-Christian society, it is possible that people believed that, as days got shorter, the Sun was dying, To a community that relied on the sun to grow all food, the rebirth of the Sun at the solstice was really something to be celebrated. Today, people all over the world celebrate the birth of Jesus Christ on Christmas Day, on December 25, both Christians and non-Christians. However, this date is not the real birth of Christas Pope Julius chose the date[28]. Some believe that date was chosen to offset pagan celebrations of Saturnalia and other pagan celebrations of solstice, as the Roman Empire officially converted to Christianity[29]. So, you could say that, without knowing it, people are still celebrating the solstice today!

Winter solstice today is sometimes called Yule. Which comes from the Norse word jól, the name given to the time between the winter solstice and the Jólablót, the Scandinavian pre-Christian winter solstice festival. It is unclear from the sources how this time was celebrated. The earliest known written reference from Hrafnsmál, by Skald Torbjørn Hornklove, to the Yule celebrations mentions the phrase 'to drink Yule'[30], so we might assume that drinking played an important part in the Norse celebrations of Yule.

In many religions winter solstice literally marks the birth of the Sun[31]. In connecting with this earth and sky event we recognise the rebirth within ourselves. After all, on a physical level, our bodies cells are constantly dying and being replaced. On Solstice Eve, if possible, try to watch the sunset say goodbye to the old Sun. Watching the sunrise can also be a beautiful way to connect with the solstice energy.

In many cultures the Sun's journey through the longest night is celebrated by lighting candles. Hanukah falls near Solstice. Also known as 'the Festival of Lights' where the eight Chanukah candles are lit during the eight days of the festival. Some modern-day Pagans have incorporated lighting a candle for the Sun on the solstice night as part of their celebrations, inspired by the Jewish festival.

---

25 ibid.
26 Forest D The Magical Year 2016 Watkins Publishing London pg 263
27 E.C. Krup Echoes of the Ancient Skies: The Astronomy of Lost Civilizations Dover Books on Astronomy Pg 165
28 Kevin Knight "Christmas" www.newadvent.org
29 Greg Dues Catholic Customs and Traditions. Advent and Christmas pg. 4
30 Soldiser "Yule celebrations in ancient Scandinavia." www.soldiser.com
31 Edain McCoy The Sabbats A New Approach to Living the Old Ways pp. 53–55

GROWING WITH THE SEASON

Light a Candle on Solstice Night

In the dark of this night, you can better see the inner light — the Jew's call this the "Divine Spark". Answers come in the quiet. You can use solstice night as an opportunity to meditate on you, where you are and where you want to go.

The Gifts in Our Lives

At Samhain, we honoured those that have passed on. Yule has been, and still is, a time of celebrating the people in our lives that we love. Both friends and family. In fact, even today, Yule is one of the only times families gather together and one of the only times we consciously make it important to show the people we care about that they are special to us.

A huge theme that has survived throughout history is the tradition of giving gifts. The people we give gifts to over Yule tend to be our nearest and dearest. There are accounts of Romans giving gifts at Saturnalia[32] and, as you know, that tradition continues with Christmas today.

Giving gifts can be seen as a way to honour the gifts that the people we love bring to our lives. By consciously looking at the gifts they gift us (the gifts they bring into to our lives, not the ones under the Christmas tree), we can begin to identify not only why people are important to us, but also why we need to learn the teachings their gifts bring to us. Taking the premise that every person in our life is a teacher and has something to share with us, and we with them.

For example, although I had a sometimes challenging relationship with my mother (who hasn't), when I really looked at the gifts of the teaching she gave me, I rediscovered her overwhelming sense of empathy and kindness. Meditating on this, I can see how this has influenced me in nearly every human interaction I have had in my life, as well as preparing me for my path as both woman, teacher and coach. I am incredibly grateful for these gifts.

At Yule, I like to honour one of the special people in my life, whose presence brings me a gift of learning. Maybe the one whose lesson is so valuable for me at that moment in time, I write them a letter thanking them for the gift they bring to my life and telling them how much they mean to me. It is a deeply enriching practice both for strengthening the relationship, but also for learning about myself.

Look at the people on your gift list. Ask yourself:

- Who are these people?

- What is their relationship to you?

- What gifts have they brought to your life (this can be stability, lessons, love)?

---

32 Joseph J. Walsh Were They Wise Men or Kings: The Book of Christmas Questions Pg 74

- For each gift, think about your life and why is this teaching necessary to your life today?
- I would highly recommend both writing them a letter (it is so much nicer than an email) and, if possible, spend time with them over the holidays, get to know them on a deeper level and you may find that you have only just scratched the surface in your understanding of the gifts they bring to your life.

Celebrating Community – Mitakuye Oyasin, All My Relations

As humans, we need our interconnected web of support and comfort around us, in the form of other people, like the web of roots connecting the trees in the forest. In the past, a community would be essential to survival throughout the winter months. In short, people need people, we need to be connected. It is one of the reasons social media is so popular.

The Lakota Sioux, as do many other tribes; have an understanding of this connection and relation we all have. They understand that, although we enter and exit this world alone, in order to grow we have need of sustenance in many forms, the most important is the community we have around us.

We rarely stop to thank or honour the people in our lives and Yule is a wonderful time to do this. In the Lakota Sioux the words Mitakuye Oyasin mean 'all my relations'[33]. Below is the version of the Lakota Sioux prayer I use honouring relations on every level. It makes a beautiful addition to any Yule celebration and a fantastic reminder to all that, to be human, we need to be nurtured and supported.

You can use this prayer in many ways, writing it in a Yule card, in your notebook. Or simply reading it out loud both alone, or with others, as a prayer of gratitude giving thanks for each other at this time of celebration.

MITAKUYE OYASIN

The Prayer:

Aho Mitakuye Oyasin …All my relations.

I honour you in this circle of life with me today. I am grateful for this opportunity to acknowledge you in this prayer….

To the Creator, for the ultimate gift of life, I thank you.

To the mineral nation that has built and maintained my bones and all foundations of life experience, I thank you.

---

[33] Joe Jackson Black Elk: The Life of an American Visionary pg 564

To the plant nation that sustains my organs and body and gives me healing herbs for sickness, I thank you.

To the animal nation that feeds me from your own flesh and offers your loyal companionship in this walk of life, I thank you.

To the human nation that shares my path as a soul upon the sacred wheel of Earthly life, I thank you.

To the spirit nation that guides me invisibly through the ups and downs of life and for carrying the torch of light through the ages, I thank you.

To the Winds of Change and Growth, I thank you.

You are all my relations, my relatives, without whom I would not live. We are in the circle of life together, co-existing, co-dependent, co-creating our destiny. One not more important than the other. One nation evolving from the other and yet each dependent upon the one above and the one below. All of us a part of the Great Mystery.

Thank you for this life.

THE GIFTS YOU BRING TO THE WORLD

As I said before, gifts do not only travel one way. As we receive from people in our lives, we also give them gifts and teachings, both consciously and unconsciously. It can often be a challenge to recognise the strength and inspiration we bring to others lives. However, your gifts are as unique as you are and they light up the world in their own way. Yule is a wonderful time to recognise this within yourself.

Finding Your Gifts

What gifts do you give to others? Brainstorm these in your journal, if it's hard to think of, you can ask your family and friends to help you here.

In your journal (or on a piece of paper) draw three candles. On each candle write the gifts that you give to people and the world.

A simple and empowering solstice eve ceremony/ tradition can include acknowledging your gifts in a more physical way.

Use three candles. Each candle represents one of the gifts you have drawn on your candles in your journal.

As you light each candle, say out loud:

I bring the gift of ………………….to the world. I am grateful for this gift and proud of myself for sharing it.

Repeat this for the three gifts you identified

Take time to meditate upon your gifts and appreciate you. This is a moment where you can truly feel proud, of yourself and your gifts. Acknowledging that you are unique, an amazing, powerful being. If you like you can leave the candles in a safe place to burn down, mirroring an old folk custom of lighting a candle on the longest night to guide the new sun to return.

THE LONGEST NIGHT

In times past, stories were told around the fire during the winter. In the Celtic and Nordic cultures it was part of the winter solstice longest night celebrations. Stories and legends are among the oldest forms of teaching known to mankind. Stories pass down the generations, changing, evolving to fit the times. In many countries, it is an old tradition to gather around the fire on Yule Eve and tell stories. Most legends or folktales contain a moral and a teaching, sometimes obvious, sometimes hidden.

A scary Yuletide teaching tale from Iceland is about the Yule Cat, perpetuated in the early 19th century poem by Johannes ur Kotlum, who will eat you if you don't have new clothes on Yule night! It is believed that Icelandic female farm workers in the old days worked on making one piece of clothing after another during the advent period, to save their family from the Yule Cat[34]. The story is a moral teaching tale. It is possible to speculate that the origin of the Yule Cat myth was to encourage farm labourers to perform well before Christmas and, as a reward, they would receive a new item of clothing from their masters. Those who did not complete their work, however, received no gift from their master, thus "ending up in the Yule Cat". However the story began, the moral of the tale was to prevent laziness and apathy.

Connecting with Your Inner Child at Yule

The child of light is a recurring theme at Yule, mirroring the idea of the birth of the new sun or sun god. This is really apparent within early Celtic tales with the theme of a child being born and then disappearing. Such as the Welsh tale of the the god Mabon, the Divine Son of the Divine Mother, who is kidnapped when he is three days old and then later 'reborn' three days after the mid-winter solstice. Or the tale of Pryderi, son of Rhiannon[35]. These tales give us a precedent for connecting to our inner child at Yule. Yule is the perfect time to connect with our inner child. So much of our lives are filled with work and responsibilities, it's vital to take a time out and healthily shake ourselves free to rediscover what gives us joy and hope.

Another Icelandic Yule tradition is to give each other a book on Christmas Eve, so the evening is spent immersed in a new story. Stories change us on a subtle level. As Terry Pratchett said, "People think that stories are shaped by people. In fact, it's the other way around."[36] Stories make an impact on us that

---

34 Haukur Magnússon,. "The Christmas Cat".www. grapevine.is.
35 Celtic Rituals. An authentic guide to Celtic Spirituality Alexi Kondratiev Pp. 127–134
36 Terry Pratchett Witches Abroad: (Discworld Novel 12) p.12,

no other form of learning can, especially the stories we hear as children. A great way to connect with Yule birth energy is to reconnect with your inner child. A great way to learn more about yourself is to revisit the stories of your childhood.

CHILDHOOD STORIES

Think back to the stories you loved as a child, the stories that have stayed with you. Choose the one that is most memorable to you right now. If possible, tell someone the story as you remember it (not as it was written). Then reflect on the following questions:

- What did one of these stories teach you?
- Did this lesson stay with you throughout your life or just a period of your life?
- Has the emphasis on the lesson changed from when you were a child to now as an adult?
- What story would you pass on to another generation and why?

Write the story and your observations in your journal and, throughout the Wheel, return to reading them, see if the meaning changes for you. This is a great exercise to do every Yule as different stories are apparent at different times. The story you tell this Yule might not be the same story you tell next Yule.

YULE TRADITIONS

As Yule has been such a significant time for centuries, so there are many Yule traditions worldwide. In this book, I try to concentrate on the western world traditions (simply because I have personal experience of these).

Bringing in the Green

Hopefully you have been out in nature as the Wheel has turned, taking walks to enjoy the winter sunlight. You may have noticed on your walks that some plants and trees do stay green throughout the winter. These trees were held sacred in the past as they maintained life whilst the rest of the world was dying. To me, they represent the coming of life and the perseverance we have to survive and evolve.

The Romans celebrated Saturnalia at winter solstice and homes were decorated with greenery. People would go out to "bring in the green" to fill their homes with this eternal life, and to welcome the spirits of nature to their home, preparing for the coming light[37]. This tradition was also found in Ireland where people went out to find holly and ivy to decorate the home. A holly bush with many berries on it was thought to be good luck. This may be connected to

---

37 Secunda Floria Zonara."Saturnalia Practices of Nova Romans" www.novaroma.org

an earlier Druidic practice of honouring the holly as a special plant because it stayed green throughout the winter. Folklore tells us that the Druids wore holly in their hair when cutting mistletoe[38].

One of the most common and persistent Yule traditions to survive is the decorating of the Yule tree, popularly known today as the Christmas tree. Evergreens such as pine were seen to symbolize protection, prosperity and the continuity of life during a season that was so often represented with darkness and death. At the Roman Saturnalia, trees in the woods were decorated with sun symbols[39]. However, the origin of the modern-day Christmas tree is given to Germany in the 16th century[40].

In Denmark, the Christmas tree tradition was officially adopted in 1808, but often the poorer families who could not afford a tree decorated a beam in the house with cabbage leaves. The cabbage leaves were then decorated with food and sometimes with paper cones containing treats [41]. The focus on food might have developed from an earlier time where the rebirth of the Sun would bring an increase of food and fertility to the land. It may also have been a way of eating up the winter greens!

In my family, we still bring in the green each and every year. Some winters it is hard to find through the thick snow, in milder winters it is easy. When we come home, we make mulled wine and hot chocolate as we used the green to make decorations and bring the spirit of nature into our home. It's a special way to honour the land, spending time together and the greenery in the home reminds us of the coming spring.

Mistletoe

A Yuletide tradition that has survived today is the honouring of mistletoe. From the earliest times, mistletoe has been one of the most magical, mysterious and sacred plants of European folklore. The Roman author Pliny the Elder wrote that the Druids knew of nothing more sacred than mistletoe[42]. The plant was believed to grow between the worlds, since it grew on trees instead of the ground so mistletoe was held very sacred. It was seen as incredibly lucky if to find mistletoe growing on an oak tree. Because oak has antibiotic properties, the Druid's called it the "cure-all". Surprisingly mistletoe features in many cultures. In fact, mistletoe's association with peace and good will is so strong that once, if enemies met under a tree that by chance had mistletoe growing on it, they were required to lay down their arms and declare a truce until the following day[43]. The best-known mistletoe myth is the death of Balder in Northern Europe. In one

---

38 Ireland Fun Facts "Irish Christmas Facts – Traditions of the Celtic Holiday Season" www.ireland-fun-facts.com
39 Secunda Floria Zonara."Saturnalia Practices of Nova Romans" www.novaroma.org
40 Carol Taylor Treasures for the Christmas Tree: 101 Festive Ornaments to Make & Enjoy 1994 Pg 7
41 Hisotrie online" Juletræets historie" www.historie-online.dk
42 Pliny the Elder: Natural history. Book XVI, chapter 95.
43 Dr Leonard P. Perry "Mistletoe Myths and Medicines" www.uvm.edu

version of this legend Frigga (Balder's mother), after foreseeing his death, asked all the creatures of the world not to harm him, yet she overlooked mistletoe, who she believed too small to be important. Balder is killed by a mistletoe javelin (of course with a hand from the infamous Loki, god of mischief). The tears of grieving Frigga are supposed to have formed the berries of the mistletoe.

The tradition of kissing under the mistletoe came from Tudor England. Mistletoe was part of the kissing bough[44]. A decoration made of woven wooden hoops that were hung with greenery, with a small effigy of the infant Jesus in the middle. Kissing Boughs were placed by the front door, and everyone was kissed by the household when they entered by the Kissing Bough. Over time, the mistletoe became associated with kissing. In some places the tradition of kissing under the mistletoe and removing one berry with each kiss arose. Once none remained, there were no more kisses. As remembered in this rhyme:

"Pick a berry off the mistletoe,
For every kiss that's given.
When the berries have all gone,
There's an end to kissing."

Wassailing

Wassailing is a very ancient custom. The word 'wassail' comes from the Anglo-Saxon phrase 'waes hael', which means 'good health". The tradition of wassailing is basically about toasting with a warm alcoholic drink. It was a tradition which marked the beginning of each year. The lord would greet his people with a toast of waes hael, meaning "be well." The watching crowd would reply drink hael; "drink well" [45].

Originally, the wassail was a drink made of mulled ale, curdled cream, roasted apples, eggs, cloves, ginger, nutmeg and sugar. It was served from huge bowls, often made of silver or pewter. Jesus College, in Oxford University, has a silver-plated Wassail bowl that can hold 10 gallons[46]!

Later, there became two ways of wassailing. The house-visiting wassail and the orchard-visiting wassail. In the house-visiting wassail people go door-to-door, singing and offering a drink from the wassail bowl in exchange for gifts (just as we carol sing and collect for charities today).

The orchard-visiting wassail refers to the ancient custom of visiting orchards in cider-producing regions of England, sprinkling cider, speaking prayers and singing to the trees to promote a good harvest for the coming year, such as:

"Apple tree, apple tree we all come to wassail thee,
Bear this year and next year to bloom and blow."

---

44   Claire Ridgway "The Tradition of Kissing Under the Mistletoe" www.tudorsociety.com
45   Melusine Draco Pagan Portals – Have a Cool Yule: How-To Survive (and Enjoy) the Mid-Winter Festival Pg 11https://www.ool.co.uk/blog/what-is-wassailing/
46   Dan Rabin, Carl Forget The Dictionary of Beer and Brewing Pg 276

A legend about how wassailing was created, says a beautiful maiden named Rowena presented Prince Vortigern with a bowl of wine while toasting him with the words 'waes hael'[47].

From this, it developed into another way of saying Merry Christmas to each other! In Denmark, the tradition of wassailing has transformed to a Yule tradition of drinking glogg (mulled wine) with apple cakes.

The tradition of wassailing continues in some parts of Britain today. Where they sing many traditional wassailing songs such as:

"Here we come a-wassailing
Among the leaves so green,
Here we come a-wassailing,
So fair to be seen.
Love and joy come to you,
And to you your wassail too."[48]

Lord of Misrule

In Edward VI's Britain, a tradition arose to appoint a Lord of Misrule[49]. At this time, Christmas was celebrated over a few days, up to a full month in the richer houses. The Lord of Misrule was both in charge of the celebration games and was responsible for the mischief in the house.

This tradition possibly has its origins in Rome. During Saturnalia, a peasant or slave was appointed to represent Saturn as the Lord of Misrule or the King of Saturnalia. At this time, the roles between Master and slave were reversed. The Lord of Misrule could order anyone to do anything despite being a slave the rest of the year [50].

Mumming

Mumming, is a type of folk play that was performed by male amateur actors; is also an ancient custom at Christmas, traced back to the time of King Edward III of England. Also called 'masking' as people disguised themselves by swapping clothes, putting on masks and visiting their neighbours, putting on a play with a silly plot followed by a procession[51].

Mumming was originally an oral tradition and has developed with each generation. One poem that people said when mumming around the 1800s was:

"Christmas is coming, the beef is getting fat,

---

47 Richard Sermon "Wassail! The origins of a drinking toast" Pp. 1–5
48 Brian Scott But Do You Recall? 25 Days of Christmas Carols and the Stories Behind Them Pg 2–3
49 John Stow, The Annales, or a Generall Chronicle of England … pp. 609–610.
50 Robert Parker On Greek Religion. p. 211.
51 Clement A. Miles Christmas Customs and Traditions, Their History and Significance Pg 297

Please drop a penny in the old man's hat.[52]"

Over the years, as Christmas traditions changed the poems change too. So today carol singers sing:

"Christmas is coming, the goose is getting fat,
Please put a penny in the old man's hat.[53]"

The tradition of Mumming still exists in Britain, Canada and USA and it is also done at Easter.

Yule Log

Today in Britain in many shops you can buy a chocolate Yule log cake. However, the Yule log tradition was originally a Nordic tradition. The Yule log was an entire tree, carefully chosen and brought into the long house with great ceremony. The largest end of the log would be placed into the fire hearth while the rest of the tree stuck out into the room! The log would be lit from the remains of the previous year's log which had been carefully stored away and slowly fed into the fire through the Twelve Days of Christmas. After the twelve days, the ashes would be spread on the fields where the new seeds were planted for fertility.

The Yule log tradition spread all over Europe. Different kinds of wood are used in different countries. In England, oak is traditional; in Scotland, it is birch; while in France, it's cherry. Also, in France, the log is sprinkled with wine before it is burnt, so that it smells nice when it is lit[54].

Volunteering

At Yule, the majority of us are blessed. We are surrounded by people we love, eat richly and get and give gifts. Yule is a celebration of abundance in our lives. But, of course, there are others not as fortunate. Of course, their suffering is all year round but at Yule it is harder to be poor, homeless, sick, alone or even in danger. It is at this time of year, more than ever, that these people need our help. A modern-day Yule tradition of volunteering to help the homeless, the lonely and the hungry, I think is one of the most relevant ways of giving the Yule gift of kindness.

So, make some time to volunteer at Yule, not only to help others, but also to be reminded of how abundant and fortunate you are (if you really don't have time make a donation to a food bank or a charity shop, put not only your money but your effort into giving the gift of kindness at Yule).

---

52   Thomas G. Crippen Christmas and Christmas lore Pg 97
53   Alfred L. Shoemaker, Don Yoder Christmas in Pennsylvania 50th Anniversary Edition Pg 24
54   James Cooper "The History of the Yule Log" www.whychristmas.com

CONNECTING WITH THE SEASON

Reflect on Your Journey in Nature:

At Yule, take a walk to connect with the winter energy. As you walk, look for the changes in the landscape. Ask yourself, how is the land different now from how it was at Samhain? How are you different from the person you were at Samhain? Reflect upon how the changes in nature since Samhain reflect on your own personal journey to the winter solstice.

Make a Sunwheel

If you have brought in the green on a Yuletide walk you can make yourself a Sunwheel to remind you of the importance of the winter solstice.

The Sunwheel is an ancient symbol. It is found amongst stone age carvings and in cave paintings. The cross in the middle represents the four phases of the Sun or the solar festivals, winter solstice, spring equinox, summer solstice and autumn equinox. The outer circle represents both the Sun and the Wheel of the Year.

Make a Sunwheel

You will need:

- Ivy, willow or flexible thin branches (to weave your circle)
- two sturdy sticks
- Twine or string
- Winter greenery such as holly, ivy and pine
- Some red ribbon (optional)

How to make:

- With your flexible bits of ivy, willow (or similar) weave a circle, just as though you were making a flower crown. Don't worry if it doesn't hold at first, just keep weaving and weaving until the circle holds together. If you can't get it to stay then you can bind it with some twine
- Form a cross from the two sticks
- Then add the cross in the middle of the Sunwheel, (again, you can either fix these naturally or tie them to the circle with twine)
- Now the fun part, begin to weave in the winter greenery you found on your walk
- Form a loop from the ribbon and hang your Sunwheel up by a window to greet the solstice sun!

Make this a cosy experience, have music on, drink hot chocolate or mulled wine if you prefer it. In doing this craft you are connecting with a human experience that is as old as mankind itself. And by doing this every year you will get to see first-hand the subtle changes between the seasons each year.

I keep our Sunwheel each year for the entire year and then burn it on the longest night.

Solstice Sunrise

One of the most magical ways of connecting with the solstice energy is to observe the sunrise on the morning of its rebirth, after staying awake on the longest night. The date and time of solstice varies as it is a natural phenomenon, not calendar specific. However, with the wonderful Google it's easy to find out when the sunrise is. The solstice sunrise can be a moving and wondrous thing to see, it gives a sense of the world around us awakening anew and is a perfect way to mark the occasion.

YULE CRAFTS

Ice Lanterns

Beautiful and magical ice lanterns to light up outside your home and maybe light a candle to guide the sun on the longest night.

You will need (for one lantern):

- Two containers of different sizes, that will fit into a freezer
- Electrical tape
- Water
- D natural materials or food colouring
- A freezer
- Tealights /flameless outdoor tea lights

How to make:

- Use electrical tape to centre the smaller container inside the larger one. N.B. The water will keep the container afloat, but you'll need the tape to keep it centred
- After you have your centre container in place, add natural materials
- Add the water but don't fill it up so that the water spills into the central container

- Freeze for six hours or longer, if necessary (the more materials you put in, the longer your lantern will take to freeze)
- Pour a little warm water into the central container to loosen it and remove it
- Run the jar under lukewarm water and slide the lanterns out
- Add a tealight and put them outside (if you use a real tealight, the ice will melt quickly and put out the light, but the effect of fire and ice is beautiful).

Birdseed Cookies

Not only do people have a hard time outside during the cold winter, the winter animals not hibernating also need a helping hand. Birdseed cookies are easy to make and fun for all the family.

Ingredients:
- Baking paper
- Chopping board
- Hard white fat warmed at room temperature (shop bought or can be saved from frying bacon)
- Bird seeds
- Cookie cutters
- Straws
- String
- How to make:
- Lay a sheet of baking paper on a chopping board
- Mix in the bowl the fat and seeds
- Put the cookie cutters on baking paper and press the seed mixture into the form
- Place the straw where you would like to put the string through the cookie
- Put the cookies in the fridge for a few hours
- Remove cookies from the fridge and make a string loop
- Hang the cookies in the trees

WINTER SOLSTICE JOURNEY

This winter solstice journey is to meet your inner child in his or her most joyful state, to connect to your simplest joy and renew your energy by seeing the world anew through refreshed eyes.

Breathe deeply and slowly, sitting or lying in a comfortable position. Make sure you're warm enough and have a glass of water close by. As you breathe feel your surroundings slip away.

In your mind, begin to see yourself standing high on a hill. The night is dark and only a few stars glint in the deep black sky. Before you there are snow covered fields, and a landscape glistening in the light of the Moon.

As you walk higher up the hill, you see a lone tree standing. An ancient oak. The wind bustles around it but the oak stands strong as you walk a circle around the tree.

At the bottom of the oak, almost hidden in the trunk, you can see a wooden door, half covered with ivy. Slowly you walk towards the door. It opens with a creak and you can make out dimly lit stairs spiralling up into the tree and spiralling down. Tentatively, you begin to make your way down the stairs. To each side of you is earth and roots. You can smell the frost of chilled decaying earth around you.

Further and further down you travel until, at the bottom of the stairs you, find another door, the door to your cave, bigger than the last. Slowly, you open this door. It opens to your cave. It is warm and well lit, a fire burning in the centre. There is a stone altar beside the fire, If you have brought your offering place on the altar and sit beside the fire.

Sit here for a while, contemplating the reason for your journey. See if any messages or spirit folk come to you. Receive their messages with gratitude and store them away for reflection.

When the time is right, explore the cave further. You will find two more doors. One leads to a river where you can see a ferryman waiting to help you travel. You board his boat and he sails you downriver until you reach the river's end. There you can see a wood. Grey pastel in colour. You step onto the land. The ferryman will wait. In the centre of the woods you find a cottage, the door is open and you can see the warm glow of a fireplace and hear the laughter of a child. Knock on the door and wait to be allowed to enter. By the fire, playing on the rug, is a child. This child is you.

Play, talk and hug your inner child for a while, reconnect with your inner child once more.

* * *

Now it is time to return. Say farewell to your inner child. And return to the ferryman. Travel the river back to your cave.

The fire is still burning, sit a while and contemplate the journey you have taken. Give thanks for the new knowledge you have gained. When the time is right for you, take one last look at your cave. This place is always here, you can always find it again. Open the door to the stairway spiralling up.

When you open the door you feel a slight warmth in the air, at the top of the stairs you can smell dew. You step out into a glorious sunrise. A new day has begun. You are alone and can see the landscape rolling away before you, the ice glinting in the sunlight.

Slowly become aware of the place in which your body lies or sits and allow your spirit self to step into your body and become one again. Gently allow the circle to slip away and bring yourself back to consciousness.

Drink some water, eat some chocolate, record your journey and get some fresh air.

For the rest of the Wheel, we will not be returning to your cave. However, this does not mean you cannot return and explore further or visit your inner child again. This place is yours and you can visit it whenever you want.

WINTER SOLSTICE CEREMONY

Here is an example of my winter solstice ceremony. Honouring the gifts in your life here and now:

Put the altar in the north (if that works for you).

Walk the circle three times imagining a boundary of pure energy around and above you.

"I am in a time that is not a time, in a place that is not a place".
At the north point of the circle invite the elements of earth.
At the east point of the circle invite the elements of air.
At the south point of the circle invite the elements of fire.
At the west point of the circle invite the elements of water.

Within the centre, invite spirits, ancestors and guides to be with you.

"Yule is here, the birth of the Sun.
In this midwinter, the light of new life has begun,
The shortest day, the longest night,
Weave hearthside tales to keep out fright.
Fill the table with feast foods, the hall with good cheer,
Laugh with your loved ones, the new dawn is here!"

"In my circle, I come to be thankful for the gifts of my friends and family and to celebrate the rebirth of the Sun!"

Name those that bring life gifts to you, say the gifts they bring out loud.

"I give thanks for you all, for the gifts you have brought me, the lessons that have inspired me and the love and laughter we have shared."

Toast the born sun and give thanks for the new light.

Put the Sunwheel in the centre of the circle and draw energy from the new sun up into your body and release this into the Sunwheel (using dance is a fun way of energising at this time of year!)

To close the ceremony alone, or in a group, share cakes and wine, or juice.

Thank the elements, guides and your ancestors for joining and walk the circle round in the opposite direction from the start.

Now it's time to celebrate!

AFTER SOLSTICE, TAKING CARE AND GATHERING WINTER INSPIRATION

The time after winter solstice, I believe, is incredibly important. At this time, we can gather winter inspiration and at the same time we often risk burn out, so it is important to take care of ourselves.

Take Care of You

As the Wheel turns, the earth is under a blanket of snow and frost, the trees and creatures of the land are sleeping, the world around us is stiller. After the busy time pre-Yule, the period after winter's solstice is the time of dreaming and taking time to appreciate your dreams. After all hibernating animals emerge slowly from their rest, allowing their bodies to reconnect hormonal patterns slowly. Be kind to yourself at this time and allow yourself to do the same. You can stop doing and focus on being. Be mindful, be aware of your actions.

If your energy is low, remember it's perfectly natural at this point in the Wheel. Keep an eye on your energy and take the time to check in with yourself.

Good questions to ask yourself at this time are:

- Which actions do not serve me?
- What does serve me?

By being conscious of your energy and what is affecting you at this time, you will find the winter blues are not as unbearable as you think!

Do what keeps you cosy and conserve your energy at this time. It's allowed!

Gathering Inspiration

As the new sun's light grows it brings us new inspiration for dreams and plans that we will begin to act upon in the spring. It could be that this is where the tradition of making New Year's resolutions came from. If you wish to make New Year's resolutions, you are welcome to. Richard Wiseman, a psychologist and author, discovered that 52 percent of people making New Year's resolutions were confident they'd stick it out. Yet only 12 percent really did[55]. Growth within

---

55 The Guardian "New year resolution? Don't wait until New Year's Eve" www.theguardian.com

nature is slower, more gradual, almost unnoticeable. Natural growth of a goal allows your plans and visions to become clearer, sharper, so you are able to focus on the end result and the impacts it will have on your life, as well as the steps you will take to achieve it. In the Wheel of the Year we begin to grow our goals at Imbolc, not in the new year. However, in order to set new goals and dreams into action we need to first collect our inspiration. There are many forms of inspiration and each is a good teaching, one of the best is actually dissatisfaction.

Low winter energy

Personally, I find that after winter solstice I often hit a low point in both my energy and motivation. Typically, I become dissatisfied with my current position in my life. Although this sounds as though this feeling is negative, it can actually be used positively. Remember, the dark in nature has its uses just as much as the light. This sense of dissatisfaction can guide you to be inspired to make changes in your life for the better, if observed and analysed carefully. One way to do this is the positive /negative energy list.

Positive/Negative energy list

If you also feel this sense of dissatisfaction during the time following winter solstice make a positive and negative energy list. Under positive, make a list of things that give you energy and under negative, make a list of the things that affect you negatively. For example, I surprisingly found that washing clothes gives me energy, whereas not having enough time with my boyfriend frustrates me therefore it is an energy drain and so, a negative energy. This list will show you in a glaringly obvious way where you want to make changes.

Dream and Inspiration Diary

Of course, winter is not all doom, gloom and dissatisfaction. From the winter solstice to the coming of spring, glimmers of ideas appear, inspirations arise. If possible do not yet act upon these ideas. Hide them away somewhere and allow the picture of these ideas to emerge gently. Make a running list of awesome ideas, so that you can return and look at them with perspective. Some of your ideas will be ones that you choose to forget or store away for another time. Some of these ideas will become your focus for the rest of the year.

Throughout winter, keep a dream diary. Record both sleeping and waking dreams as these can bring inspiration and insight to the coming year. As you become clearer about your upcoming goals and projects for the rest of the Wheel, begin to gather images or words which represent your ideas. We will use these at Imbolc to help you visualise more clearly the work you have to do.

Watching and Waiting

Yule marks the beginning of the darker time. From now on, you will find yourself slowly beginning to wake up energetically. Surrender to this rhythm and enjoy it. As winter is not the time for overworking, from now until Imbolc in February, just take it slowly energetically. Gather your inspiration for the coming Wheel. Take time to get as much sunlight as you can, to observe the world around you and your feelings. This is a time of watching and waiting. Slowly you will see the world around you awaken, the daytime is lit for longer. Enjoy the last beauty of the winter and the gentle emergence from the dark. Have a magical Yule!

Now it's time to celebrate Yule!

> *The longest night, the shortest day,*
> *The Sun's light is on the way.*
> *The hall full of laughter and good cheer,*
> *Warmth in our hearts, to last all year.*

> *A celebration of life and light,*
> *Loved ones sharing the longest night.*
> *The winter ends at solstice's dawn,*
> *In frost and ice, the summer's born.*

> *The Wheel turns...*

CHAPTER 7

Imbolc – infinite New Beginnings and Possibilities

Imbolc is one of my favourite points in the year. In contrast to some of society who at this point in their year are bogged down with the misery of the continuing cold, complaining of the lack of sun; those of us that walk in harmony with nature's cycle, see before us the bursting possibilities. Spring is already subtly surrounding us. The air is warmer, with a hint of frost, and the snow has melted away leaving the land beneath rich and fertile. Colour is beginning to come back to the land, pale and misty. Birds are beginning to sing once more and all around there is a feeling of freshness, of excitement. New life is coming, it's exciting to think what will it bring?

Imbolc is the festival of new beginnings. In ancient days, bardic inspiration was a primary focus at Imbolc, celebrating both gods and goddesses of poetry such as Bragi[56] and Brigid[57]. Imbolc is about being inspired, deciding and creating what will come. Imbolc is the perfect time to start creating the life you have always imagined for yourself. By connecting with the energy of the new life emerging from the ground at Imbolc, you can harness this energy to begin living the life you imagine for yourself. As the spring bubbles beneath the surface of the land, you can bring forth the vision within you. The vision of the life you want and the vision that will create it.

It is at Imbolc that we begin to set our intentions and goals which we will work with until Samhain. Imbolc inspires the seeds we will plant and the harvest we will reap. Imbolc energy influences and shapes our personal journey and development every Wheel.

---

56 Raven Kaldera "Seasonal Holidays and Blóts" http://www.northernpaganism.org
57 Teresa Moorey. Jane Brideson Wheel of the Year Myth and Magic through the seasons Pg 59

History of Imbolc

Imbolc is considered to be the Celtic celebration of the end of winter, and the imminent beginning of the light half of the year. It's coming signified that the hardest, coldest part of the year was almost over. The land was once again showing the first signs of spring, in the new shoots on the ground and in buds just beginning to appear upon the trees. Food was once again becoming available in nature assuring the continuation of life[58].

Imbolc is considered the first day of spring in the Wheel of the Year and, in my understanding of the wheel, the first of the three fertility festivals. Imbolc was the second of the four quarterly fire festivals within the Celtic year[59]. At this time, Celtic society farmers were getting ready to go back to work, preparing animals for breeding, warriors were picking up their weapons again, and the political and social aspects of life that had been put on hold for winter began once more.

The name Imbolc originates from 'i mbolg', which translates as 'in the belly'[60]. This possibly refers to the pregnant ewes at this time of year, which was one of the focal points of the celebration. Because the festival was so associated with this, its timing often varied. Today it is celebrated on February 2nd.

Imbolc was celebrated all across Ireland, Scotland, the Isle of Man and Wales, with each region having slightly different variations in name and customs[61]. After the onset of Christianity, the festival was tied into Christian celebrations such as the Welsh Gwyl Fair y Canhwyllau or "Mary's Festival of the Candles", St Brigid's Day in Ireland and Candlemas; the Christian festival of lights that commemorates the ritual purification of Mary forty days after the birth of her son Jesus.

In the Nordic calendar, Imbolc seems to have been a regular feast only in Sweden. The Icelandic historian Snorri Sturluson in Heimskringla visited and recorded Dísablót, a sacrificial holiday also known as The Thing of all Swedes. He recorded that in Uppsala a blessing took place in early or mid-February combined with the first public moot/fair of the year[62].

In Anglo-Saxon England, the second month of the Anglo-Saxon year, corresponding roughly to February was called Sólmónað[63]. The venerable Bede observed that this was called the 'month of cakes', where cakes were offered to the gods by the Angles. One theory suggests the month name actually comes from sulh, "plough". The cakes are thought to have been offered by leaving them in the furrows; and they were called "plough-cakes".

---

58   Sharon Paice MacLeod Celtic Cosmology and the Otherworld: Mythic Origins, Sovereignty and Liminality pg 80
59   Alexi Kondratiev Celtic Rituals. An authentic guide to Celtic Spirituality Pg 135
60   Ibid.
61   Ibid. pg 138
62   Snorri Sturluson Saga of Olaf Herladson, Heimskringla Part II (Translated by Kim Lembek Rolf Stavnem Snorris Edda på dansk pp 222–248)
63   Shirley Two Feathers "The Charming of the Plough" www.shirleytwofeathers.com

Another interpretation calls this the 'month of mud'[64], which ties in with the other Anglo-Saxon activity of Blessing/Charming of the Plow[65] also referred to as Éowemeolc (ewe's milk). The Blessing/Charming of the Plow was done at this time of year before the first furrows were ploughed in the fields.

In the 11th century the Æcerbót, an Anglo-Saxon charm, was recorded. It was used when blessing the plough before furrowing the fields. It is an interesting mix of Pagan and Christian prayer to bless the land to produce fruitful crops. It was accompanied by a full days procedure and included intricate ceremonial activities, such as: cutting out four sods from the four sides of the field, marking where they were cut from; treating the soil sides of these with oil, honey, yeast or milk from the cattle on the land and having them blessed in church; then replacing them in their original positions. Collecting all your ploughing implements, making a hole in the plough-tail, and pouring in incense, fennel and hallowed materials; putting the seed on the body of the plough. Finally, baking a palm-sized loaf of breadflour of every kind and kneading it into milk and holy water, then putting it under that first furrow, and blessing the field[66].

In almost all celebrations of Imbolc throughout history the themes of purification, light, new beginnings, and ultimately the blessing of the beginning of the work of the coming year

GROWING WITH THE SEASON

New Beginnings – Setting Goals for Personal Manifestation this Wheel

Imbolc is a busy and important time in the Wheel of the Year for nature and for us. It is at Imbolc we begin to set our intentions and goals that we will work with until Samhain. Imbolc inspires the seeds we will plant and the harvest we will reap later in the Wheel. The energy at Imbolc is the most important to connect with if you wish to learn to manifest your dreams and create the life you imagine for yourself. Do not be concerned or pressured by this idea. Remember, if you set goals that are in contrast to your path in life, this will become apparent throughout the coming months, goals and intentions that are right for you will flow more easily. As we reconnect with the world around us, it becomes clearer as to the path we need and want to take in life. Your senses will attune to what is right or wrong for you. For now, follow the inspirations that feel right to you.

It can be extremely easy to become overly motivated during this time, especially if this is your first time setting goals at Imbolc. With the returning of spring millions of ideas surface and it can be impossible to give concentration

---

64 Wyrd Designs "The Holy Tides: Charming of the Plough / Disting / Solmonaþ " www.wyrddesigns.wordpress.com
65 ibid.
66 Karen Louise Jolly Popular Religion in Late Saxon England: Elf Charms in Context Pp. 113 – 132

and energy to them all. If we tried to do it all, nothing would succeed. This is known as setting yourself up for a fail. The goals you set need to be achievable and manageable to have a successful experience of manifesting the life you want for yourself. Remember, the new energy you feel now will be tested and throughout your journey, will disappear at times, so it is important to keep your goals realistic.

SETTING GOALS

So now, with the inspirations from your winter dreaming, it is time to pick which projects or goals are the most relevant for your journey during this Wheel.

To ensure you achieve your goals this Wheel, set boundaries for yourself. Choose a minimum of four and a maximum of eight things you wish to concentrate on from now until next Samhain. These boundaries will help you avoid setting yourself up for a fail. For example, if your dream is to move from the country to the city, this may not be achievable immediately. However, you can begin to save money towards this goal or the much needed driving license. Small steps grow strong roots from which to bloom. Within your journal, write down your goals, make them clear and succinct.

Remember when making your goals, this is about your life journey. You may have goals for your relationship or your family. However, these should not be the only focus of your life. You can only ever work on yourself. So, remember to do just that. From there you will become a stronger being within your relationships. So maybe focusing on self-love will manifest the right kind of partner in your life, or creating time for you to relax will make you a better parent. Focus on the change you need and can make yourself in your relationships.

Your goals can be practical, spiritual, personal growth based or whatever it is you need. I often find that my goals are a combination of all three. I have very practical goals for work and home and then personal goals, such as setting boundaries or connecting with nature.

I like to go on my Imbolc journey before setting my goals for the Wheel. On my journey, I ask if there is anything I really need to work on in this Wheel and by doing this I allow my subconscious needs to be part of my goal setting.

CLARIFYING THE VISION

Imbolc is all about inspiration and this activity will really connect your personal journey to nature's energy. Here and now, you are going to clarify your vision. The best way to do this is to make a vision board. I make one each year to help inspire me and focus my energy. It is also a great way to look back through the years as a record of my journey in life and my own personal growth. Plus, it's fun to do!

To make your vision board, collect images, words or quotations that will help you visualise your dreams and goals. On a large sheet of paper or cardboard,

IMBOLC – INFINITE NEW BEGINNINGS AND POSSIBILITIES

begin to paste these images around a picture of you in the centre. Choose a picture of you that is a happy one. After all, in the journey of your life, the founding intention of all development and growth you do is ultimately aimed at you enjoying your life and being happy. The picture of you is to remind you that your journey is about you, and most importantly your happiness.

Your vision board is your personal visual reminder of your dreams. There is no right or wrong way to create it and if, like me, you choose to do this every Wheel, you will build your own method of creating them. Personally, I group my images around the picture of me rather like a mind map.

Have fun with this activity. As children, we played with paper and glue, cutting and sticking enjoying the simple pleasure of creating. There is no unspoken rule that says all adult experiences should be serious. So, break out the scissors, glitter, glue and felt tips (these may be hidden somewhere in your child's bedroom) and enjoy!

Eventually you will have your Wheel's vision board. At this time of year, your work is to focus upon these intentions, to make a clear picture within your mind as to the outcome of your efforts.

When working with this process, it is very important that you believe in yourself and your ability to affect change within your life. To work with the Wheel and connect your personal growth with the energy of nature's rhythm, is to step into living consciously and being empowered by that. When you work with the Wheel and natural flow, you take the stance of taking charge of your life. I tell myself, "I know I can create my universe and have the ability to make changes and decisions for the better in my life,"

This can be hard to do at first, but as the Wheel turns to Beltane in May and the summer solstice in June, we will work with loving ourselves, as well as realising and honouring our power. For now, you simply have to accept the fact that you can do this. It is, after all, the first step of the journey and one you in fact already have made by working with this process.

Put your vision board in a place where you can see it every day. I have mine on the front door, so I can be reminded of my dreams every time I go out of the house and every time I come home. It is an empowering and joyful process to look at your board as the Wheel turns and realise that it is you and your efforts that are manifesting your dreams.

A great way to help you believe in your power of manifestation is to write a letter to yourself in your notebook as though you are your future self and have already achieved your goals or are living the lifestyle you dreamt of. Start each sentence with, "I am so happy and grateful now that I have ……….". Imagine how happy and proud you will feel when this is your reality. Use this to remind yourself when you don't think you can get there.

As the Wheel turns from Imbolc to the spring equinox and as you begin to work upon your goals and dreams, think of it as slowly stretching out your wings and trying to fly. By trying, you will get a feeling if this goal is right for your life. It may be that some of your projects are tough to begin with or you have some false starts. That's ok. Remember that, although the first signs of spring are with us, the frost does return throughout February, even the earth has some false starts! It is up to you to decide if this means you should not continue with a particular goal this Wheel or at this point in this Wheel.

Listen to your instinct and inner guidance and trust yourself. You have all the tools inside you to guide you on your path in life, you just need to trust and believe in yourself to follow them. Each day, choose one of your dreams or goals to work upon. Record your progress to help you focus and assess if these actions are right for you. Remember along the way, you will find guidance if you need it so listen for those chance encounters and universal signs and be thankful for them.

A LITTLE HELP TO MANIFEST YOUR GOALS

Obviously, at Imbolc we feel inspired and full of energy. However, during the coming year, you may feel despondent, as though you are not making headway as much or progress with the goals as you imagined. At these times, a little support or boost of energy can help you remain focused. In my time working with a women's circle, we worked with the Imbolc tradition of making or blessing new candles as a way of calling on the inspiring Imbolc energy when we needed it.

We made our candles together and later in the Wheel, at the harder times, we lit our candles to shine a little light into the darkness to help us. I now do this every wheel and bless my candles in my Imbolc ceremony. I have included my favourite method of making candles in the crafting section ff you would like to try this tradition. When you make your Imbolc candles, focus upon your intentions and goals in your vision board for this Wheel.

IMBOLC TRADITIONS

Imbolc Candles

Imbolc, in many spiritual calendars and folklore, is traditionally associated with candles. I believe this is because Imbolc was the time where people would melt down the old candle ends from the long winter indoors and would make new candles for the new part of the Wheel. However, we do know that Alfred the Great created a law that no candle should be lit after Candlemas[67]. Perhaps it was thought that, as the daylight hours should begin to lengthen and so there was less of a need for candles, hence the saying, "You should on Candlemas Day, throw candle and candlestick away." Imbolc survived as Candlemas in the Christian calendar. It was also celebrated by the blessing of candles to bring new light into the home, such as in Wales where candles were blessed at this time and carried throughout the villages in a procession[68].

---

67 Paddy Slade Seasonal Magic Diary of a Village Witch Pg 85
68 Mara Freeman "February the Festival of Imbolc" www.chalicecentre.net

Bride Doll Procession

Around 2000 years ago, Imbolc was a time in Celtic cultures to celebrate the Celtic Goddess Bride or Brigit, later known as St Brighid, whose feast day is on the 1st February[69]. Brigid was the Celtic goddess of inspiration, healing and smith craft, with associations to fire, the hearth and poetry[70].

On Imbolc Eve, Brigid was said to visit households and bless the families. As Brigid represented the light half of the year, and the power that will bring people from the dark season of winter into spring, her presence was very important at this time of year.

The girls of the village would make a "bride doll" out of straw, symbolizing the Goddess/ saint Brighid (Irish) or Bride (Scottish), out of the last sheaf of the previous year's grain harvest, which they would carry from house to house. In this way, they, brought the blessings of Bride and of the fertility of the last year's harvest to every home. The girls collected cakes, bread and butter as they went.

When they were done, they would put the doll into a bed of rushes by a hearth. A stick of birch called a "slachdan" was placed in the bride doll's hands. Brighid, or Bride, was the summer face of the Winter Hag or Cailleach, she who controls the weather. The wand symbolized her magical ability to influence storms and climate[71].

Weather Divination

Imbolc was traditionally a time of weather divination. The Celts believed that the Hag Goddess, the Cailleach; gathered her firewood at Imbolc for the rest of the winter. The folk tale says that if she wanted to prolong the winter, she would make sure Imbolc had good weather, so she could collect all the firewood she needed. Therefore, it stands to reason that people would be relieved if Imbolc was a day of bad weather. This would mean that the Cailleach was asleep and winter was almost over[72]. This old tale is remembered in a Candlemas weather proverb:

If Candlemas day be sunny and bright, Winter again will show its might.
If Candlemas day be cloudy and grey, Winter soon will pass away.
If Candlemas day be fair and bright, Winter will have another flight.
If Candlemas day be shower and rain, Winter is gone and will not come again.

---

69 R.J. Stewart Celtic Gods Celtic Goddesses Pg 96
70 Teresa Moorey. Jane Brideson Wheel of the Year Myth and Magic through the seasons pg 59
71 Alexi Kondratiev Celtic Rituals An authentic guide to ancient Celtic Spirituality pg 140 -143
72 Katharine Briggs,An Encyclopedia of Fairies. pp. 57–60

Imbolc – a Time of Creativity

The Goddess Brigid was also a goddess of creativity[73]. She supports all matters of inspiration and also encourages the continuation and improvement of talent. In the County of Limerick, folklore tells that Brigid visited the household of a chieftain, and asked that his foster father and his sons play the harps that were hanging on the wall. She was told that the chief's bard was away, and the children did not know how to play. Thereupon, she blessed their hands, and they played the harp with such skill that they became famous harpers, and the bards of kings for generations[74].

As the patroness of poetry, she provided the 'fire in the head' of poetic inspiration and was celebrated in poems at Imbolc. Imbolc as a time of creativity is also echoed in Nordic culture as the god of poetry, Braggi, was celebrated in Blot where the Skalds (bards) would tell poetic sagas[75].

Imbolc and Milk

For the Celts, the ewes lactating at Imbolc renewed the dwindling food supply with milk, butter and soft cheese. Milk was traditionally part of the fertility rituals held at Imbolc, blessing the land and animals. Buttermilk was added to the St Bride's Bannocks, the traditional bread baked for Candlemas.

Even though the world has turned from the past to the present day, the ewes still give birth at this time of year. So, for those of you who love dairy products, this is the perfect time to indulge in your favourite dairy treat! (Of course, if you are lactose intolerant or vegan you can use lactose free and soya or nut milk as an alternative.) Although drinking a glass of milk at this time of year may not feel as though you are connecting with nature, you are. Because, drinking it and focusing on why you are drinking, keeps your connection to the natural world, heightening your connection by your conscious awareness.

Dressing Wells and Springs

Water played a significant role in Celtic mysticism and religion[76]. We know that natural springs and wells were honoured as sacred places both in and before the Celtic times and prehistoric times by the archaeological finds of offerings. Water not only symbolises new life, ergo fertility, but is also cleansing and purifying. Visiting the springs also served the practical purpose of making sure that you knew your geographical water sources. Springs and wells were visited at all the Celtic cross quarter festivals and offerings were made for the continuing

---

73 R.J. Stewart Celtic Gods Celtic Goddesses Pg 95–96

74 Patrick Kennedy "St Brigid and the Harps" www.libraryireland.com

75 John Lindow, Handbook of Norse mythology. pp. 12–23

76 Montague Whitsel "Springs and Wells in Celtic Spirituality" www.store.isisbooks.com https://store.isisbooks.com/Springs_and_Wells_s/402.htm

fertility of the land. The practice of offering still exists today in the folk custom of dressing the well with flowers, pictures and, in some places, fabric dipped in the water and hung in the trees. Yearly 'dressing the well' celebrations are held in Derbyshire, Staffordshire and at the Chalice Well in Glastonbury.

CONNECTING WITH THE SEASON

Going Outside

If you haven't been outside much during the winter, Imbolc is the time to take a walk in the first spring light. As always, notice how the world around you has changed. What signs of the coming spring can you see? I find this time of year fascinating. The dream of the summer to come. Each year, this time is different. Sometimes the shoots are far out of the ground, sometimes the trees are just starting to bud. It is wondrous to behold and truly a miracle of the wonderful lives we are blessed with. With the warmth coming back to our bones, we slowly emerge from our winter hibernation, reenergised and ready to begin the work and fun ahead. Take time to reflect upon your journey from winter solstice to now. Before you walk, read through the dreams you collected from after Yule until now. Ask yourself:

- Do these dreams still seem relevant and inspiring now?
- What periods of low energy did you experience?
- How did these points of low energy inspire you to make changes within your life?
- Write your reflections in your journal after your walk.

Release Your Creativity

Imbolc is the time to allow your inner bard, artist, musician or writer loose. Often adults are afraid to dive into their creative natures. Putting up false statements such as "oh I can't draw", the dramas and judgements show us both our creative desires and how much as adults we compare our talents to others. There will always be someone better than us and someone worse than us, with everything in life. It is only your own belief that stops you from opening this part of you. As children, we created without judgement, we created for the pure pleasure of the process.

If you feel as though you are not creative, connect with your inner child and allow it take over for an evening. The results may surprise you and the experience brings with it a reminder of the freedom and joy in experiencing life as we did as a child. A reminder that we stuffy busy grownups really need to play once in a while!

Visit Water

Take a walk to a local well, spring or river. You can leave an offering in the old way by dipping fabric in the water (be careful while you do this!) and hanging it in a nearby tree as a thank you for the first signs of the spring. You could also do a Tree of Life meditation by the water to revive you from your winter's sleep.

Prepare Your Tools

Like the Anglo-Saxons, with the coming of the spring, we also have new work to do. As a gardener, I can truly relate to the idea of preparing my tools and even doing a ceremony to bless my garden for a good harvest. If you would like to try, you could use this Anglo-Saxon blessing prayer:

Erce, erce, erce, Mother of Earth,
May the Almighty, the eternal Lord, grant you,
Fields flourishing and bountiful.
Fruitful and sustaining,
Abundance of bright millet harvests,
And of broad barley harvests.
And of white wheat harvests.
And all the harvests of the Earth!
Grant him, O Eternal Lord,
And his saints in Heaven that be,
That his farm be kept from every foe,
And guarded from each harmful thing,
Of witchcrafts sown throughout the land[77].

However, as a writer, I also know that, at this time of the year, I will probably be really inspired to write. So, a practical way for me to connect with the preparation energy at Imbolc is for me to tidy up my office, getting myself and my space ready for work. The possibilities are endless and personal – try and find yours!

IMBOLC CRAFTS

Make Imbolc Candles

Candles can be made in many different ways – the internet has many options so be as creative as you like. The key to this crafting is immersion. The easiest and most simple candles to make are beeswax rolled candles. Sheets of beeswax and wicks can be easily bought at most hobby suppliers.

---

[77] Diana L. Paxson Taking Up the Runes: A Complete Guide to Using Runes in Spells, Rituals …Pp.124–125

Spiral beeswax candles

Materials:

- Beeswax sheets
- Chopping board
- Hobby knife
- Wick, enough length to make the number of candles (the same height as the edge on your wax sheet plus 2in.)
- Hair dryer, if wax is very hard, although leaving them at room temperature can help solve this without the hair dryer

How to make:

- Place the sheet on a cutting mat and, using a sharp knife, make a diagonal cut from corner to corner
- If the wax is very cold and hard, warm it with a hairdryer to make it soft and pliable (be careful not to warm it too much!)
- Lay the wick along the edge of the beeswax sheet and carefully fold the edge over the wick. Leave 2in. of the wick uncovered at the lighting end of the candle
- Applying even pressure with both hands, begin to roll the candle. Make sure to keep it straight at the bottom of the candle so it will be even when it is completely rolled
- Once the candle has been rolled, gently run your finger along the inside seam of the wax, spirally around the candle, pulling the wax out to create a fluted taper

I do not recommend adding fragrance oils to the beeswax sheet candles as the natural scent of the beeswax is quite strong and will blend with whatever scent you add, creating a different aroma from that which you may desire. Never put scent directly on the wick. This will cause the candle to smoke. If you want to add some scent, either add a drop to the pool of melted wax while the candle is burning or add a few drops along the sheet while rolling it (only in honeycomb sheets as the cell structure will hold the scent).

This the simplest way of making candles. However, if you look online there are many ways for you to try, such as recycled or dip candles.

However you make your candles do remember to use them throughout the year. Only yesterday I had a moment of doubt in my ability to reach my goals this Wheel. I was tired, stressed and unable to think positively no matter what I tried. Eventually, I lit my candle and went about my home trying to achieve manageable small victories, such as the washing up. By the end of the evening, I felt lighter and recharged. I once again believed I can create my reality.

MAKE A BRIGID'S CROSS

A traditional craft at this time of year in Ireland is the making of Brigid's crosses to honour the goddess Brigid[78]. The crosses are hung at the door to welcome Brigid into the home. The Brigid's cross can be considered a Christian symbol for protection. However, I make them to remind me of the four pathways from my sacred grove.

(Both the ends of the candles and the Brigid's cross can be burned before the next Imbolc.)

How to Make a Brigid's Cross

You will need:

- 12 or 16 reeds or straws 16 inches long
- 4 pieces of string 6 inches long

How to Make:

- Get at least 12 pieces of reed or straw (16 is better). Take the shortest one and hold upright.
- Take a second straw and fold it in the middle
- Wrap the second straw around the first straw at the centre so that it opens to your right. Pull it tight
- Rotate it 90 degrees counter-clockwise, holding it at the centre where the straws come together
- Take a third straw and wrap it around the second straw so that it is opens to your right. Pull it tight
- Rotate it 90 degrees counter-clockwise, holding it at the centre where the straws come together
- Take a fourth straw and wrap it around the third straw so that it opens to your right. Pull it tight
- Rotate it 90 degrees counter-clockwise, holding it at the centre where the straws come together

---

[78] Courtney Weber Brigid: History, Mystery, and Magick of the Celtic Goddess pp. 160 -161

IMBOLC – INFINITE NEW BEGINNINGS AND POSSIBILITIES

- Take a fifth straw and fold it around the fourth straw so that it opens to your right. Pull it tight
- Repeat this process until at least 12 straws are used
- You will always be adding a straw at the top so it opens to your right, then turning the entire thing 90 degrees counter-clockwise, and repeating ("add to the right, turn to the left")
- Secure the ends of the arms of the cross with the string and trim the ends of the straws so that they're even

Imbolc Journey

In the last turnings of the Wheel we have journeyed underground to our cave and explored the underworld. Now as the Wheel turns towards spring and the light, it is time to journey to the middle worlds to find our sacred grove. The purpose of your journey is to ask for any guidance about the work you have to come during this Wheel.

If you meet someone or something you are unsure of, simply ask it three times, "are you here in love and light?" If it is not, it will go away.

Now it is time to take your Imbolc journey….. Remember, be clear as to why you are journeying...

Breathe deeply and slowly, sitting or lying in a comfortable position. Make sure you're warm enough and have a glass of water close by. As you breathe feel your surroundings slip away as you cocoon yourself in a safe protective circle.

In your mind, begin to see yourself standing high on a hill. It is daytime, the pale sunlight glimmers from the frost on the ground and the air is fresh, filled with birdsong and the sense of spring and warmth just around the corner.

As you walk further up you become aware that high up on the hill a lone tree stands. An ancient oak. The branches bear no leaves but you can see buds just starting to open, snowdrops grow around the trunk and the oak stands strong as you walk in a circle around the tree.

At the bottom of the oak, almost hidden in the trunk you can see a wooden door, half covered with ivy. Slowly you walk towards the door. It opens with a creak and you can make out dimly lit stairs spiralling up into the tree and spiralling down. Tentatively, you begin to make your way up the stairs. To each side of you is earth and roots. You can smell the musty damp of the rich fertile soil around you.

Further and further up you travel until, in the middle of the tree, you find a door of gnarled and aged wood, the stairs continue upwards but this is not your journey today. Slowly you open this ancient door. As it opens, a bright white spring light fills the space around you and you step out into a wide-open field, on the horizon you can see a knoll of trees. You walk towards the trees, breathing deeply the fresh air, enjoying the birdsong. This world is similar to our own yet somehow more alive, more vivid and more beautiful.

WALK YOUR PATH

At the entrance to the woods you pause, see if you have a guide awaiting you. If you meet someone or something, greet them politely and listen to what they have to say. If no guide appears, take time to ask for permission to enter the woods. This place is special secret and ancient.

As you enter the woods you will see a path clearly outlined by tall trees and you know that you need to follow this path. You find yourself walking along the path, almost dreamlike, almost floating. At the end of the path you find a circle of trees with three paths coming away at the cross quarters.

What do you see? Walk into your grove, explore the circle but do not yet take one of the paths. Enjoy just being in this special space. It is yours and you can return here whenever you wish. Here you are safe and you are loved. Maybe you have guests within your grove, people, animals, ancestors, the fey and nature spirits can all enter your grove to connect with you and give you messages. If you find beings, talk with them, connect.

Take this time to be in your grove, there will be time to explore the pathways another time.

Remember the purpose of your journey is to find guidance for the work to come, ask your guests if they have a message for you. If you have no guests ask your grove for guidance.

Explore for a while alone.

* * *

Take time now to contemplate the journey you have taken. Give thanks for the new knowledge you have gained. When the time is right for you, take one last look at your grove. This place is always here you can always find it again.

It is time to return.

Walk through the woods and back towards the oak tree until you reach the door. Open the door to the staircase spiralling up and down and smell the rich soil once more.

Once again, you travel down to the doorway where you entered (not down to your cave). Walk away from the tree. As you stand on the hill, you can see that the frost has retreated and the air feels warmer than before.

* * *

Slowly become aware of the place in which your body lies or sits and allow your spirit self to step into your body and become one again. Gently allow the circle to slip away and bring yourself back to consciousness.

Drink some water, record your journey and get some fresh air. With your Imbolc journey it is a good idea to reflect over the goals you have made and maybe adjust them if you got a clear guidance within your journey.

From now until spring equinox return to your grove. You can begin to explore the various paths or simply use it as place to recharge, centre yourself and focus on you and your life.

IMBOLC CEREMONY

Here is a simple ceremony that you can use to inspire your own ceremony.

Put the altar in the north
Walk the circle three times imagining a boundary of pure energy.

"A time that is not a time, in a place that is not a place".

At the north point of the circle, invite the elements of earth.
At the east point of the circle, invite the elements of air.
At the south point of the circle, invite the elements of fire.
At the west point of the circle, invite the elements of water.
Within the centre, invite spirit and the ancestors.

"The light grows strong once more in the land.
Under the snow, the pulse of life quickens.
Feel the Earth beneath you, the new life quickening.
May we share in the great cycle of the universe.
And blossom with new life and creativity."

"As we move forward on the Wheel of the Year and move ever closer to spring, I ask the universe for help in manifesting my dreams for this season."

Speak out loud about your goals and how you've planned to accomplish them.

"As I work toward these goals, and as we travel toward the spring, I ask that you help me stay focused and move forward, and remember to honour myself, my family and mother earth while I do so."

Lay your candles in front of you and raise energy from the earth.

Drawing energy from the earth will help connect you closer to the Earth. To draw energy from the earth, clear your mind and then visualize energy coming up through the earth as a green coloured ball. See it rise slowly each time you inhale, until it reaches your feet. Then visualize it enter through your feet into you and travel up to your stomach. From there, visualize it dispersing throughout your body and mixing with your own personal energy. After it mixes a few moments, bring it back to your stomach where it forms a multicoloured ball. Again, you might feel a full or bubbly feeling, and this is natural. Take your time and spend however long you need to fully visualize everything as clearly as possible.

Think of the different goals and intentions you have. When the pictures of your goals and intentions are clear, send the energy from your stomach, up through your arms and into the candles. As you do this, repeat the rhyme three times:

"Candle bright, burning fire,
Shine within me and inspire.
Listen to the words I speak,

And clear a path to what I seek.
Let my dreams all come true,
As they burn so bright with you!"

Sometimes, if I am alone, then I will do a journey at this point in my ceremony. In a group, we often dance or sing to bring our energy up.

   To close my ceremony alone or in a group, I share cakes and wine.

   Thank the elements, guides and my ancestors, for joining you and walk the circle round in the opposite direction at the start.

Now it's time to celebrate Imbolc!

> *Amidst winter's brazen, bitter light,*
> *A promise of Spring bursts into sight.*
> *Snowdrops overcome the winter's cold,*
> *And gently life begins to unfold.*
>
> *Energised we wake from hibernation,*
> *Exhilarated, for the time of creation.*
> *Our souls inspired, dreams brew and bubble,*
> *We discard all of our winter's troubles.*
>
> *We begin to plan the year ahead,*
> *What seeds to pant, which roads to tread.*
> *With the growing warmth our path is clearer,*
> *As each day light grows, and spring draws nearer.*
> *The Wheel turns ...*

CHAPTER 8

Ostara and the Spring equinox – Birth and Balance

The spring equinox also known as Ostara celebrates the birth of spring and is a point of balance in the Wheel of the Year. At Imbolc, it was a time for the birth of the land. Ostara, the second of the fertility festivals, is a time for the birth of animals. Wherever we look, new life surrounds us. The colour has come back to the land with daffodils, crocuses. The spring has well and truly arrived. Each day, as new life is born the land grows stronger, more alive. In the fields and gardens, the last of the winter debris is cleared away, the earth turned and farrowed ready for the seeds to be planted. The conception of the crops to be harvested in the late summer. This is a time of cleaning, planting and bringing into existence life itself. In the solar calendar the spring equinox is one of two points in the year when day and night are equal length, balance in the wheel. At the spring equinox, we move from the dark to the light. Winter is truly behind us and from this point forwards, everything begins to move faster, as if the equinox is the spurt of growth-energy we and nature need to birth our projects, do the work and create.

HISTORY OF OSTARA

We know very little about the historical Ostara or the pre-Christian spring equinox holidays of Northern and Western Europe. The pre-Celtic inhabitants of the British Isles likely observed the spring equinox, as their surviving megaliths are aligned on a solar basis. But there is no clear evidence that the spring equinox received any special attention by the pre-Christian Celts[79], and no reference to Ostara itself can be found before 725 CE in the writings of the Christian monk Bede[80].

According to the Venerable Bede, Eostre was the Saxon version of a Germanic goddess called Ostara. Both of whom were goddesses of spring.

---
79 Alexi Kondratiev Celtic Rituals An authentic guide to Celtic Spirituality Pg. 149
80 Faith Wallis, (Trans.) Bede: The Reckoning of Time. Pp.53–54

Their feast day was held on the full moon following the spring equinox–almost the identical calculation as for the modern-day Christian Easter in the west which is calculated by the Moon. There is very little documented evidence to prove this, but one popular legend is that Eostre found a bird, wounded, on the ground late in winter. To save its life, she transformed it into a hare. But, "the transformation was not a complete one. The bird took the appearance of a hare but retained the ability to lay eggs...the hare would decorate these eggs and leave them as gifts to Eostre." Which may be the foundation of the modern-day Easter bunny!

We know from archaeological and historical records that the spring equinox has been significant throughout human history. Many ancient Indo-European and near-eastern religions, with the Romans, Persians and Babylonians, all began their calendar years around this time[81]. Ancient temples around the world were built in alignment with equinox sunrise. This can be found in the Stone Age temples of Knowth and Loughcrew in Ireland, where the light fills a 100 ft passage that lets the sunlight in to illuminate one of the chambers on the equinox dawn. Similarly, the Mayans, Egyptians and the ancient Celts built temples aligning to the four solar festivals[82]. The Mayan ruins, Chichen Itza in Mexico, one of the most famous sites to celebrate the spring equinox around the world. On the day of both the spring equinox and the autumnal equinox sunlight bathes the western side of the El Castillo pyramid's main stairway, creating seven triangles making a shadow that imitates the body of a 120 foot long rattlesnake that creeps downwards until it joins a huge serpent's head at the bottom of the stairway[83]. Scholars believe certain rites of agriculture may have been the basis for the design and concept of El Castillo.

The link between spring equinox and agriculture is still apparent today. In agriculture, the number of daylight hours are an important factor in deciding when to plant crops. This is because many plants require a specific amount of incoming solar radiation for germination. The date of the equinox helps farmers decide when the best time for planting will be. At spring equinox today, as in days past, the land is furrowed and the seeds are planted for summer wheat crops.

Playing so much importance throughout human history, it is unsurprising that today we still celebrate the spring equinox under the guise of Easter. There are many different ways to celebrate Ostara all over the world. However, most traditions include the symbols of the egg and the hare.

---

81 IDEA "Other Ancient Calendars" www.webexhibits.org
82 Danu Forest The Magical Year Pg. 53
83 Ivan Šprajc, Nava Sánchez Francisco Pedro "El Sol en Chichén Itzá y Dzibilchaltún: la supuesta importancia de los equinoccios en Mesoamérica". Arqueología Mexicana. XXV (149): Pp. 26–31.

SPRING CLEANING

In the social history of Ostara, this time of year is traditionally associated with "the spring clean". In my opinion, this tradition arises from the time when we had been staying inside the longhouses during the winter. With the arrival of spring and the new light, more time can be spent outdoors therefore it was time to clean out the house to make space for the new food and materials to be stored after the harvest.

The concept of the spring clean is so deeply ingrained in the human psyche that you can find examples all over the world. Where this tradition originates from no one really knows. It has been claimed by some that the practice of spring cleaning originated in Iran, or that maybe there is a biological and historical explanation as to why we spring clean.

Shaking the house clean in Iran

Iran celebrates their New Year with festivals, customs, rituals and symbolism that date back before the country's current Islamic culture. The day of the spring equinox, 21 March, is the day when Iranians celebrate Nowruz (Persian New Year). For two weeks, Iranians adorn their streets and houses with symbols of burning and planting to signify renewal. It's a time for refreshing, a process that is perhaps most apparent in the tradition of khooneh takouni – 'shaking the house' – a custom that apparently lives up to its name[84].

Khooneh takouni is a vigorous spring cleaning ritual. Iranians buy new clothes to wear and every corner of the family home is scoured and cleaned; nothing is missed. The scent of flowers in vases clears the air of stale odours and every household item from the rugs, curtains, bedding, floors, ceilings, windows, cupboards and shelves, down to the last ornament, receives a thorough cleaning. Once the house has been 'shaken', the Nowruz can start and spring can arrive again.

Cleaning for survival – a biological trigger

Some schools of thought suggest that the spring cleaning habit predates all cultures, with a trigger found in our biological makeup. During the shorter days of winter with less sunlight exposure, our pineal gland produces more melatonin -a hormone that induces sleepiness. Ancient humans' lack of exposure to light would have led their bodies and minds to become slower. As the days grew longer in March, the increased exposure to light caused melatonin levels to drop and energy levels to recover. During the long winter, dirt will have gathered in the home. As spring brought warmer temperatures, bacteria would begin to grow, so spring cleaning was necessary to prevent infection and disease.

---

84   Real Iran "Iranians Welcome Nowruz with Spring Cleaning" www.realiran.org http://realiran.org/iranians-welcome-nowruz-spring-cleaning/

GROWING WITH THE SEASON

Taking Action to Manifest Your Goals

"The gods help those that help themselves" is one of my favourite expressions inherited from my Mum and tweaked by me. Results often come easily and readily when working in harmony with the Wheel. However, nothing in life happens without your own energetic contribution. You can sit, pray and visualise your goals, asking the universe for what you want, but if you do not take action yourself nothing will ever change. After spring equinox comes the growth spurt in nature. If you don't believe me take a walk once a week after spring equinox and you will be amazed at how quickly leaves and blossoms appear on the trees, baby animals grow, and plants shoot up from the earth.

For me, taking action to manifest my goals is a six step process. It may seem strange to you that there is so much preparation involved in me actually working on my goals. But experience has taught me that the old adage 'preparation prevents'.... yada yada yada, you know how it goes; is ultimately true. Following this six step formula will mean that you manifest your goals and be able to appreciate and celebrate your successes along the way.

Step 1 – Spring Cleaning
At Ostara, we begin to work with our personal goals in earnest. And, although it might seem strange place to start, is with a clearing. Or in other words, a good spring clean. Following in our ancestors' footsteps. Although spring cleaning your home may seem like an arduous and strange task to be doing to help us tune into nature, it is in fact bringing us home into the cycle's rhythm.

Every new piece of work takes some clearing and preparation to begin. Just as in the garden the winter beds need to be cleared for the new plants coming, we need to clear out the dirt, dust and debris of winter to make room for the new growth we are creating within our lives.

I find that when we tidy around ourselves, we also tidy within ourselves (and in times of mind turmoil and confusion, cleaning something can be the achievable task that gets you through the day). So, grab a duster, chuck out the old bills you have no use for and, if you want a good cleansing after all that hard work, book yourself into a spa day. After all, cleaning doesn't have to be all hard work!

Step 3 – Evaluating Your Goals
Now with the bad fortune and bacteria swept away from your home, it is time to really get going on your goals for this Wheel. From Imbolc to Ostara, you will (hopefully) have been trying out and testing the waters with your projects, goals and dreams that you wove into your vision board at Imbolc. As I mentioned at Imbolc, the awakening energy is extremely inspirational. However, that can sometimes lead to being overly optimistic in our goal setting process.

- Look again at your vision boards. Ask yourself:
- What projects have started to work?
- Have any projects been challenging to begin?
- Have you forgotten any of your dreams? Which projects have been flowing naturally?
- Have you had any success so far? Or are you finding it difficult to focus and create the visions you set for yourself?

It may be that you notice that some things are working better than others. Check in with yourself by asking, is this because you are not really passionate or motivated to achieve this particular goal? Maybe it is not the right time to be working on that particular goal. It may be better to start it later in the Wheel or, in fact, at another point in your life.

Ultimately, here I am asking you to be realistic with yourself and your goals. Speaking from experience, I know this is easy to do. Nothing is more demotivating than setting yourself up for a fail. So, it is important to check in and evaluate objectively.

In your journal, write these questions and reflect over the answers. It is important from now on that you can hold your vision clearly and that you know exactly what you want to do. Ostara is action time. We all have only 24 hours a day, 7 days a week, and a certain amount of energy. So, it simply makes sense to make sure we are using our time and energy in a way that will be effective.

Step 4 – Believing You Can Do it, or Just Doing it Anyway
First things first, one of the most important factors in taking action is believing that your actions will make a difference. Believing it is possible to change your life. When you take action, you take control. You cease to be a human being and become a human doing. This can challenge all of our falsely constructive beliefs about our lack of ability to change our life. Part of the Ostara teaching is simply getting on with it anyway, despite the hurdles you have to overcome. No matter how small or limited you believe your abilities to be.

I know you can do this, and you can achieve your goals. If you don't believe me just look at the mustard seed.

Mustard seeds are the smallest seeds I have ever seen. A mustard seed is so small that if you were holding one in your hand and dropped it on the ground, you might not be able to find it. Even though the mustard seed is one of the smallest of all seeds, when it is planted in the ground, it grows into a plant so large that birds can perch on its branches and can even build their nests in it. These tiny seeds can produce a plant that grows ten feet high or more!

For our projects and ourselves to flourish, grow and blossom we need faith, we need to believe in ourselves as much as a mustard seed does.

For now, say no to all of your negative and limiting beliefs. Remove the word 'impossible' from your thoughts and replace it with 'possible'. Your mind believes what you tell it to believe. My mother always taught me "where there is a will there's a way", and as mothers tend to be, she was right. Believe, do, and the way becomes open.

Step 5 – Planning Your Actions
Probably the MOST IMPORTANT step towards manifesting your goals, is planning the actions you will take. This can sometimes be very confusing. You know what you want but haven't got a clue how to get there. The vision you are holding may seem daunting. For example, your goal may be to create a healthy economy but you feel that you are stuck in a job you hate.

As Lao Tzu said, "the journey of a thousand miles begins with a single step". He could have legitimately added and a lot of planning. Now it's time to translate all your dreams into practical actions, to make your plan and follow it. Step by step.

The guidelines for the actions you will take will keep you earthed and rooted on your journey, as well as nourishing your motivation. Ultimately, to succeed, remember to keep your plans simple, practical and achievable.

Now, to get to work. For each of your goals, you need to brainstorm / plan the dedicated actions you will take to manifest it. This makes it easy to measure your progress and keep on track.

Now say your dream is to travel to another country in this Wheel, you can break it down into actions as follows:

1. Decide where I want to go.
2. Find out how much it will cost to go there.
3. Save the money to go.
4. Book the holiday or flights.
5. Go there.

Of course, this process is easier with very practical goals. However, with more abstract goals, it can be more challenging.

For example, if your goal is to love yourself more and be more self-confident, it may seem harder to make into step by step actions. You have to really think and dig deep to break this down into actions. It could be that you will need to investigate why it is you have the lack of self-love and confidence in the first place? Or you may need to look at what does self-confidence mean to you. One client I worked with saw Lady Gaga as the epitome of self-confidence. She looked at what she admires in Lady Gaga and chose actions based on those, such as daring to wear something she thought was outrageous. Another person I worked with wanted to stop putting others before himself and came up with the following plan:

1. Do daily affirmations reinforcing my self-worth.
2. Take time each week to do something good for myself, e.g. take a bubble bath or go for a walk in nature.
3. Set myself boundaries of how much I am going to help people in my life and how much I will concentrate on me and my life.

Make an action plan for each of your goals and keep it somewhere you can return to regularly, to keep a check of your progress and remind yourself what it is you actually wanted to get done.

Step 6 – Get On With it Already!
Like a farmer planning his crops, you know what you want. You have done the preparation. So now it is just time to get on with it. Begin to follow your action plans. Spring is in full swing. No more hibernation, it is a time of action so get moving!

Aim to work on one of your goals each day or each week. Once you have completed a step, check it off on your plan and move forward. Keep a note of your progress, mentally or physically. Some people prefer using an app or an online document. For me, I like the old fashioned process of paper and pen.

Whilst working on your goals for the rest of the Wheel, change your planning if something is not working and stopping you from moving forward. Nature's process is naturally adapting, sometimes it fights for growth, but is never forced. Trust your instincts. If you feel as though you are forcing something, look at why. It could be this doesn't benefit you. Trust your instincts. When you listen to yourself and know what you want you will always make the right decisions. Remember to use your Imbolc candles if you need inspiration when it gets tough. I have burnt a few on the way to creating this book!

If you hit a bump in the road, relax, take a break from that project and work on something else. Or just relax. Remember, everything works out alright in the and if it's not alright, it's not the end.

The Lesson of the Hare

Equal opposites are one of the major themes at equinox. Storms and darkness, as well as light and calm, are part of the journey of our lives and of the natural world. As the storms and rains will surely come in April, we will have challenging times ahead in our goal manifestation process. It is par for the course. At the same time, part of the process of manifesting dreams leads to us having to make sacrifices. Sacrifices are challenging, to greater or lesser degrees. There are times where we will need encouragement and inspiration to continue.

One of the wonderful Ostara sights is seeing the hares dancing in the fields. The hare has a long-associated history with the Spring equinox and many legends and traditions associate hares with this time of year. Where I grew up in Wales we believe in the importance of stories. Every life situation and season has a tale that can inspire us and for me this West country Ostara tale always reminds me of the importance of making sacrifices and brings me inspiration to keep working on my goals.

The Story of the Hare and the Egg

Once upon a time, the animal kingdom gathered together for a meeting in a flurry of excitement. There was to be a very special party and a very special guest was coming to visit them. The very special guest was none other than the Goddess herself, and every creature wanted to give her a Very special gift.

Now, some of the animals were rich and some were poor but off they went to prepare their gifts, for only the best would do for the Goddess. Hare was excited. He dearly loved the Goddess and, although poor, he had a generous heart – he was going to give her the very finest gift he could find!

Hare rushed home to see what he could find to give to the Goddess – he looked everywhere, on the shelves and under the bed but there was nothing, even the larder was empty. He had absolutely nothing to give her. Except for one thing. On the shelf in the larder was a single egg, and that was it. It was the only thing he had left. Hare gently took the egg out of the larder and lovingly decorated it and took it to the party.

Hare was very worried, as all the other animals gave their gifts of gold and silver and all Hare had was the egg. Eventually, all the gifts had been given and Hare was the very last. Hare shyly presented the Goddess with the egg. She took it and looked at him and saw the true spirit of Hare. Then and there, the Goddess appointed Hare as her special animal – because Hare had given away everything he had...

And by giving all he had, he humbly created a beautiful path for himself and all hares.

For me, this story reminds me, that even if I feel I have very little to give, when I give it all, I give everything I have towards manifesting a project, goal or dream. Life, the Universe, will help and appreciate me. Sometimes we have to have the challenges to appreciate the reward, or give something up to make space for something new. Maybe you find a different teaching in this story. After all, stories affect us all differently.

STRENGTHENING YOUR VISION – A POWERFUL MANIFESTATION TOOL

Visualisation is one of the most powerful processes to support goal manifestation. Many elite athletes routinely use visualisation techniques as part of training and competition.

Visualisation has also been called, 'mental rehearsal'. It is the process of creating a mental image or intention of what you want to happen or feel in reality. So, an athlete might mentally go through the race and see themselves winning the gold. Remember, everything man-made in our world began as a thought inside a human being. In a nutshell, we know that visualisation works.

Visualisation works best as a daily practice to support the actions you are going to take to manifest your goals. You can choose to visualise the outcome of achieving your goal, or you can choose to visualise the positive outcome action you will take that day.

How to visualise what you want:

1. Close your eyes and think of the goal.
2. Concentrate on the image of the positive outcome of your goal, not the steps you will have to take.
3. Take several deep breaths.
4. Visualize the object or situation you desire in your mind, as clearly and with as much detail as you can.
5. Add emotion, feeling and your senses to your vision.
6. Hold the vision for 2 – 5 minutes.

WORKING WITH THE MOON AND MANIFESTATION

Spring equinox is the time of both equal day and night, equal sun and moon. It might be considered rude to not mention the Moon and lunar energy at this time.

Within many religious traditions, the Moon is still remembered and recognised as a powerful influence within our lives. To Buddhists, the Moon has significance because events connected with the life of Lord Buddha took place on full moon days. His birth and his renunciation, his enlightenment, the delivery of his first sermon and his passing away were all on the full moon[85].

Whereas in modern day Wicca, the Moon is worshipped as a goddess, the different phases of the lunar cycle representing the different stages of life.

Scientists now know that the Moon affects the liquid envelope of the Earth, and the oceanic tides in particular[86]. If you would take away the Moon suddenly, it would change the global altitude of the ocean. Right now, there is a distortion which is elongated around the equator, so if we didn't have this effect, suddenly a lot of water would be redistributed toward the polar regions.

The Moon is a stabilizing factor for the axis of rotation of the Earth. It stabilizes our planet so that its axis of rotation stays in the same direction. For this reason, we had much less climatic change than if the Earth had been alone. For centuries, it has been believed that the Moon has an effect on humans. So far, scientists have not proved or disproved that to be true. What is a fact is the

---

85 Venerable K. Sri Dhammananda Maha Thera "The Moon and Religious Observances" www.budsas.org https://www.budsas.org/ebud/whatbudbeliev/217.htm
86 Bernard Foing "If We Had No Moon" www.astrobio.net

effect that the Moon has on nature and, to my reasoning, if it affects nature, it will affect us as we are, in my opinion, just another form of animal life on Earth.

I have found that, just as there are solar times that energetically are the best time to begin working on your dreams, projects and goals, there are equally times within the lunar cycle which affect the manifestation process. Simply put, some points in the lunar cycle are better for starting and working on projects than others. The guidelines for working with the Moon are simple, however, do remember these are guidelines from my experience, not dogma to be strictly followed. If this works for you do it, if not don't).

New moon: Is a time of beginnings, renewed energy. A good time to begin working on something new or to renew your energy in ongoing work.

Full moon: This is the moon at the time of greatest power. Reflecting that this is a time where you will be focusing your maximum effort into your work.

Waning moon: As the Moon decreases in our skies, take this as a chance to relax, evaluate and allow the ebb and flow of the universe to assist your work.

Dark moon: As the Moon takes a break, take a break yourself. You cannot always be on task, it is good to give yourself a chance to rest, recharge and renew.

If you choose to, you could incorporate the lunar phases into your goal manifestation process to see if that gives you the energetic boost to complete your goals in a powerful and natural way.

SPRING EQUINOX DARK TO LIGHT AND BALANCE – OUR RELATIONSHIP WITH OUR SHADOW

The equinoxes area a very important time, in terms of our relationship with the Wheel of the Year, with the yearly solar cycle and with ourselves. It is when the Sun is directly over the equator, one of the two times in the Wheel where night and day are equal in length. In some respects, spring starts to really "kick in" after the spring equinox. The growth in the land and the changes become less sloth like and begin to speed up.

The equinoxes are the times between the balance point before a transition and, as they approach, we are reminded of the need for balance in our lives. In order to have balance in our lives and, most importantly within ourselves, we have to accept ourselves. Our entire self. The good and the bad. Our light self and our shadow self. Just as we are. For me, both the spring and autumn equinox are the perfect point in the Wheel to reconnect with myself and accept myself just as I am.

At the spring equinox, we transition from the dark half of the year to the light. I believe that, in order to truly accept our light self, we must first accept, acknowledge and integrate our darker self. Our shadow self. By working with understanding, accepting and integrating our shadow self at the spring equinox we can truly step into and own the light aspects of our personalities. For me this is one of the most essential parts of the journey of connecting and reflecting our personal growth to the Wheel's rhythm.

What is the shadow self?

Your shadow self is a part of yourself that has been in the dark for a very long time. To paraphrase Carl Jung, it is the part of us that we really don't want to be[87]. It is, in essence, the part of us we do not like. The part we are ashamed of or like to hide.

People often see the shadow self as something bad or something to cure. But without dark there would not be light. We need both dark and light to grow.

Our shadow self offers us insights into our very being on a deep level. Why we are, who we are and what makes us tick. Our shadows are our deepest, darkest secrets, and our deepest fears, there is strength to be found in these dark places. To understand your shadow is to understand yourself. Accepting your shadow as a part of you is a truly empowering process.

However, this takes work, patience and bravery. You have to be brave to face your shadow. You need patience. This journey will take, and should take, time. You cannot do it all at once, not in one Wheel. It takes work to accept your shadow self. Peeling back the layers of understanding as each Wheel turns. This is by no means an easy process. If you want to work with accepting your shadow self, you need to be non-judgmental, willing to forgive and be merciful towards yourself.

Embracing the shadow self ultimately is to embrace that you are perfectly imperfect and that is your strength, not your weakness.

Working with Embracing Your Shadow Self

The key to this work is integration. Many people believe that, by working with themselves, their shadow self will disappear. It won't, the shadow self, and our lighter self, have to be integrated to be whole. To integrate an inner quality is to take ownership and responsibility for it, rather than rejecting or denying it.

Identify your shadow self

A good place to start is to identify your shadow self. In "The Mindfulness Solution," Siegel provides a simple exercise to begin this process[88].

- Make a list of 5 **positive** qualities that you see yourself as having (e.g. being compassionate, generous, witty, etc.)

- Look at each positive quality that you wrote down – describe its **opposite** (e.g. being unfeeling, stingy, dull, etc.)

- Picture a person who embodies these negative qualities vividly in your mind

---

87 Adler G Hull EFC The collected works of CG Jung Complete Digital Edition Practice of Psychotherapy Vol 16 Pp. 53–75
88 Ronald. D. Siegel, The mindfulness solution: everyday practices for everyday problems. Pg 224

Roughly, this is your shadow self. The version of you which you don't want to be and secretly feel you are.

Another way to identify your shadow self is to see the reflection of your shadow self in another person. A person you don't like.

We have all met people that irritate us. Sometimes we can meet someone who we take an instant dislike to. Unconsciously and without knowing it, this person is mirroring or reflecting something back to you. Something you dislike about yourself. When we dig deeper than the surface of not liking them, we often find that it resonates with things within yourself that you dislike or which lie within your shadow self.

Try to mindfully pay attention to each time someone around you does something, says something, or "is" a certain way that irritates you or upsets you. When you notice that someone is affecting you negatively (or getting under your skin), try this process:

- Make a list of the qualities that you vehemently dislike in this person
- Why are these certain qualities so bothersome to you?
- What is it about yourself that you dislike that you can see reflected in the other person?

You don't necessarily need to do anything with this information. Just examining, becoming aware, and owning these parts of you allows shadow integration to begin to occur. If you are feeling brave, you can take this exercise to the next level and investigate deeper.

Try arranging some time with a person who challenges you the most in your life. Be honest explain that you are challenged by them and you understand that this is a reflection of a part of you that you are not comfortable with. It is here you need to ask for their help to work out this issue within you (I did say you needed to be brave). Make sure you put emphasis on your gratitude for their help. Ask if they are also challenged by you. Talk together and try to find what challenges you about each other and honour each other, for telling it to each other. This may seem like a frightening and overwhelming exercise. In practise, and when open and honest, this is an empowering and enlightening experience.

Accepting and Integrating the Shadow Self

Once you have identified your shadow self, you are ready to work on accepting your shadow self. This can be an ongoing life process. However, once accepted, you will find that, as you integrate your shadow self, you have a strength. By facing your fears, you own them. By acknowledging that your personally judged negative qualities are part and parcel of you, you begin to integrate and accept yourself more.

There are many ways to accept your shadow self. Creativity is one of the most therapeutic methods, for example, writing, painting and dancing with your shadow self. You can also use meditation, breathwork, walks in nature or any other way that makes you connect with your inner self/higher self.

The most powerful exercise I use is to write my shadow self a letter using a process called automatic writing.

On a sheet of paper or in your journal, write:

- Please reveal to me what I am not seeing about myself... about my relationship, my work, my ability to earn more money (any issue you want answers or information about)
- Also write; "please answer me through my pen"
- On the next line, write "Dear _____" (your name)
- Take a few more breaths and start writing anything that comes through your pen

Don't look for anything to make sense. Just let a stream of thought come through your pen. When the stream of thought ends, read what you have written. You might be surprised. When working with your shadow self, I recommend practicing automatic writing often. The more you do it, the clearer the messages become.

Wholeness, personal power, unbounded creative energy – these are the gifts of shadow work. When you know your shadow, you know yourself. As you begin to know, accept and integrate your shadow self, you will find you begin to find balance.

During this work, the most important thing to remember is that, in nature nothing is bad, nothing is good, it just is. We are part of nature, so there is nothing bad or good within us, we just are. Our shadow and our light is not bad or good. It just is. We just are.

TRADITIONS

Ostara and Eggs

Ostara is the second of the fertility festivals in the modern Wheel of the Year, celebrating the births in the animal kingdom. It is a time of lambs and chicks. Animal's fertility roles can be overlooked when working with nature. People often tend to think of nature as just the land and forget the life part.

Eggs are a traditional symbol of Ostara representing fertility and reproduction. Eggs (as well as all seeds) contain 'all potential'. For me the symbology of the Ostara egg reminds and reconnects us with this time of birth in the animal's Wheel of the Year.

An egg is a symbol full of promise and new life. It symbolises the fertility of the Earth and all Creation. In some traditions, the egg is a symbol for the whole Universe. The 'cosmic' egg contains a balance of male and female, light and dark, in the egg yolk and egg white. In another interpretation, the golden orb of the yolk is seen to represent the Sun God held by the White Goddess. So, the egg can be said to be a particularly appropriate symbol for Ostara and the spring equinox, when the world is in balance for just a moment, with the underlying energy being one of growth, potential and expansion.

In some parts of Scandinavia and Ireland, people still put eggs out in the holes and crevices of standing stones as an offering to encourage fertility and a good harvest. Another egg tradition which remains in many Scandinavian and European countries, is the art of egg painting. This tradition lies deep in the realms of human history and the oldest examples are over 5,000 years old: eggs with decorations were found in Assyria, ancient Mesopotamia[89].

Today in Poland, the Easter eggs or Pisanki are painted with motifs that have a deep symbolic meaning, connected to rebirth, fertility, beauty, protection and sun symbolism (vitality). I like to incorporate this practice into my goal manifestation process. Not only is it great to refocus, it can also become a wonderful tradition that brings you closer to the turning of the seasons.

Needless to say, there are endless egg traditions around the world today that people use to celebrate Easter and Ostara.

Gækkebrev (Fools letter)

Since at least 1660 in Denmark the Easter tradition is to send a gækkebreve, a fool's letter. The rules of a gækkebrev are simple. You cut out a gækkebrev in a similar form to paper snowflakes and write a rhyme which hints at who it is from and has dots representing the number of letters in the sender's name. Then leave it where it can easily be found. If you cannot guess the sender of the gækkebreve then you have to give a gift. If you guess the sender then it is them that gives the gift, usually an Easter egg[90].

The most common rhyme used in a Gækkebrev is

Gæk, gæk, gæk – Mit navn det står med prikker pas på det ikke stikker!

Guess, guess, guess – my name is in the dots be careful they don't sting!

Egg Rolling

Egg rolling has been a traditional activity for hundreds of years. In the United Kingdom, the tradition of rolling decorated eggs down hills goes back hundreds of years and is known as "pace-egging". It takes place on Easter Sunday or Monday, where decorated hard-boiled eggs are rolled down a slope until they are cracked and broken, then they are eaten by their owners. Of course, in some places this can be a competitive game! In Germany, prizes are awarded to the person whose egg rolls fastest down a track made of sticks. In Denmark, decorated

---

89 Richard L. Zettler, Lee Horne, Donald P. Hansen, Holly Pittman Treasures from the Royal Tombs of Ur Pp. 70–72
90 Videnskab.dk "Historien om gækkebrevet: Startede som små valentinskort" www.videnskab.dk

eggs are rolled down slopes in grassland or forest and, if not broken, the eggs are eaten after the game. In Egypt, children bowl red and yellow eggs toward another row of eggs and whoever's egg cracks one egg, they may claim them all. This tradition spread to America and still today an egg rolling competition is held on the White House South Lawn for children by the President and the First Lady[91].

Egg Jarping

In the UK a traditional activity is egg jarping. Two players smash hard-boiled eggs together, and whoever has the egg that's still intact is the winner[92]. The World Jarping Championships are held each Easter in Durham, England. Following, of course, the official rules...

Pomlázka

The origin of the Czech Republic's pomlázka tradition (pomlázka, meaning both the whip and the tradition itself) is said to date back to pagan times. Symbolically pomlázka's meaning is to chase away illness, bringing health and youth for the rest of the year to everyone who is whipped with the young pussy willow twigs. Boys would whip girls lightly on the legs and possibly douse them with water, which had a similar symbolic meaning. The boy then sang an Easter carol and the girl would reward him with a painted egg or candy and tie a ribbon around his pomlázka[93]. The tradition is still popular in the Czech Republic today.

Predicting the Summer Weather to Come

As with Imbolc, Ostara has weather predicting traditions. You may have heard, "April showers bring May flowers," but what about," If it thunders on All Fool's Day, it brings good crops of corn and hay" Or "A cold and moist April fills the cellar and fattens the cow."

In Denmark, farmers believed that weather conditions on Easter holidays showed how the summer's harvest and weather would turn out. For example, if rain dripped from the trees on Easter morning the year would be fruitful, and if the Sun shined on Good Friday, as long as a man could rise to horse, then it would also be a good year.

---

91 Saffy "Curiosities, Grotesqueries, Follies & Strange Customs No 7 Customs Associated with Eggs and Eastertide" www.web.archive.org
92 Venetia Newall An Egg at Easter: A Folklore StudyPg. 344
93 Czech Gallery"Czech Easter (Velikonoce)" http://www.czechgallery.com

CONNECTING WITH THE SEASON

Reflect on Your Winter's Journey in Nature:

At Ostara, take a walk looking for signs of rebirth and spring. The land will have rapidly transformed since Imbolc. We are now half way through the Wheel's journey. At lot has happened to you and to the land since Samhain. As you walk, look for the changes in the landscape. Ask yourself:

- How is the land different now from how it was at Samhain?
- How are you different from the person you were at Samhain?

Once again, meditate and reflect upon these changes. See if you can make the correspondence between your own internal and external growth, and the internal and external growth in the world around you. How has your life's journey been reflected in the journey of nature?

Write your thoughts, reflections and observations in your journal when you come home.

Clear the Garden

In Scandinavia and some parts of Europe, Ostara is the time where the fields are cleared of winter debris. The land is fertilised for planting. Around April in Jutland, when the muck has been spread, you will hear people saying, "Det lugter af guld," roughly translated it means, the land stinks of money/ manure. The newly fertilised earth bringing the crops and the family finances later in the year. At this time of year, farmers furrow the land and plant the new seeds. So, another way to connect with spring equinox energy is to get outside and get your fingers in some soil. You can even spread some muck if you like!

Plant Seeds

After the spring equinox, farmers will begin to plant the summer crops. I love to plant seeds at spring equinox. And, as you will see in my ceremony, I like to use the seeds to represent my goals. The tending of these plants reminds me to tend to my goals during the summer and autumn. A few years ago, I still had blooms at winter solstice as my goals from the previous Wheel manifested in my life. But even if you don't want to do that, you can plant seeds at spring equinox. Nothing will connect you to nature more than spending time outside, helping plants grow.

Visit a Farm

If you can, go and visit a farm. There may even be an urban farm in your city. Coming from Wales, I love to see the daffodils and lambs at spring equinox. It just confirms for me that spring is truly here. In Denmark around spring equinox, the cows are returned to the fields after the long winter indoors. Necessary in the harsh Scandinavian environment. When the cows are returned to the fields, they 'dance' by leaping and jumping for joy. It is a Danish tradition to go and watch the cows dance to celebrate the return of spring. I wonder what traditions the farmers have in your country at this time of year?

OSTARA CRAFTS

Painting Eggs (and Manifesting Goals)

It's time to get your creative hat on and allow your inner child to guide you as you paint eggs for Ostara. I love to combine this with my process of setting goals. Now you might be saying to yourself: this is childish, why do it? The answer is simple. When setting goals and focusing on personal growth, we adults have a tendency to become overly serious. Life is also about enjoyment and having fun. Children know this and, by taking part in activities that can appear childish, we remind ourselves of the simple joys in life.

I have found that you don't need to paint an egg for each goal. In order to help you focus upon your vision, and to help you not set yourself up for a fail by trying to achieve too many goals, a little preparation goes a long way in this Ostara manifestation process.

Step 1

- Group your goals into a maximum of three distinct and clear groups
- Try, if you can, to define them in one sentence / word. For example, one of your goals could be to hold your responsibility in agreements you make and to take responsibility for your own health. These two goals could be grouped under responsibility.

Step 2
Blow a maximum of three eggs and paint each egg to represent your goals

- REMEMBER your paintings do not have to be a masterpiece, it is perfectly acceptable to use stick figures, abstract patterns, whatever makes sense to you. As I constantly repeat in workshops; there is no right or wrong, there just is
- Put these eggs in your sacred space to serve as a reminder throughout the year.

Each year, I leave my eggs in my sacred space and then at the next Ostara, I grind the old egg shells down and add them to the earth where I plant my new seeds. Each dream fertilising the next.

Natural Dyed Eggs with Leaf Prints

You will need:

- 1 Dozen (or more) white eggs (brown will not work so well)
- Large pots (2 or more for dyeing, 1 for boiling eggs)
- Water
- 1/4 cup distilled white vinegar
- 1 head of red cabbage (blue, purple dye)
- 1 beet (red, pink dye)
- Jars for dyes
- Old tights
- Twist ties
- Leaves, flowers, stickers – whatever you'd like to imprint on the egg

How to make:

Step 1 – Make the dye

- In a large pot, mix 8 cups of water and 1/4 cup white distilled vinegar
- Add 1 head of chopped red cabbage. This will make purple and blue dye
- Bring the mixture to a boil and then let simmer for several hours until you get desired colour
- In another pot, mix 4 cups of water and 1/4 cup white distilled vinegar with 1 chopped beet for red and pink dye

Step 2 – Boil the eggs

- In a large pot, add cold water and your eggs. Then bring to a boil over medium heat
- Once the water comes to a hard boil, let your eggs boil for 10 minutes
- Take out and cool
- Be careful to not break the eggs

Step 3 – Decorate with leaves

- Take your tights and lay them flat not doubled.
- Cut 10 cm squares

- Then lay the leaves on the tights
- Lay your egg on top of the leaf then cover it with the tights.
- Make sure it is tight!
- Then use your twist tie to secure.
- Make sure your leaf is tight on the egg, if not, the dye will seep into the spots and bleed colour where your leaf print should be.

Step 4 – Dye the eggs

- Divide the dye into the jam jars.
- Put the eggs into the dye and let sit for at least 30–45 minutes – or longer if you want darker colours.
- Allow the egg to dry and remove the tights and leaves.

SPRING EQUINOX JOURNEY

At Imbolc, we journeyed to our sacred grove. In between Imbolc and now you will hopefully have returned there and explored some of the pathways from your sacred grove. The purpose of this journey is to meet your shadow self in a safe place. In this journey, you are not going to go in to the deeper shadow work. This journey is to acknowledge your shadow self. To be less afraid of him/her. To see if you are ready to accept and love your shadow self.

Remember, if you meet someone or something you are unsure of, simply ask it three times, "Are you here in love and light?" If it is not, it will go away.

Now it is time to take your Ostara journey ... remember to be clear as to why you are journeying...

Breathe deeply and slowly, sitting or lying in a comfortable position. Make sure you're warm enough and have a glass of water close by. As you breathe feel your surroundings slip away, as you cocoon yourself in a safe protective circle.

In your mind, begin to see yourself standing high on a hill. It is daytime, the golden sunlight warms the cold air and the grass is green, the earth rich and fertile, birds sing, golden daffodils and crocuses paint the ground, in the fields you can see sheep, lambs and hares dancing. Spring is here and the land is awake!

As you walk further up the hill you become aware that, high up on the hill, a lone tree stands. An ancient oak. The branches bear no leaves yet but you can see buds are opening. Daffodils and crocuses grow around the trunk and the oak stands strong as you walk in a circle around the tree.

At the bottom of the oak, almost hidden in the trunk you can see a wooden door, half covered with ivy. Slowly, you walk towards the door. It opens with a creak and you can make out dimly lit stairs spiralling up into the tree and spiralling down. Tentatively, you begin to make your way up the stairs. To each side of you is earth and roots. You can smell the musty rich, fertile and damp soil around you.

Further and further up you travel until, in the middle of the tree, you find a door made of gnarled and aged wood. The stairs continue upwards, but this is not your journey today. Slowly, you open this ancient door. As it opens, a bright white spring light fills the space around you and you step out onto a wide open field and, on the horizon, you can see a knoll of trees. You walk towards the trees, breathing deeply the fresh air, enjoying the birdsong. This world is similar to our own yet somehow more alive, more vivid, more beautiful and shimmering.

At the entrance to the woods you pause, see if you have a guide waiting for you. If you meet someone or something then greet them politely, and listen to what they have to say. If no guide appears, take time to ask for permission to enter the woods.

As you enter the woods, you will see a path clearly outlined by tall trees and you know that you need to follow this path. You find yourself walking along the path, almost dreamlike, almost floating. At the end of the path, you find your grove, with a circle of trees with three paths coming away at the cross quarters.

What do you see? Walk into your grove and explore the circle, but do not yet take one of the paths. Enjoy being in your special space. Remember, your grove is yours. You can return here whenever you wish. Here you are safe and you are loved. Maybe you have guests you have met before within your grove, people, animals, ancestors, the fey or nature spirits. Greet them and explain the purpose of your journey today.

As you look around your grove, a pathway you have not walked before becomes more apparent and inviting. It is here you will travel today.

You walk along the tree lined path until there is a lake before you, the golden Ostara light dancing across the water. In the centre, you can see a small island. A thick wood in the middle with a spiral of smoke from a fire, curling up into the sky. Before you, a small row boat is tethered to an old worn jetty.

Step into the boat and row towards the island. Hear the water lapping at the oars. Feel the coldish air on your face and hands. As you approach the island, you can see there is someone waiting for you. As you get closer, you can see that this person looks just like you, identical in every way. As you pull the boat to shore, the person meets and says, "Hi, I am part of your shadow self."

What does he/she look like? Ask her what he/she is called. How do you feel toward him/her? What is their mood and body language telling you?

Your shadow-self beckons to you that you should follow through the thin woods. At the centre is his/her home. Be with this part of your shadow self. Listen to and respect it. Your shadow self may have a gift for you? Or may have something to tell you.

Now it is time to leave the island and head to your grove. Thank your shadow self for your time together. Walk to the boat together and, if you feel comfortable, give your shadow self a hug.

Row back across the lake, walk along the path that leads to your grove. Spend some time in your grove contemplating your meeting with your shadow self.

Take time now to contemplate the journey you have taken. Give thanks for the new knowledge you have gained.

* * *

When the time is right for you, take one last look at your grove.

The Sun is beginning to set. It is time to return.

Walk through the woods and back towards the oak tree until you reach the door.

Open the door to the staircase spiralling up and down and smell the rich soil once more.

Once again you travel down to the doorway you entered by (not down to your cave). Walk away from the tree. As you look up to the sky, on one side of you is the setting Sun, on the other side the rising Moon. You stand perfectly between day and night. Take a moment to feel this balance around you and within you.

Slowly become aware of the place in which your body lies or sits and allow your spirit self to step into your body and become one again. Gently allow the circle to slip away and bring yourself back to consciousness.

Drink some water, record your journey and get some fresh air.

From now until Beltane, you can return to visit your shadow self at least twice. When you are complete with your journeys, write your experiences down in your notebook.

Ostara Ceremony

Put the altar in the north (if that works for you).

Walk the circle three times imagining a boundary of pure energy around and above you.

"I am in a time that is not a time, in a place that is not a place."

At the north point of the circle invite the elements of earth.
At the east point of the circle invite the elements of air.
At the south point of the circle invite the elements of fire.
At the west point of the circle invite the elements of water.

Within the centre, invite spirit, ancestors and guides.
Put your eggs and your seeds on the altar.

Hold each seed in your hand. What does this seed represent to you? Which of your goals? Remember that you are not just holding "seeds" – you are holding marigold seeds or cherry tomato seeds or English lavender seeds. These seeds have within them all they need to become plants, trees, herbs and food.

Think about your goals and visualise the final, successful outcome of your efforts. The more specific you make your intention, the greater likelihood that what grows will be what you actually want and need. Whatever you choose to plant, think of it now and meditate on what it will bring into the world.

As you visualise, plant the seed and say:

"Awaken, stir, and swell.
Grow strong, grow well."

Don't forget to pour a bit of water onto the seeds, and, if you have them, mix the shells from your previous year's eggs into the soil.

Hold the container in front of you. In your mind's eye, see what will happen to this seed: darkness, new shoots, a growing blooming plant. See yourself tending the plant, and see the flowers or fruits that will come from it.

Contemplate the growth – all the growth – that is beginning here and now.

When you are ready say, "I ask for blessings on these seeds. May they grow strong and true."

Give thanks and share cakes and wine.

Thank the elements, guides and ancestors for joining you and walk the circle round in the opposite direction at the start.

Now it's time to celebrate Ostara!

The spring is here, the land is alive,
The birds have returned, new life has arrived.
The daffodils paint the grass with gold,
While new born lambs become more bold.

The fertile land is tilled and furrowed,
We say farewell to our winter shadows.
We plant our seeds and work for future yields,
As the mad March hare dances over the fields.

A spirit of youth is in everything,
As we create our dreams, our hearts sing.
The point of balance between day and night,
Here and now begins the time of light.
The Wheel turns...

CHAPTER 9

Beltane – Love and Sensuality – The Dance of Life

At Beltane, the land is bubbling, but not the fresh bubbling of Ostara. Beltane brings with it a deep humming, the throbbing of the pulse of the Earth. The colours of the land are bright and strong, emerald green, clear bright blue skies, the trees full of blossom. It is time for the dance of life, the mating dance. We feel alive again.

Beltane is the last of the three fertility festivals of the Wheel. At Imbolc it was the lands fertility, at Ostara the animals joined in the growing fertility. Beltane is the time of human fertility. The time where we begin to have our sexual awakening once more. Have you ever noticed how, around May, people begin to feel frisky, flirty and playful? May heralds the beginning of the mating dance of man. In the growing light and warmth we desire a partner. We desire fun, flirting and romance. With our winter layers removed, we show more of our bodies. The sunlight inspiring confidence and the extra burst of Vitamin D lifts our moods. People's faces change with the seasons, try watching the people you are closest to (or yourself) over the Wheel and you will see it. At Beltane we lose our dark, winter faces. Radiant and beautiful we blossom like the flowers around us.

Although Beltane is a time of love and couples coming together, it is not entirely a time for meaningful deep relationships. Of course, I am speaking generally. However, often at this time of year, couples who have been together for a long time sometimes have a resurgence of romance and sex within their relationship. Or they decide to part, new relationships begin and the world begins to fall in love once more.

For me, love is the primal theme to this time of year. In Celtic legends, it is the time where goddesses and gods find each other and fall in love[94]. At Beltane there was, throughout human history, a tradition of young people spending the night in the arms of a lover, perhaps found at the Beltane fires[95].

---

94 Alexi Kondratiev Celtic Rituals An authentic guide to ancient Celtic Spirituality Pp. 157–160
95 Ibid. pg 161

Working with the energy of Beltane in this interpretation of the Wheel of the Year, our theme and focus is love. And the most important love of all is the love of yourself. After all, if you can't love yourself, how can you expect to love and be loved yourself? Nothing is more attractive than a person that loves themselves, truly comfortable with their soul. Oscar Wilde said, "To love yourself is the beginning of a life-long romance." The most important relationship you can have is with you. At Beltane, it is the perfect time to heal the love within all of our relationships. And especially in your relationship with yourself.

Beltane reawakens our sensuality. We feel alive once more. We are in our skin. Beltane is the time of the year where we really connect with our physical blood, skin and bone. Our primal self. It is a time to connect with this feeling. The throbbing rhythm awakening in the land connects us with our power which grows to its fullest at the summer solstice. We connect with our core human essence, the fire in our hearts ignites our passion and we begin to dance again.

HISTORY OF BELTANE

Beltane is the third of the fire festivals in the Wheel of the Year and is the equal opposite to Samhain. This festival marked the start of the Celtic summer[96] and was celebrated all over the Celtic world. The name of the festival 'Beltane' is believed to originate from the Celtic god 'Bel', meaning 'the bright one', and the Gaelic word 'teine', Beltane can be interpreted as meaning 'Bel's fire' or 'goodly fire'[97].

Beltane is first mentioned by Cormac, Bishop of Cashel and King of Munster, who was killed in 908. Cormac describes how cattle were driven between two bonfires on Beltane as a magical means of protecting them from disease before they were led into summer pastures. On Beltane Eve, all fires in the community were put out and a special communal fire was kindled for Beltane. This was called the 'Tein-eigen', the 'need fire' or the 'Bel fire'. People jumped the fire to purify, cleanse and to bring fertility. According to historical texts, such as Sonas Cormaic, the Druids would light two fires 'idir dha thine Bheltaine' and the cattle and people moved between the flames of the fires as part of a purification ritual[98]. At the end of the evening, the villagers would take some of the communal fire to start their hearth fires anew[99].

Like at Samhain, the Celts believed that this was a time of year when the veils between the worlds are thin. But at Beltane, it is the veil to the underworld of the fae that is said to be open. According to folklore, the faery folk, also known as the fae; are an ancient race of people who lived in Britain long before the Celts. In Ireland, stories tell that the fae are descendants of the Tuatha De Danann, of the tribe of Dana. These are a magical race who flew into Ireland in ships from

---

96   Alexi Kondratiev Celtic Rituals An authentic guide to ancient Celtic Spirituality pp.155–160
97   Danu Forest The Magical Year Pp. 86–87
98   Paul Russell. "Sanas Chormaic." In Celtic Culture. An Encyclopedia, (ed. J.T. Koch) Pg 201
99   Edain McCoy. The Sabbats A New Approach to Living the Old Ways pg 124

the clouds on Beltane[100]. In all the myths from Ireland and Wales, the Fae are often known to be mischievous and tricksy, and love to deceive humans. One folk tradition said that, by having no light or fire in the home on Beltane Eve, that the fae would not be attracted to people's homes and so they would be free of mischievous misfortune.

The eve of Beltane is known as Walpurgis Night in German folklore and is surrounded by a tradition of mischief too. Walpurgis means "Witches Night". It was believed that, on this night, witches would meet with the Devil atop the Blocksberg, the highest peak of the mountains in central Germany. On Walpurgis Night, people would dress up in costumes and make loud noises. To ward off malevolent forces, blessed sprigs of foliage were hung from houses or offerings of bread with butter and honey (known as 'ankenschnitt') were left out for the tricksy fae[101].

In Scandinavian countries, such as Sweden and other Eastern European countries, the eve of Beltane is a farewell to the last day of April and the welcoming of bountiful crops, sunshine and romantic courtship, which they symbolise by lighting the baelfire with 2 flints to represent the spark of life between lovers coming together[102].

GROWING WITH THE SEASON

Reflections on Working with the Shadow Self

At the turning of each season, there is a time where you feel as though the world stops still. It is the time to reflect upon your growth. From beginning your work with your shadow self at Ostara, you know that, in order to love yourself, you have to accept, respect and honour the parts of you that you do not like.

From Ostara to now you have been journeying to visit, and working with, your shadow self. Your understanding of your shadow will have empowered you, giving you a deeper understanding of yourself. It may have opened old wounds, or led you to investigate early experiences in your life. If you have peeled back to the deeper layers, you may have found the root of your insecurities and fears.

Now it is time to move forwards (unless of course, you feel the need/desire to continue working with a particular aspect of your shadow, especially if this connects with your Wheel's goals).

Ask yourself the following questions:

- How has my relationship with my shadow self developed?

- Has it changed from my first meeting?

- What have I learnt about my shadow self?

---
100 Frédéric Armo. "La Charniere De Mai: Beltaine, Fete Celtique ou Fete Irlandaise?" Pg 103
101 Javier A.Galván, They Do What? A Cultural Encyclopedia of Extraordinary and Exotic Customs from around the World. p. 51.
102 Edain McCoy. The Sabbats a New Approach to Living the Old Ways pg 124

- How has my understanding and awareness of my shadow self manifested or been apparent in my daily life?
- What tools have I used to connect with my shadow self? Have they all been effective?
- Do I need to continue working with my shadow self for the remainder of this Wheel?
- Can I accept all that I have learnt and understood about my shadow self at this moment?
- Can I now understand where my shadow self is limiting /holding me back in my life?
- Can I love my shadow self at this moment in time?

By assessing your progress, you become conscious of the journey you have taken and the consequential growth. Record your reflections in your journal and reread them. Remember to reward yourself for the work you are doing. Be proud of yourself and thankful to yourself for making the difference in your own life.

Improving Your Relationship with Yourself – Working with Self-love

There is a common myth in our society that there is such a thing as 'perfect' and we should all strive to be it. The truth is we are all human, flawed and prone to making mistakes as we navigate the world and learn and grow from our experiences. I was once told that the ancient Egyptians recognised this. Apparently, whenever anything was man made, they built a deliberate flaw into it. In their opinion the only thing that was 100% perfect was made by the gods. I love this idea. The concept that I am not supposed to be perfect. That, in my natural state, I am supposed to be truly imperfectly perfect.

True self love, self-acceptance, is a hard place to get too. It has taken me many years, hours of work and tears to get to where I am right now on this journey. I found that one of the worst things about having negative self-image or not being able to love ourselves, is that we feel so alone. As though we are the only one who feels this way. Even though you may feel like this, I promise you that you are not the only person who feels vulnerable, insecure and self-critical at times. We're all fighting our own demons and trying to do our best. The first step to loving yourself is realising that everyone feels this way at times. By doing this you immediately take the pressure off yourself and no longer feel so isolated and alone.

It is easier for EVERYONE to focus on the negative aspects about themselves. Our inner critic, our inner judge, are loud voices and if you give them your energy and believe they become increasingly louder. We believe them of course, because it is the voice in our head that we hear the most. Our inner critic creates angst, paranoia and feeds every fear you ever had about yourself. If you allow them to run free these voices eat away at your self-confidence.

At Beltane, I like to dedicate the entire month to quieting those voices and indulging in 31 days of self-love practice. To reprogram my brain to stop the negative cycle and remind myself how truly beautiful, unique and imperfectly perfect I am. I invite you, at this time of love and sensuality, to do the same. There are many different tools you can try. Some will work for you, some won't. The following is a list of my favourite self-love practices for you to try at Beltane.

Your Past Inspiring You in the Now

The first step to self-love is finding something to love, and it is here where your past can help you. It is sometimes easier to look back on the past and find positives than to find positives, in the now. Your past is full of incidents and memories that created the person you are today. Although some of those incidents were not pleasant, you survived and grew, you had good experiences and grew. To help you love you now, it can sometimes help to look at why you loved yourself before.

Find pictures of you when you were younger and happy. Make these pictures from a broad range of your life, such as a baby, toddler, starting school age, then at 11, 13, 16, 18, 21, 30, 40 and so on. Also, if you have them, choose pictures of significant moments or memories from your life. Look at the pictures you have found of the younger you. For now, look at the pictures in age order.

As you look at each picture reflect upon:

- What do you love about this version of you?
- Do you still have or recognise this quality within you today?
- If not, do you want this quality in you today?

Write the qualities you love in your journal or upon the back of each picture and put them where you can see them every day. These things you love about yourself have brought you to where you are today, and they are still here in you today. They are part of the intrinsic fabric of your soul.

Now, individually look at each picture again and feel love for the person in the picture. You can return to these pictures whenever you need to remember the beautiful person you have grown to be and the beautiful person you are.

Changing Your Thought Patterns

One of the biggest hindrances to loving ourselves is our chatterbox of an inner critic. The negative statements running around in our brains constantly re enforcing the negative beliefs we have about ourselves. The first hurdle is to stop the negative inner critic in its tracks.

The Power of NO

To shut up the inner critic I recommend using the power of NO! When the negative cycle begins, just say 'NO'. No to those thoughts that harm you and pull you down. Say 'No' out loud. Clearly and definitely. Whenever my ugly judge, or critic pops up I find myself imagining that I bop it on the head (with an oversized comedy judge's gavel) and flatten it completely. Afterwards it is good to do or think about something else, cleaning the car, washing up, any small task that is achievable. Distract your brain. This is challenging to do at first. However, it becomes easier with time. Until you get to the point where it becomes so automatic that you won't ever notice it.

Changing the Record

Now you know when your negative voices pop up, it is time to change the record. It is good to have given some thought as to how you can change these thoughts beforehand.

An easy way to do this is to divide a piece of paper in two. In one column, write all of the negative statements you currently make and believe about yourself. In the other column, rewrite these statements in a positive way. So, for example, if you had written:

'No one could love me'.

Write instead:

'My family and friends love me and show me that it is possible for others to love me.'

Now tear away the negative column and throw it away. It is rubbish, untrue and not worthy of your energy anymore. Read the positive statements out loud to yourself every day, (I recommend in the mornings). The more you tell your brain the positive statements, the more your brain will believe it.

Affirmations

Daily affirmations are a powerful tool to reprogram negative thinking patterns. Remember, the brain believes what we tell it. So, affirming your new positive thoughts about yourself daily will make them more real to you.

You can say an affirmation looking into a mirror (or not, if you find it is too challenging). You can say them internally, or externally. It is entirely up to you. For an affirmation to really succeed it is best said over a period of time, a minimum of five minutes a day will really make an impact on your self-love.

- I love and accept myself
- I accept myself for what I am

- I am constantly showing myself and the world the beautiful person I am
- I am unique and perfect in all my imperfections

Another way to remind yourself how beautiful and wonderful you are, is to put quotes that remind you of this around your home, on your phone and computer background. One of my favourites is in my bathroom by the mirror I have a beautiful quote. Every day it reminds how perfectly imperfect I am.

If you cannot find affirmations that inspire you, then look again at your positive statements list, you already have a list of new positive affirmations right in front of you!

Loving Your Body

In a society focused on personal appearance, it is easy to focus on what we don't like about our body. I personally have battled all of my life with eating disorders and for many, many years hated mirrors so much that I wouldn't sleep in a room with a mirror in it. The only way to love your body is to grip these feelings of self-hate and turn them around.

So, go and look at yourself in the mirror. See all the parts of you that you don't like. Now look for the things you do like, there will be something.

Say to yourself out loud:

I don't like my .... but I do love my ....

For example:

I don't like my bum but I do love my eyes.

Try this with your entire body at least five times in one week. Eventually, you will begin to focus on the things you like about yourself every time you look into the mirror.

Forgiving Yourself

Forgiving yourself is part of 'the learning to love yourself' process. No matter who you are and what has happened in your past, there will be things that you are not proud of, things you feel guilty about. Your feelings about these incidents or actions can have a negative effect on your sense of self -worth and your sense of love. You might even think, because I did X, I am not a person that can be loved. This is you being your own worst enemy. To truly love yourself, you have to accept what has happened and forgive yourself. After all, you cannot change your past, you can only change your future. One process, evolved from the ancient Hawaiian spiritual tradition of Ho'oponopono, consists of mindfully repeating four simple phrases:

I love you.
I am sorry.
Please forgive me.
Thank you.

It doesn't matter whether you think you are saying them to God, Source, Spirit, the Universe, your higher self, or your inner mind, it only matters that you say them sincerely, from your heart. Direct them in a way that has the most meaning for you. You can chant all four together as a mantra, or repeat a single phrase in response to whatever perception or thought you find yourself entertaining. Some people do this for five minutes, some for longer. Take the time you need to forgive yourself.

Taking Time to Love Yourself

How often do you dedicate time to loving and appreciating yourself? Think about it, ask yourself.

- What do I do to show myself that I love me?
- Do I make time for myself?

If it's hard to answer these questions, then you are way overdue on some time for loving yourself. In today's society, there can be a taboo about putting yourself first. However, how do you honestly think you can be there for everyone else if you don't make time for you? Putting yourself second only tells the world that you think you are not good enough or important enough, and the world will only reflect back to you what you believe. Self-love can be challenging, so take baby steps.

Make You time

I have a dear friend who is constantly saying "I must do something good for myself soon", It occurred to me recently that she never actually said what she would do, or when. If you relate to my friend, try the following exercise:

- What is it that you will do to be good to yourself? Make a list
- Now look at your diary and plan exactly when you are going to take the time to do this for yourself

Personally, I dedicate one day or afternoon each month to pampering and loving myself, it gives me the greatest energy boost.

Caring for you

It is often so easy to care for others more than we care for ourselves. Taking care of yourself is a way of showing yourself some self-love. There are many small ways you can care for yourself. Eating healthily, exercise, meditation, laughing, going out in nature or having a spa day at home.

In a busy life, keep it simple (don't set yourself up for a fail). At a time in my life where financially I was on my arse, I made a commitment to eating organic food, which often meant going to three or more different supermarkets to find offers I could afford. Putting the best and most natural food in my body was, and still is, a constant reminder that I am worth the best. It also had the added bonus that I was living my beliefs, regarding caring for the planet, which increased my self-respect.

Small caring and loving actions you can easily do during a day are:

- Giving yourself a gentle hand massage
- Five mins of yoga stretching and breathing at your desk
- Watching a short comedy show to make you laugh
- Begin a positive bank where you write down and store positive memories, reading them when you need a positivity boost
- Hugging yourself
- Massage your earlobes (especially when feeling down as it comforts and release endorphins into the body)

Write Yourself a Love Letter

As children, we get a lot of positive reinforcement but, as adults, this tends to lessen. Yet, consciously or unconsciously, we still crave that acknowledgement that we are loved. Self-love is about getting into and strengthening the relationship you have with yourself. After all, you're the person you have to sleep with every single night, for the rest of your life. So, nurturing that relationship is crucial. Remembering that the voices we hear the most are the ones we believe, then it is logical that you need to hear words of love from yourself to yourself.

One of the most powerful ways you can do this, is to write yourself a love letter. A letter where you tell yourself the things you love most about yourself. I find that writing it and then reading it aloud is an empowering and uplifting process.

Showing Love in Your Relationships

How often do you tell the people you love that you love them? How often do you honour them? People reflect what they see and feel from us. How often in a relationship, be it lover, family or friend, do we tend to put the blame on the other person and not take responsibility for the part of the situation we created, then do not understand when the other person does not take responsibility for their own actions. Simply said, what you give is what you get.

So, at Beltane, after giving yourself some love, it is time to share it around. I had a particularly challenging relationship with my mother (who doesn't?) until it was suggested to me, how often did I acknowledge the great gift she gave to me. The gift, of course, is my life. On my birthday, her birthday or Mother's Day, I write and thank her for the gift of my life and for being my mum. We have a much better relationship these days. A little reminder of love and gratitude can go a long way.

My partner and I have very different ideas on how to keep our house clean and cosy. He is very messy, can't remember where things live and doesn't care about the environment around him. I am also messy but do my best to keep our home tidy and nice to look at. We understand this about each other. Every day, when he has had a nap, he makes the bed for me because he knows I like to see the bed made. When he couldn't remember where things lived in the kitchen I made picture signs on the cupboards to help him. Small actions that make us both feel loved, honoured and appreciated.

A friend who lives in the UK, who I am unable to see often, knows that I love Cadbury's cream eggs (we all have our guilty pleasures!) and I cannot buy them here in Denmark. Every year at Ostara, she sends me an egg box with six cream eggs, a loving gesture that reminds me of my friend, how much I love her and often leads to a skype session with wine to catch up and reconnect.

So, think of a relationship you have with someone you love and take a few moments to find a small way you can show that person you love them, that you are thankful for them and that you want to honour them. Then do it. The results may surprise you.

Ideas to honour someone you have a relationship with:

- Set a day aside to spend with that person, doing something you know they will enjoy. Creating memories strengthens relationships

- Write a letter to that person and post it. In this technological age it is exciting and feels more caring to receive letters by snail mail

- Ask them what small thing you can do to show them your love for them daily, and make sure that they also make an agreement to do something for you

- Practise daily gratitude with your lover and, each day, maybe over a meal, tell them three things you are thankful for that they have done on that day

Awakening Your Senses at Beltane

Awakening your sensuality is about getting into your body, and awakening your inner fire. What better time than the passionate fire festival Beltane to connect your physical self?

You might ask why it is it important to do this? The answer is simple. Stress. Today we live in a society where chronic stress is on the rise. When we live our lives under chronic stress, we are not able to fully experience the simple pleasures in every moment. We are perfectly designed to experience pleasure without guilt or shame just as we are perfectly designed to experience stress under short term durations. Too often we associate pleasure with pain or pleasure as something we are not worthy of, or that is not a priority in our lives. A person that takes in more fully the experience of the NOW through their five senses is a sensual person.

The word sensuality is very much associated with sex or being sexy. But is that what it means to be sensual? In western philosophy the ability to sense, to experience sensation, is called sentience. Sentience in Buddhism is the state of having senses. In Buddhism, there are six senses, the sixth being the subjective experience of the mind[103]. The very root of the word sensual comes from the medieval word sensory, denoting the animal side of human nature[104]. Ultimately, I interpret being sensual as stimulating and experiencing my senses.

Take a moment to think what does sensuality mean to you?

One of the definitions of sensual is, "exciting the senses". Do not be afraid of your sensuality, do not judge it as something dirty or only as sexual. Every creature in nature uses their senses, unconsciously. To consciously connect with them is to bring yourself closer to your primal natural state. It gives a deeper connection to yourself and to others, as well as reminding you on every level how beautiful, unique and alive you are, stimulating more opportunities for loving yourself. By becoming mindful of our sensory experience, we activate parts of our brain that are involved with feeling and experiencing, and this helps anchor our awareness to the here-and-now. We become more self-aware as we work with the senses.

Try these different exercises to activate and become mindful of yourself as a sensual and sensory being:

Touch: Look in front of the mirror and give yourself a hug of appreciation for you, while you give yourself a smile in the mirror with a thank you for being you! EXTRA TIP: Put music on… dance and get into your body and experience joy once more. Feel the joy and passion of being in your most natural state.

Sight: Look for opportunities to see the small beauties in the world. The sunlight on a tree, the flight pattern of a bird, look up at the sky instead of straight ahead, even seeing a child's blissful state of contentment during rush hour in the metro. To see these beautiful things makes you happy and feel blessed to have observed these intimate moments just for you.

Smell and Taste: See the apple before you. Close your eyes before you eat it. Give thanks for the food and all the people and hands who prepared it. Sense the smell, taste, temperature and texture of the food on your plate. Bring it close to your mouth to feel it with your tongue, then slowly place it in your mouth. Feel the salivary glands bursting with liquids, all dancing in harmony with the food in

---

103 Red Pine. The Heart Sutra: The Womb of the Buddhas pg 103
104 Lexico Dictionary s.v. "Sensuality" www.lexico.com

your mouth. Notice the sensations in your mouth. Notice the pleasure of eating, and tasting. Notice how you feel from eating mindfully and sensually. EXTRA TIP: This is an amazing exercise to do with chocolate!

Sound: Music is one of the most uplifting creations of nature and man. No matter what you are feeling music can change that emotion. Whether it is bird song or your favourite pop song. Listen to music that makes you happy, that makes you feel passion and gives you energy. Happiness and contentment are both keys to sensuality and self-love.

Mindfulness practice for awakening and exploring the senses

This exercise is a powerful way to experience both your senses and sensory capabilities, as well as becoming entirely present in the moment.

Sit comfortably and breathe deeply. Keep your eyes open.

Begin to focus on the smallest thing you can see. Experience it. See every detail. Do this for a period of no less than three minutes.

Now begin to focus on the next smallest thing you can see. Experience it. See every detail. Do this for a period of no less than three minutes.

Now begin to focus on the largest thing you can see. Experience it. See every detail. Do this for a period of no less than three minutes.

Now begin to focus on everything you can see. Experience it. See every detail. Do this for a period of no less than three minutes.

Close your eyes. Take three deep breaths.

Begin to focus on the smallest noise you can hear. Experience it. Hear every detail. Do this for a period of no less than three minutes.

Begin to focus on the noises you can hear in the room or space you are in. Experience them. Hear every detail. Do this for a period of no less than three minutes.

Begin to focus on the noises you can hear far away from the room or space you are in. Experience them. Hear every detail. Do this for a period of no less than three minutes.

Begin to focus on all of the noises you can hear in the room or space you are in. Experience them. Hear every detail. Do this for a period of no less than three minutes.

Keep your eyes closed. Take three deep breaths.

Focus on your mouth. Taste and sense the feeling inside your mouth. Do this for a period of no less than three minutes

Keep your eyes closed. Take three deep breaths.

Focus on your body. Feel your connection to the ground. Feel the air on your skin. The warmth. Do this for a period of no less than three minutes.

Now take your hands to your heart and feel your heartbeat.

When you are ready, begin to move your body and stretch out.

BELTANE TRADITIONS

Bringing in the May

In The Court of Love, written in 1561, possibly by Geoffrey Chaucer, it says that in medieval England, people would celebrate the start of spring by going out to the country or woods and gathering greenery and flowers, 'bringing in the may'[105]. Just like at winter solstice, bringing in the May is to bring the new season into your home and your awareness. In England, for centuries up to today on May Day a girl in the village is crowned as the May Queen and becomes queen for a day[106]. Often the May blossoms would be woven into garlands decorating ships[107] and homes, also the blossom garlands were worn as a crown by the village maidens[108].

Dancing the Maypole

If you live in Europe, North America, you may have seen, or participated in dancing around the maypole, on May Day. According to historians, maypole dancing originated in Germany and was taken to the British Isles and became part of spring fertility ceremonies, both Pagan and Christian. Like many mayday customs, the tradition survives today.

It is believed that the earliest maypoles were actually living trees, rather than the pole we have today. It has been suggested by Oxford professor and anthropologist, E.O. James, that the maypole tradition has a possible connection to Roman traditions connected to the Floralia, which began on April 28[109]. James suggests that trees were stripped of their leaves and limbs, and then decorated with garlands of ivy, vines and flowers to honour the mythological couple Attis and Cybele[110]. Today in Sweden people still make and decorate their own maypole for the 'Midsommersfesten' (Mid-Summer festival) now celebrated on summer solstice[111].

---

[105] Shmuel Ross "What You Might Not Know About May Day" www.infoplease.com
[106] Rev. T. F. Thiselton-Dyer, M.A British popular customs, present and past; Pg 252
[107] William Hone Hone, William, The Table book: or, Daily recreation... Pp. 315 – 316.
[108] C. Bladey "Folklore Accounts- III May Games" www.cbladey.com
[109] Edwin O. James "The Influence of Folklore on the History of Religion." Numen 9, no. 1 Pp. 1–16
[110] ibid.
[111] Visit Sweden "Midsommer i Sverige" www.visitsweden.dk

A theme of Beltane mythology and traditions is the union of the masculine and feminine. Most historians and scholars agree that the maypole is a lasting symbol of this. Within Neo-pagan circles the pole is thought to represent the god planting his phallus within the goddess earth, as her body. With a wreath of flowers symbolising the feminine, the ribbons are woven in different directions as people dance around the maypole, thought to symbolise the union of man and woman[112].

Belfire

A Beltane custom was to leap over the Beltane bonfire. Young people jumped the fire for luck in finding a spouse or for good health. Travelers jumped the fire to ensure a safe journey[113].

A belfire is traditionally built using nine different types of wood

- Alder
- Hawthorn
- Oak
- Ash
- Hazel
- Rowan
- Birch
- Holly
- Willow

Although if you do decide to spend an evening around the Belfire, it does not have to be made of specific woods. Do what is practical and simplest for you. Jumping a fire is exhilarating, although it is good to remember safety and not to wear easily flammable clothing or jump the fire when it is burning high. You don't want to spend Beltane Eve at the A&E department.

To emphasise your work with loving yourself, you could jump the Bel fire to dedicate the start of a new relationship with yourself!

May Day Love Charms

A Swedish verse says, "Midsummer night is not long but it sets many cradles to rock." Unsurprisingly, with the themes of love and romance at the core of Beltane, there exists still many traditional activities and customs for finding a partner at Beltane. For unmarried girls, it's said that if you pick seven (or sometimes nine) types of flowers and place them under your pillow, you'll dream of your future husband[114]. In France, jilted men would lay in a field on May Day and pretend to sleep. If a girl wanted to marry him, she would awaken him with a kiss. The pair then went to the local inn and led a dance to announce their betrothal. The boy was called the betrothed of May[115].

---

112 Edain McCoy . The Sabbats a New Aproach to Living in the Old Ways. pg130
113 Teresa Moorey. Jane Brideson Wheel of the Year Myth and Magic through the seasons pg 86
114 Daisy Carrington "Summer solstice: Traditions around the world" www.edition.cnn.com
115 Various Authors "History of Witchcraft Internet Book of Shadows" www.sacred-texts.com Pg 807

CONNECTING WITH THE SEASON

Take a Walk and Connect with Your Senses

Take a walk out in the sunshine, or even the fresh rain of Beltane. As always, reflect upon how nature has changed since Ostara, and ask yourself how do these changes reflect your own life? At Beltane it is a great time to connect and engage your senses within nature. Smell the flowers, touch the bark, lie down and listen to the sounds of the birds and people around you. At Beltane, give yourself the time to 'feel' that you are alive in nature. A great way to do this is to do the mindfulness method for awakening the sense.

Record your reflections in your journal.

Dance

You may not have a maypole or even space for one at home. However, if there is ever time to celebrate the season with dance, it is at Beltane. The land energy is beating like a drum. Releasing and embracing this energy connects us with our roots, with the very essence of being alive, in a way no ceremony can. Beltane dancing is a freeing experience. Dancing in nature is of course best. But if that is too outside your comfort zone then crank up the volume, close your eyes and lose yourself in a wild Beltane dance!

Make a May Crown

At Beltane you can bring in May and welcome summer to your home. A lovely way of connecting with the Wheel is to weave a flower crown to honour your beauty and the things you love about yourself. As you weave, think about the qualities you love about you. See your beauty represented in these crowns. This is a beautiful ritual to do with friends or family. You can wear your crown on Beltane Day and then place it in you sacred space. The flowers will of course wilt eventually but as you look upon your garland/crown throughout the next part of the Wheel remember your beauty and take a moment to feel love for you.

You will need:

- Thin ivy willow branches
- May flowers
- Twine

How to make:

- Create a circle a little smaller than the size of your head from the ivy or willow branches. You can weave it together or tie it together with twine

- Weave in the flowers. If you feel they are not secure then you can tie them with twine and hide that under other flowers
- Wear it with your favourite clothes to a Beltane party!
- The flower crown will wilt the day after but you can hang it up to dry over your sacred space

May Day Dew Bath

According to folklore, the dew on 1st May has magical properties and anyone who washes their face in it will have a flawless complexion for the entire year. May dew is also said to be able to remove spots, freckles and pimples. A traditional rhyme says that the maid who rises early on May morning "and washes in dew from the hawthorn tree, will ever after handsome be." Apparently, the dew only works at or just before sunrise[116].

BELTANE CRAFTS

May Day Cone Baskets

May Day cones are a rural tradition that became popular in North America. The idea was to send a love message in the form of a May cone. A paper cone filled with May flowers was hung on the door of the loved one's house and the door was knocked upon before running away. The difference between this and a Valentine is that in a May cone the identity of the sender is not hidden. You could send someone you love a May cone at Beltane and brighten their day.

You will need:

- Medium-weight paper
- Decorative scissors
- Pencil
- Craft glue
- Hole punch
- 20 inches of 1 inch wide ribbon
- May flowers

How to make:

- Cut medium-weight paper into a seven inch square

---

[116] Rev. T. F. Thiselton-Dyer, M.A British popular customs, present and past; pg 237

- Use decorative scissors to scallop edge and a pencil to form tip.
- Secure outer flap of cone with craft glue
- Punch six holes, 1 inch apart, beginning at the top front centre; thread the ribbon through holes
- Tie bow at front, and leave a seven inch loop at the back
- Add fresh or dry flowers

If you don't know which flowers to send, then the 19th century language of flowers will give you inspiration. In the late 19th century, the romantic ideal was medieval chivalry and courtly love. It became popular to send people you loved a message in the language of flowers.

- Ivy leaf – Friendship
- Apple blossom – Preference
- Rhododendron – Danger, flee
- Myrtle – Good luck and love in marriage
- Passion flower – Mourning over the death of a loved one
- Rose – Love
- Lily-of-the-valley – Purity
- Bluebells – Kindness
- Peonies – Bashfulness
- Rosemary – Remembrance
- Tulips – Passion
- Wallflowers – Faithfulness in adversity
- Aloe – Bitterness
- Pomegranate – Conceit
- Purple violet – Thoughts occupied with love

Beltane Journey

Make sure you are comfortable and will not be interrupted. Have a glass of water to hand.

Now it's time to return to your sacred grove. The purpose of this journey is to connect with the Beltane energy and your own sensuality.

Remember, if you meet someone or something you are unsure of, simply ask it three times, "are you here in love and light?" If it is not, it will go away. Beltane is truly the time of the fey, and they can be tricksy.

Now it is time to take your Beltane journey...... Remember be clear as to why you are journeying...

Breathe deeply and slowly, sitting or lying in a comfortable position. Make sure you're warm enough and have a glass of water close by. As you breathe feel your surroundings slip away, as you cocoon yourself in a safe protective circle.

In your mind, begin to see yourself standing high on a hill. It is dusk, the red blazing sunset burns across the emerald fields, birds sing the dusk chorus, you can see flowers all over the ground starting to close up for the night. The land, the air, is bubbling with excitement. It is Beltane Eve.

As you walk further up you become aware, that high up on the hill, a lone tree stands. An ancient oak. The leaves are easy to see, now small, fresh and new. Opening the oak stands strong as you walk in a circle around the tree.

At the bottom of the oak, almost hidden in the trunk, you can see a wooden door, half covered with ivy. Slowly, you walk towards the door. It opens with a creak and you can make out dimly lit stairs spiralling up into the tree and spiralling down. Tentatively, you begin to make your way up the stairs. To each side of you is earth and roots. You can smell the musty dampness of the rich fertile and damp soil around you.

Further and further up you travel until, in the middle of the tree, you find a door made of gnarled and aged wood, the stairs continue upwards but this is not your journey today. Slowly, you open this ancient door. As it opens, a bright white spring light fills the space around you and you step out into a wide open field and, on the horizon, you can see a knoll of trees. You walk towards the trees, breathing deeply the fresh air, enjoying the birdsong. This world is similar to our own, yet somehow more alive, more vivid, more beautiful, shimmering.

At the entrance to the woods you pause, you can hear music and smell a bonfire. The woods seem full of voices and hustle and bustle. As you walk to your grove, you can see peopleand creatures moving around your grove, dancing and laughing. You can see ancestors, guides, animals and the land spirits all coming together to dance and celebrate. Walk around and see who is there. Tonight all of these beings love you and are part of your life and you. Do not be afraid. Greet them and smile. At this party, you belong. This is your Beltane party.

As you feel the music in your soul and the warmth of the Belfire, you begin to dance. Slowly at first, then faster and faster until you are swept away with the music in the wild dance of life.

Enjoy this dance.

Now you see in the centre of the fire that the embers are dying down a little and, one by one, the beings begin to jump the Belfire to be cleansed. You know you will not get burned. Heart pumping, blood rushing, drums pounding in your ears, you leap through the flames.

As you land, you are caught by someone. As you look up, you can see he is half man, half stag / she is part woman, part dryad. You smell a musky smell. He /she lowers you to the ground and beckons to you to follow him/ her through the woods. He/ she begins to run through the woods and you run beside him/her, wild and free.

Eventually you come to a clearing. Spend time with him/her here, be with him/ her until the dawn, listen to what he/she has to tell you...

The sunlight begins to fill the clearing, the morning dew upon the ground. You are alone. You reach down and wash your face in the dew. You feel fresh and alive. You begin to walk to your grove. The visitors are gone and the fire has burnt down to embers. Take a moment to contemplate your Beltane fire.

It is time to return. When the time is right for you, take one last look at your grove.

Walk through the woods and back towards the oak tree until you reach the door.

Open the door to the staircase spiralling up and down and smell the rich soil once more.

Once again you travel down to the doorway you entered by (not down to your cave). Walk away from the tree. As you look up to the sky in the fresh dawn light you can still feel a bubbling energy in the land, gentler than Beltane Eve but it still energises you in every part of your being.

Slowly become aware of the place in which your body lies or sits and allow your spirit self to step into your body and become one again. Gently allow the circle to slip away and bring yourself back to consciousness.

Drink some water, eat some chocolate, record your journey and get some fresh air.

Beltane Ceremony

Have some music playing for this ceremony.

Put the altar in the north

I walk the circle three times imagining a boundary of pure energy around me.

"A time that is not a time, in a place that is not a place."

At the north point of the circle, I invite the elements of earth to join me.
At the east point of the circle, I invite the elements of air to join me.
At the south point of the circle, I invite the elements of fire to join me.
At the west point of the circle, I invite the elements of water to join me.

Within the centre, I invite spirit to join me.

Silently, I invite my ancestors and guides to be with me.

Place your full attention on your heart, in the middle of your chest. Usually, most of our attention is placed around our eyes (since our eyesight is our most active sense), but imagine now that you lower your attention from your eyes and down into your chest. Here is the seat for healing and love – self-love, friendly love, romantic love, and universal love. Imagine that you are breathing straight into your heart.

Feel a ball of light in your chest which grows for each breath – for every in-breath, you suck up energy around you, and for every out-breath, your heart chakra becomes bigger and bigger, until it spills out into the room as a bright, warm, healing, loving light. You can enhance this loving energy by thinking about things, people, or animals that you love unconditionally.

When you are in the middle of this energy burst, read aloud the following words, slowly and gently, really feeling every word:

"There is abundant love in all creation.
There is abundant love in me.
I see myself as the eternal beautiful soul I really am.
I know I play an important part in this world.
I love myself deeply.
I am worthy of the love of others.

Breathe slowly and let the power of those words sink in. If you feel any resistance coming up when reading, find out where in your body you feel the resistance, and direct your heart energy towards it. Once it feels soothed and diminished, start reading again from the beginning.

Now breathe deep into your womb or groin. As you inhale, imagine pure gold energy circling through it. As you exhale, imagine that energy flowing through your whole body, nourishing you and allowing you to magnetize and create all that you want and more. Feel the music. Slowly, with your eyes closed, begin to move to the music sensually. Move from your womb from you heart. As you move, remind yourself of the qualities you love about yourself. Whisper to yourself, "I am ... [sensitive, kind, compassionate, generous, loving, well-meaning, creative, curious, inspiring, caring ... etc."

Allow the energy of self-love and sensuality to flow over you, gently embracing you, until you land inside your body again and are ready to open your eyes.

Give thanks and have cake and wine.

Thank the elements, guides and ancestors for joining you and walk the circle round in the opposite direction at the start.

Now it's time to celebrate Beltane!

> *The land is rainbow painted in flowers,*
> *Beautiful blossoms fertile with life's power.*
> *The air heavy and joyful, summer has begun,*
> *Passions awaken with the setting of the sun.*

BELTANE – LOVE AND SENSUALITY – THE DANCE OF LIFE

'Tis Beltane Eve, no time for sleep,
The Bel-fire calls, will you take the leap?
The flames burn bright, cleansing the tribe,
Your heart set free you jump the divide!

Senses aflame, your heartbeat pounds,
Surrendering to the dance your soul demands.
The call of the wild rushes through your blood,
You relinquish all to the power of love.

The Wheel turns...

CHAPTER 10

Summer solstice – the height of power

At the summer solstice, also known as Litha, the Sun comes to the height of its journey in the Wheel. Full of power, it shines upon us through the longest day. Around us, the land is fast becoming green, luscious and full of growth energy. The land's dance, which began at Beltane, builds to a passionate fury. A final burst of growth energy to the crops and also to our projects, our dreams and ourselves.

At solstice we experience not only the height of our power on a primal level, but the transition from the height of our power to the next phase. The winding down. Like winter solstice, the summer solstice marks a turning point in the Wheel of the Year. And, although it is the height of summer, it is here in the heat that the winter is born. It is the equal opposite of the winter solstice. In their own way, the solstices are as much about balance as the equinoxes. Solstices symbolise the extreme turning points between transition and growth. Without experience of these extremes, we would not fully understand balance.

At summer solstice, you can harness the power of the Sun to reflect your own power. At Beltane, you explored your self-love, the root of your relationship with the self. At Litha, it is time to turn your attention to your power and abilities. To acknowledge, appreciate and take responsibility for allowing yourself to shine at the height of your own power. Reflecting the Sun's journey.

Around us, in the corporate and private world, there is an almost manic rush for completion. An intense pushing to complete work, take exams or finish projects before the summer holidays. Everyone is rushing for deadlines and trying to do all the odds and ends that need to be done before the break. But this is not the energy rush of summer solstice. Solstice power is deep rooted. Steady. Like a mountain or the strength of the tide. At summer solstice nature is at its most powerful point, the height of its energy. The land and Sun together have an energy surge giving us a boost of power, but it is not a manic, frantic, stressful energy. If you observe the animals born at spring equinox or the plants that bloomed at Beltane, they are not rushing. They are slowly growing and working on their life's purpose, existing and evolving. I believe that the reason this time is so stressful for humans, is because we are working against nature's rhythm. Instead of enjoying and harnessing our

SUMMER SOLSTICE – THE HEIGHT OF POWER

steady, powerful energy, we push it. We try to force progress into a deadline, rather than encouraging it to evolve.

When connected to the land's journey, the period from now until Lammas (August 1st), can be the most productive time of the Wheel. Our ancestors did not have 'a summer holiday'. In fact, the modern concept of a summer holiday is a 19th century invention[117]. With the Sun out, our bodies are replenished with vitamin D and the longer days gives us both the energy and the time to focus deeply and take the actions needed to manifest our dreams. It is here at the heart of summer that our Imbolc goals and dreams get the chance to expand and ripen before the first harvest at Lammas. summer solstice is a time where you will have the energy to make progress, reflecting the crops in the field which, within six weeks, will transition from green fresh plants to ripe golden heads of corn, ready to harvest.

HISTORY OF SUMMER SOLSTICE

The word solstice means to stand still[118]. Astronomically the summer solstice (in the northern hemisphere) is the point when the Sun is farthest north from the celestial equator, creating the longest day of the year.

Today, summer solstice is also called Midsummer or Litha, meaning 'mildest, most pleasant time of the year'. According to the author the venerable Bede, Litha isn't the name of a particular holiday, it was the Anglo-Saxon for the months of June and July[119].

What makes summer solstice so famous, and in my mind so fascinating, is that it has been celebrated in many different ways for many different reasons throughout human history. With many Neolithic monuments such as Stonehenge, Callanish and Bryn Celli Ddu aligned to the summer solstice sunrise, there is much evidence that the summer solstice was important to mankind from the days when we were still semi-nomadic groups with an emerging agricultural economy[120]. Some historians theorise that summer solstice was part of the guiding system for farmers with regards to the planting and harvesting cycle[121].

In Egypt, the Nile river rises at summer solstice. It's observance may have helped to predict annual flooding[122]. In ancient Greece they celebrated Kronia, a festival celebrating the titan god Cronus, the god of time and agriculture. Similar to the Roman festival Saturnalia held at winter solstice, Kronia was a festival of reversal. The social code was temporarily turned upside down during Kronia, with slaves participating and sometimes taking on the identity of their masters[123].

---

117 Tim Lambert "A Brief History of Holidays" www.localhistories.org/
118 Danu Forest The Magical Year 2016 Watkins London pg 122
119 Faith Wallis, (Trans.) Bede: The Reckoning of Time. Pp.53
120 Bradshaw Foundation "Stonehenge the Age of Megalithas – When was Stonehenge built? " www.bradshawfoundation.com http://www.bradshawfoundation.com/stonehenge/stonehenge.php
121 Gerald Hawkins. Stonehenge Decoded pg 150
122 Robert Carter Ancient History Vol I Ancient Eygyptians New York: RobPg 14
123 Atlantic Religion "The days of Kronos and Saturn" www.atlanticreligion.com

In ancient China, the solstices were associated with the turning points between the balance of Yin and Yang. After summer solstice they believed that the "yin", the feminine force emerged. The three day festival celebrated Earth, femininity, and the "yin" force. Women gave each other beautiful fans and pouches of sweet-smelling herbs to cover bad smells and cool themselves in the heat[124].

In the Nordic calendar, summer solstice was a crucial time of year for the Vikings, who would meet to discuss legal matters and resolve disputes. There is evidence that they celebrated Midsummer with bonfires and sometimes mock marriages called Jonsokbryllup (Jonsok weddings)[125]. After Christianity spread across Europe and into parts of Scandinavia, the Midsummer celebration continued. Today in Denmark, they celebrate St Hans Aften (St John's Night) by burning a bonfire topped with a witch figure. This probably comes from folk superstitions surrounding witches at this time of year or a left over tradition from when witches were burnt at the stake.

Some Native American tribes hold ritual dances to honour the Sun. The Sioux called this 'Wi wanyang wacipi' or 'sun gazing dance'[126]. Preparations included cutting and raising a tree, and then building a circular structure, open to the sky with an entrance to the east. The dancing takes place within a central arena that is completely open to the sky and to sun gazing. Participants abstained from food and drink during the dance. Their bodies were decorated in the symbolic colours of red (sunset), blue (sky), yellow (lightning), white (light) and black (night). The Sun Dance was not a tradition held only on summer solstice. However, in many parts of the world the Sun Dance has been incorporated into summer solstice celebrations.

GROWING WITH THE SEASON

With the Sun at its fullest point, radiating its full power upon the longest day, what better time of year for us to reflect upon our own power and to recharge that power by connecting with the Sun's energy at summer solstice.

The word 'power' often gets a bad reputation with negative connotations. However, I believe that this depends on your perspective. To recognise one's own power can be seen as being big headed. To be proud of one's abilities and power can initiate the "pride comes before a fall" feedback from others. Of course, there is a place in life for humility. But having an understanding of and claiming your own self-power gives a solid foundation for confidence, self-acceptance and being able to create and live the life you want. There is nothing wrong about acknowledging your own strengths.

At the summer solstice, the Sun is at the height of its power, but how can we be at the height of our power? Do we know what the source of personal power

---

[124] Moreen Liao "Summer solstice Marks Shorter Days and Yin's Rising" www.theepochtimes.com

[125] Joshua Rood J. "The Festival Year A Survey of the Annual Festival Cycle and Its Relation to the Heathen Lunisolar Calendar" Pg 25

[126] David J. Wishart "Sun Dance" www.plainshumanities.unl.edu

is? And, most importantly, how can we embrace that power and live a powerful life? summer solstice is the time to find out.

LIVING A LIFE – EMBRACING YOUR POWER

I know that you were born to be a powerful person and live a powerful life. Don't believe me? Well think about this: the fact that you were born here and now, where you are, your DNA, who your parents are by a 1 in 400 trillion chance, and you made it to here[127]. THAT IS AMAZING! I mean seriously mind boggling. You made it through all of the possible hinderances and arrived here and now, at this moment, as a sentient human being. For me, this revelation was one of the most powerful I ever had. When I realised this, I said to myself, "You owe it to yourself to live a powerful life and make the most of the opportunity you were given to be you and live out the potential you have within you". The same goes for you.

Living powerfully is a choice, It is also the key to achieving your dreams, not just keeping them as 'wouldn't that be lovely' wishes. YOU have within YOU the power to create your world, your reality. When you begin to live your life acknowledging your own power, your own strength, you find freedom in life. It took me some time to believe this and a long time to implement it within my own life. However, it's the best thing I have ever done for myself.

There is a key step that can help you live your life from a place of power.

Take responsibility for your life

This is the hardest concept to take in. It was my biggest stumbling block for many years. However, the day you begin to live this truth and take conscious control of your thoughts, is the day you declare your freedom and begin your mastery of life.

It's the day you cease to be a victim.

James Redfield in his enlightening book The Celestine Prophecies (which, if you haven't read, I highly HIGHLY recommend), named four control dramas which originate from our childhoods. The 'Poor Me's' is the drama that makes people feel guilty. A 'poor me' is a victim. And, if we are honest with ourselves, we have all played the victim card.

Typical victim thoughts are: why does this always happen to me? What did I do to deserve this? Why can't I have/ get/ do…, you did this to me, it's your fault that I feel so bad. Sound familiar? We all do it. Even when you are consciously aware of it, this behavioural pattern is so easy to fall into. However, it's not real. Life didn't do this to you, your partner didn't make you feel bad. Every situation in your life, you have chosen and created. I was so mad the first time I heard this. I was angry. I didn't create it that I grew up in discord, or that I ended up living

---

127 TED X Talks "How to stop screwing yourself over | Mel Robbins | TEDxSF" https://www.youtube.com/watch?v=Lp7E973zozc&t=17s

on the streets, or that I developed type 1 diabetes! How could anyone say that! I believed that all of these things happened to me, that I was the victim.

However, when I started to look at it from the perspective of taking responsibility, I could see that actually I did create these things. I did choose my path and I choose my reactions to these events, and I am responsible for the consequences of those actions and my intentions. Whether consciously or unconsciously. This may seem unbelievable to you. How can someone create diabetes type 1? It's a genetic condition. However, when I looked from a position of taking responsibility, I realised that I had called my diabetes into my own life by the abuse I gave my body. I was unable to accept the sweetness in life because I didn't believe that I deserved it. Type 1 diabetes lay in my DNA but my actions, my love of and excessive use of sugar and other harmful things helped bring it on. If I had taken care of myself, it could have been avoided. Once I acknowledged that I created my illness, I could also begin to take responsibility to take care of myself and honour myself, thus I became powerful.

In taking responsibility for my choices, I stepped out of the' poor me' role with the realisation that my actions create my world, my life and my path. If I had continued down that path, playing the it's unfair to poor little me role, I wouldn't be here today. As long as you think that how your reality turns out is due to someone or something else, you are still not taking 100% responsibility for the fact that YOU create your own life. You will remain in the victim role, and nothing changes that way. Victims have no power to do anything, for that is the belief they operate from.

In reality, the only thing you can really change is yourself, and to do that, one must move into the role of creator rather than victim. To be a clear, functional, healthy human being, always bring what is happening in your life back to you and look at how you created it. Especially whenever you think it's about someone or something else, or you feel that it's someone else's fault or the Universe getting at you. If you refocus on your actions, ask yourself why you are creating, this your life operates without blame or victimization and that frees you up to look for teachings and solutions.

You have control of only one thing in your life, you and your perspective. Remember, IT'S NEVER ABOUT ANOTHER PERSON, PLACE, OR THING. IT'S ENTIRELY UP TO YOU.

There are many, many ways to understand this concept. Don't worry if you don't get it all at once, I didn't.

One way is to think of it is that everything in this world, our human world; starts with intention. Everything you can see, started with an idea and intention. Your intention can create your experiences. Everything happens inside us, every experience you create, it all comes from our intention. Take the experience you are having right now, as it is created by two intentions. I had the intention I wanted to share my learnings, and so I wrote this book. You maybe had an intention that you wanted to get in touch with nature, yourself and your life and are reading it.

Another way is to look at it like this – you are like a computer. The computer depends upon what you type into it, and that determines what it will print out, correct? It's the same with your life. Whatever you type into yourself – that is, whatever perceptions or beliefs YOU have put inside you, or, "programmed into your computer" – that is what will get printed out and become your life. This printout is like a script available for other people to read. They read it, and simply respond to what you have typed out, to YOUR printout.

For instance, if what you have typed into your computer is: "Oh, I'm selfish. That means I'm a bad person," someone will read this in your printout (your energy field) and you will imagine them saying something like this to you: "You are so selfish!! Why don't you ever think of me? Why don't you make me happy?!" When you change what you type into yourself, when you change the energy that is in your energy field, when you change the thoughts and beliefs and emotions that you carry around, your printout will be different. Then everyone will read that new printout and respond to it differently.

Remember, if you can create the bad, you CAN create the good. Dreams, words, actions and choice beget reality, you are the architect of your life.

Live your life by taking responsibility for yourself, and you will live your life from a place of power. Here are a few of the tools I have used to take responsibility for my own life.

Accept where you are and look for teachings

Part of accepting responsibility for your life and living from a place of power is to accept responsibility for your past. You have to accept your previous actions, and I don't mean beating yourself up with guilt about it, I mean just accepting it, for what it was. Now you may have made what you consider to be bad choices, but they were the choices you made. You have to accept it and let go. You can't change it. You can really only do anything about it now. If you don't accept you and your choices from the past, how the heck is anyone else supposed to? So, make peace with the you of your past. Tell yourself that you did your best and accept that whatever you did, you did.

The most important thing about your past is to learn from it. Yes, you have made choices but everything in life is an opportunity to learn. When you look back at your life, there will be repeating patterns. These are a huge opportunity for learning. Four times in my life I had the pattern of bad relationships leading to sickness and homelessness. Each time was harder than the next, until I started to look at the patterns. I could see that all of it, all of the things I had done, came from a place of self-hate. Once I realised that and began working on my relationship with myself, raising my own opinion of my self-worth, life got better.

'Why did I create this?' An exercise to help you find the teachings

Think back to something that has happened in your life. Not a good situation, not the worst experience you have ever had however, choose a not great situation.

Write a short sentence explaining what happened.
Write why and how this happened to you, whose fault you thought it was.

Now we are going to look at your responsibility in this situation. Ask yourself:

- Why and how did you create this event?

Write down in a list the actions you took in this situation:

- What choices did you make?
- What was the outcome of these choices?

Now write what happened in your life after this event:

- Why was this event necessary in your life?
- Where did it lead you to?

Look again at your first description of why and how – do you agree with your first reaction or can you now see your role in this?

By looking at how we created a situation, we give ourselves an opportunity to learn. Learning empowers us to grow and evolve.

Find and Acknowledge Your Power

Just as trying to find things we love about ourselves can be challenging, so is admitting and owning our own personal power. Try these exercises to help you find out how powerful you are:

- Brainstorm keywords that describe the strengths you can see in yourself (if you like you can also name the sources of these strengths if they are external, it's good to know the source of your power).
- Ask close friends and family to give you three words that describe you as a person. Other people will have more of an objective perspective than you will. Collect this information. You will be surprised how the world sees you.

Your Past Inspiring Your Now

Even with your keywords from the people you love, it can still be hard to see your power when you look in the mirror, or even at your life. Sometimes it's easier to look back at your past and see where you have shown the world your powerful you. Take a look at the pictures of yourself you used to identify you from Beltane, the photographs of you in the past where you identified something you loved about you then. Now look for the power you embodied at this time.

For each picture, write a sentence about your strength at this time. Can you see this strength in you now?

Search for Your Power

One of the best ways to learn about your power is to recognise someone else's power. When we learn to appreciate other people for their unique talents, we also increase our own personal power as well as acknowledging the personal power of others.

Find someone you can interview. Take five minutes to ask each other these questions (with a timer):

- What makes you truly happy?
- What are your core personal values?
- What have you done in your life that you are most proud of?
- What is the second thing that you are most proud of?
- What empowers you?
- How do you describe your powerful self?

Now read the other person's answers to them. It is amazing that when we hear our own thoughts aloud, how differently we perceive them. Reverse the process and listen to your own answers. It is amazing when we look at how uniquely, and fantastic, we truly are.

Look at the person you have found yourself to be today. This person is strong, has individual talents and gifts, has survived and learnt and, most importantly, is consciously choosing to change their life and create and follow their dreams. This person needs to be honoured.

Be Your Own Personal Team Coach

If you have been working through some of the process described you hopefully will be feeling ultra-powerful right now! However, that can be challenging to do in the darker times when you are tired, alone or just having a crappy day. It's on days like these that we need to feel our power the most. One of the best ways to do that is to become your own coach and fan club!

In every team, be it sales, football or theatre the leader or coach will often give pep talks to his or her team. Compliments, and belief, boosts our confidence and reminds us how competent we are. You are your own team. SO, you need to become your coach and give yourself a pep talk. An exercise I found in the Magic of Thinking Big by David Schwart PhD, showed me the perfect way to do this

You need to write and read your own team pep talk! When we write and put conscious effort into creating, it becomes more believable. Rereading your writing and your words makes them believable.

Create your pep talk

Begin your pep talk by introducing you to yourself then, starting as many sentences as possible with your name, tell yourself about all the amazing things about you. Here is one of mine to get you started. I write a new pep talk every summer solstice. It will feel as though you are selling yourself. But it's ok to big yourself up once in a while!

Emma, this is Emma.
Emma is a wonderful person.

Emma connects with people. Emma inspires people and helps them with their lives. Emma brings people back to living with nature, to appreciate the world around them. Emma loves the world around her and is loved in her life. Emma has had adventures that no-one else has had. Emma is living an exciting life, learning every day. Emma has left legacies behind in her life already and will continue to do so.

Emma is a wonderful, amazing and beautiful person.

Use 'I am' Statements

One of the most powerful statements in the world is "I AM". In saying "I am", we are defining ourselves. There is no uncertainty. No room for doubt. "I am" is a 100% statement of creation. By stating what we are, we are bringing it into reality. Create I am statements for the strengths you see, in yourself or, if you dare, the strengths other people see in you for example:

I am brave.
I am strong.
I am kind.
I am caring.

Make a list. Pin it by your bathroom mirror and read them out loud every morning from now until Lammas. See how much stronger you feel.

   I like to combine my "I am" statements with the craft of making a solstice sun wheel.

TOOLS TO SUPPORT YOU TO LIVE A POWERFUL LIFE

There are many tools out there to support you to live a powerful life. Here are some that I have found that work for me. Try them and take what works for you.

Remove the Three C's from Your Life

Stop **comparing, competing, and criticizing**. There will always be greater and lesser persons than yourself. There will always be someone better or worse at doing the thing you want to do.

When you use the three c's, you waste SO much energy.

- Instead of complaining, do something positive.
- When you see someone doing something better than you, be inspired.
- Likewise, if you see someone struggling or doing something badly, help.

Smile

As a child I remember clearly watching one smile light up and change the mood and environment of an entire train carriage. One man, sat facing me, was sitting smiling. It made me smile. Opposite me, a lady caught the smile and slowly the smile travelled through the carriage. It felt good. Although I had been training all day in the ballet studio and was exhausted, that smile changed my day. It made me feel content and, to this day, I will always remember the power of that one smile.

Although not yet conclusively defined, it is known that it takes more muscles to frown than to smile. Smiling makes us feel better. If you smile, it helps you to change your mood. Try smiling at yourself in the mirror, you will feel better. When you feel down, try to laugh. See the humour in a situation. Make someone else laugh. If that doesn't work, watch or read something funny. Smiling and laughing releases dopamine which will make you feel better.

Powerful Body Language

Another way to change your own energy is to change the way you move your body. My favourite is the Peter Pan stance. The Peter Pan stance has changed my energy more times than I can count. Peter Pan stands with legs wide, hands in fists on hips and with his head and chin up and proud. The Peter Pan stance releases dopamine, by making you smile, and feels great. It's not possible not to smile after doing it and the best part is that it takes three seconds! So, stand legs wide apart hands on hips, throw your head back (mind your neck) and say loudly, "HA!" I challenge you not to feel good afterwards!

The way we use our body has a huge impact on the way other people perceive us and, more importantly, how we perceive ourselves. Dr. Albert Mehrabian, author of Silent Messages, discovered that 55% of our communication is through body language[128]. If you stand with your head and shoulders wilting, people will perceive you as a wilted flower. If you stand strong and upright, you seem more confident. When you seem confident, people treat you in that way.

---

128 Michela Rimondini (Editor) Communication in Cognitive Behavioral Therapy Pg 111

Analyse your own body language. By standing a little straighter with wider legs, people respond differently to you. Another way of changing your own confidence levels is to walk faster than you would normally. When you walk with purpose, slightly faster than the average pace, you create a field of importance. If you are in a room where you don't know many people, see who is mimicking your body language. That person feels comfortable with you. That is the person you can naturally talk with. At the same time, if you want to make an impression on someone, for example, a boss or interviewer, subtly copy their body language and they will feel more comfortable with you. Body language is a fascinating study, but you don't need to go so deeply into the subject. Find the few changes you need to make yourself feel positive and consequently more powerful.

Set Your Intentions – End of Day Thinking

A method of setting clear intentions for your day is called 'end of day thinking'. I step away from my desk for a moment and put the list of possible tasks for the day out of my mind. I then imagine myself sat in front of my evening meal that day and focus my attention on how I want to feel at that point in the day.

So, for me to feel like I have made the most of my time, and that I have had a powerful day, I visualise the feeling I want to achieve. Today I am going to choose the feelings 'calm and satisfied'. Now, I spend a little bit of time really making that visualisation clear. Imagining myself sat down, about to eat my meal and sensing the calm and satisfied feelings in my body. It feels attainable. I then go back to my desk with a clear destination for the day. I make a plan and I focus on the feelings that I visualised, into the now. I choose to approach the day feeling calm.

End of day thinking can be used for any chosen time frame. It is selfcoaching at its best.

Serve Others

Remember, a tree whose branches are numerous but whose roots are few, the wind will come along and uproot it. We are only as strong as the community or roots we grow. Make it a goal to help or serve someone every day. Expect nothing in return and you will find that you have around you strong roots to support you to reach for the Sun.

Lastly, FACE YOUR FEARS!

Although some fears are rational and serve to defend us, a survival instinct, some are simply blockers to our development. Fear can be your mind's way of tricking you to remain in old, comfortable and familiar patterns. I truly believe in challenging these fears. If I get scared, I remember my favourite saying paraphrased from Nelson Mandela; "Bravery is not the absence of fear, it is having a fear and doing it anyway." So, if something scares me and is not life threatening, I do it anyway. Whether it's taking that conflict, putting myself out there or simply trying to do something I have never tried before, I do it. By doing it I feel empowered!

SUMMER SOLSTICE TRADITIONS

Despite the many early temples aligned to summer solstice or the carvings of sun wheels on stones, we know relatively little about early pagan ceremonial practices, folk traditions or beliefs surrounding the summer solstice. The majority of these traditions survive in the Christian tradition of St John's Day the Christian festival that overtook the pagan celebration.

The Burning Wheel

We do know that the most celebrations included a bonfire[129]. In Europe, there was a tradition called the Burning Wheel – a burning cart wheel or sometimes a big ball of straw, was lit on fire and rolled down a hill into a river. The burned remnants were taken to the local temple and put on display. Records of this go back to the 4th century[130]. In Wales, it was believed that, if the fire went out before the wheel hit the water, a good crop was guaranteed for the season[131].

Collecting Medicinal Herbs

From Celtic times onwards summer solstice seems to have been the best time to pick medicinal plants as they were believed to be most potent during the summer solstice[132]. In Wales summer solstice is called 'gathering day' and in Sweden, mistletoe was also gathered and displayed on summer solstice eve possibly to honour Baldar and Frigg, as mistletoe contributes to Baldar's death, thought to have occurred on summer solstice[133].

There are many folk charms connecting summer solstice and St John's wort. If you wish to get pregnant then one charm has it that you should walk naked in a vegetable garden and pick some St John's wort! Another charm suggests that wearing St John's Wort picked on Midsummer's Day keeps depression at bay[134].

A Neighbourhood Feast

In Yorkshire, it was customary for someone who had moved to a new neighbourhood to put a table outside their home with bread, cheese and ale to

---

129 Edain McCoy The Sabbats a new Approach to living the Old Ways pg 153
130 West M.L. Indo-European Poetry and Myth Pg 214
131 Sir James Frazer The Golden Bough. Pg 630
132 Edain McCoy The Sabbats a New Approach to Living the Old Ways Pp 153–154
133 Edain McCoy The Sabbats a New Approach to Living the Old Ways pg 154
134 Teresa Moorey. Jane Brideson Wheel of the Year Myth and Magic through the seasons Pg 104

share with people that chose to partake of it. The guests were then invited to share supper with their new neighbours[135].

The Oak King and the Holly King

This folk story is for both of the solstices. The tale of the Oak King and the Holly King, the brothers who fought each other every solstice. The Holly King winning at Midsummer the Oak King at Midwinter. Each ruling a half of the year.[136] Here is a variation of Erica Barton's interpretation of that tale.

Once there were two brothers.

One brother was the king of life, light and warmth. He wore a crown made of green oak branches and brought with him all growth and vitality, fertility and abundance. He was called the Oak King.

His brother was the king of death, cold and darkness. He wore a crown made of holly branches and brought with him all withering and decay, stillness and hibernation. He was called the Holly King.

Each year, the Oak King would grow strong and mighty and during his time the light would gradually increase bringing with it abundance. But each year, at summer solstice, he would be thrown down by the Holly King. In the wake of the Holly King's victory, the light would gradually wane, and, as it did, the cold would come and the land would go to sleep. But at the height of the Holly King's power, he was challenged by the Oak King and would fall at the winter solstice. Each and every year the cycle repeated. Again, and again and again.

Alone, the brothers were equals, but there came into the world a new race known as people. The people watched the battle of the Oak King and the Holly King, and they began to take sides. They loved light and warmth, and they feared darkness and cold. So, they would celebrate the Oak King's victory and they mourned the victory of the Holly King. Every summer solstice, as the brothers battled, the people would lend the strength of their voices and their bodies, their minds by cheering for the Oak King. To the Holly King they gave no support.

Over time, the people's adoration of warmth and light only grew, and they invented new ways to keep warm in the cold, to see in the dark. Finally, they could spend their time in the light and warmth all year long. As this happened, the Holly King ever so quietly withdrew from the land. Time passed and at first the people did not notice the shifts in the world around them. The world filled with artificial light and heat. They did not mourn the loss of the darkness.

Generations passed, and as time went on, they began to notice that animals, birds, plants, even people, began to suffer the effects of light unbalanced by darkness. The people began to see that their support of warmth and light over cold and darkness had altered the balance of the whole world. The Holly King was dying. For the first time, this thought filled the people with fear. Could

---
135 Rev. T. F. Thiselton-Dyer, M.A British popular customs, present and past; Pg 319
136 Robert Graves The White Goddess; a historical grammar of poetic myth. Pg 173

they even survive in a world without the Holly King where the darkness was destroyed?

In the world of the gods, the Oak King realized it too. He realized that he loved his brother deeply, and could not live without him despite their competition. The longest night came, and the Oak King and the Holly King met again, but this time, the Oak King did not want to fight. He laid down his weapons and greeted his brother open handed.

The Oak King promised to help his brother heal. On the winter solstice night when he usually claimed ascendance, the Oak King realized that the world was already too warm and too light. So, he put the oak crown on the head of his brother and, each supporting the other, they went out into the world to see what could be done to restore balance once more...

CONNECTING WITH THE SEASON

Visit Your Powerful Place in Nature

Go somewhere that is a powerful place for you in nature. I am fortunate, as throughout my years of travelling, I have found many of these places, such as my childhood forest (complete with a ruined castle!), Tintagel beach and, of course Avebury. However, when I moved to Scandinavia, I lost my connection to the land and I had to find new places. This led me on some great adventures of exploration and now I have power places all over the world, such as a hawthorn on the banks of a fjord, the stone ship setting in Gammel Lejre, or a great willow in a public park in Copenhagen. So, if you don't have a place you can get to around summer solstice that feels like a place of power and rejuvenation for you, take some time at this time of year to go and find one! In your power place reflect on your personal power and what it is about this space that makes you feel powerful?

While you are there, as always; notice the changes in nature and the changes in your own life and how they correlate. Remind yourself of how the world looked at winter solstice and how your life was. You have travelled six months, so has nature. Ask yourself, how do those journey's mirror each other?

Record your reflections in your journal.

Summer Solstice Gathering

Social gathering as celebration is very much a part of summer solstice energy. Today, around the world at ancient places, people gather to celebrate, to give thanks for life and watch the summer solstice sunrise. It is an amazing experience to stand in one of these ancient places and watch the sunrise, if you have the chance do it (although be aware that the more well-known sites like Avebury and Stonehenge have a lot of people attending, so parking can be a nightmare!).

If you can't make it to an ancient site, then find a place where you can observe and enjoy the solstice sunrise. I find that spending the night with friends around the fire or going to a park for sunrise is just as powerful. It's also a really good excuse to schedule the overdue family camping trip!

Make a Sunwheel Personal Power Catcher

This Sunwheel is to act as a personal power catcher. I do this every Wheel. My strengths and sources of personal power are always changing with each Wheel. This is a great way to acknowledge that journey.

You will need:

- Small pieces of card
- 8 long sticks
- One long, bendable branch such as willow
- Twine
- Strips of fabric, raffia ribbons or wool in sun colours

How to make:

- On the small pieces of card, write down your 'I am' statements
- Cross the long branches in the middle, to form the wheel spokes and arrange them evenly
- Tie them together securely with twine
- Take your long, bendable branch and begin to bend it gently, to form a circle. Don't rush it, otherwise you'll get kinks. Just work your way along the branch until you can tie both ends together. Tie them securely and don't economize on the twine
- Tie your circle to the crossed branches, creating a wheel. Just be sure to align both pieces Now the base for your Sunwheel should have sufficient stability
- Tie each branch individually from the spokes to the circle
- Now to the fun part! (And the part that takes longest) Start to cross the raffia ribbons or wool in sun colours over the middle and cover the part where the branches cross completely Continue to weave your ribbon for a few rounds and secure it
- Then you start with the special weaving technique for your Sunwheel. Instead of just weaving your ribbon over and under the branches, you have to wrap your raffia, fabric or wool around each branch. Continue on wrapping until your Sunwheel is finished

- Decorate your Sunwheel by tying your 'I am' statements to the wheel and hang it in the window to catch the solstice sunlight

Find your Totem Animal

We have looked so far at the very practical real-world ways to access your self-power. However, there is another way to find the source or sources of your personal power. That is to connect with your totem animal. Over the centuries, there have been many different ways suggested to do this and many different opinions about which is right and how your relationship works with your spirit animal. I can offer my own opinion and guide. This may not be right for you, as it is my truth. I have two beautiful totems I work with. They change with the seasons as to which is dominant. However, I do not believe that these are the only totems who walk with me. I find that different animals walk in and out of my life, guiding my journey on both the spiritual and physical plane. So, I believe that we have a plethora of guides throughout our journey. Some just stay with us for longer than others. I use the signs around me in the physical world when certain animals begin to appear continuously in my life as well as the Druid animal oracle to see who is walking with me. In my shamanic journeys I often travel with and talk to my totems, they are a constant source of inspiration, guidance and comfort.

When planting a wood in Wiltshire with an older shaman, I was taught a simple and effective method of connecting with your totem animal, and this I would like to share with you.

Lay still and comfortable in a quiet space. Light candles and incense if you wish. Make sure you have some water and a notebook to hand. Allow your breathing to slow and, as you breathe out, relax.

Focus and set your intention on meeting your totem animal, the animal that represents your power and strength.

Now in your mind's eye, begin to see your cave at the bottom of your ancient tree. You are sitting comfortably in your cave. Warming yourself by the fire. Invite your spirit animal, your power animal to sit with you.

Wait to see who appears. Spend some time with your totem. Maybe they will speak, maybe not. You may feel their communications with you. You might spend time grooming your totem. Or they may wish to take you on a journey.

Be with them. Ask them to help you return to your body when you feel it is time to return.

When you have returned, remember to record your journey, eat some chocolate and drink some water.

It is a good idea to research the symbology of your totem. This animal represents your power your personality in its rawest, most beautiful form. Connect with this in both your spiritual and physical worlds. You will benefit greatly from connecting with your totem as often as you can. It is one of the keys to understanding yourself and your purpose on this earth walk. Not to mention a wonderful way to reclaim and acknowledge your own personal power.

Collect Summer Herbs

Around the summer solstice, the herbs are ripe to be harvested and dried, especially lavender. One of the most pungent and relaxing flowers on the planet. Lavender is great for inducing sleep and lessening anxiety. As you will probably be taking some R and R in the coming summer, you can make yourself a gorgeous smelling lavender pillow or tincture. In this way your summer solstice harvest will help you boost your power in the months to come.

SUMMER SOLSTICE CRAFTS

Dream Pillows

You'll need:

- Fabric in pattern of your choice
- Pins
- Cotton, polyfill, or other stuffing material
- Dried lavender
- Needle, thread, scissors

How to make:

- Place the fabric with the right sides together
- Cut out the shape you'd like your pillow to be -- square, circle, whatever
- Pin the material together, and sew most of the way around the edges. Be sure to leave a gap where you can stuff the pillow
- Turn the material right side out, and fill with cotton or polyfill
- Add a few handfuls of dried lavender, and stitch the opening closed

Easy Lavender Tincture

Lavender tincture has many uses. I like mine added to baths, as a light perfume (dab on the wrists), to refresh sachets. You can add tinctures to a range of body care products (soap, lotion, massage oil, toner) or you might add it to your washing liquid to give a lovely smell to your clean clothes!

    A non-distilling approach to make tincture of lavender is easier than the boiling and steaming process.

SUMMER SOLSTICE – THE HEIGHT OF POWER

You'll need:

- Lavender buds. I collect mine from home (if you are going to add your tincture to body care products, make sure you use organic lavender)
- Grain alcohol or cheap vodka
- Mortar and pestle (alternatively you can use a bowl and spoon)
- Coffee filters
- Two jars, one with a tight-fitting lid
- A dark colour jar for storing

(NOTE: do not substitute isopropyl / rubbing alcohol for this project. Rubbing alcohol has its own overpowering disinfectant smell that will overpower your lavender essence.)

How to make:

- Gently wash and dry your lavender buds
- Put lavender buds into your bowl or mortar, and crush lightly to release the aromatic oil
- Just bruise the flowers with the back of the spoon or pestle. Do this gently. Too much agitation will give you lavender soup — and that's not how to make lavender essential oil
- Transfer the lavender to a jar with a tight-fitting lid
- Cover entirely with the grain alcohol or vodka
- Shake the jar to release more oil, several times a day, for several days in a row
- After a week or so of this – (a shortcut during this phase of how to make lavender essential oil is to leave the "brewing" jar on a sunny kitchen counter for a weekend) you're ready to refine. Use a coffee filter to strain the liquid into the second jar, (the pour-off is technically lavender-infused vodka, though I don't recommend drinking it)
- Place a clean coffee filter or cloth on top of the jar of liquid and allow it to sit undisturbed for about one week. This will allow the alcohol to evaporate from the jar, leaving essential oil as the result
- There may be sediment at the bottom, which is no big deal. (if it bothers you strain it again with a clean coffee filter into a lidded storage jar). Use dark-coloured glass to protect the actives in the oil
- Store out of direct sunlight

SUMMER SOLSTICE JOURNEY

The purpose of this journey is to connect with the solstice energy, the source of your own power and to ask for guidance to reveal your life purpose or how you can use your power in your life wisely.

Remember, if you meet someone or something you are unsure of, simply ask it three times "Are you here in love and light?" If it is not, it will go away. Beltane is truly the time of the fey and they can be tricksy.

Now it is time to take your solstice journey….. Remember, be clear as to why you are journeying…

Breathe deeply and slowly, sitting or lying in a comfortable position. Make sure you're warm enough and have a glass of water close by. As you breathe feel your surroundings slip away, as you cocoon yourself in a safe protective circle.

In your mind, begin to see yourself standing high on a hill. The golden sun warms the earth, you are surrounded by green in the trees, the grass. In the fields you can see the green wheat stalks ready to ripen. The land hums deeply with activity.

As you walk further up you become aware that, high up on the hill, a lone tree stands. An ancient oak. The leaves are easy to see now small, fresh and new, opening. The oak stands strong as you walk in a circle around the tree.

At the bottom of the oak, almost hidden in the trunk you can see a wooden door, half covered with ivy. Slowly, you walk towards the door. It opens with a creak and you can make out dimly lit stairs spiralling up into the tree and spiralling down. You begin to make your way up the stairs. To each side of you is soil and roots. You can smell the musty damp of the rich fertile and damp earth around you.

Further and further up you go passing the middle of the tree you see the door to your grove but this is not your destination today. The stairs continue upwards, this is your journey today. Today we are travelling to our higher planes. At the top of the staircase is a door made of gnarled and aged wood. Slowly you open this ancient door. As it opens, a bright golden summer light fills the space around you and you step out onto a wide open field and, on the horizon, you can see a circle of stones. The colours here are richer and deeper. You walk towards the stones and, as you walk, you call your animal guide to meet with you in the circle. The land here is alive, more vivid, electric.

At the entrance to the circle you pause, ask for permission to enter, and give thanks to those who built the circle.

Sit in the centre, close your eyes and breathe deeply. Call your animal spirit to you, call the one spirit that is the essence of you. As you open your eyes, you are sitting opposite the animal. You are looking deep into each other's eyes. Quietly you ask, show me.

This picks up as you become your animal spirit, allow yourself to blend with your totem. Do not try to control it. You are along for the ride today. Allow your animal to become your guide. Ask him/her to show you your strength. As they move, feel the power within you both, the strength you have. I will call you back to the circle in a while. Enjoy this time in the pure essence of your strength.

SUMMER SOLSTICE – THE HEIGHT OF POWER

* * *

Now it is time to return to the circle. Once again in the centre, you step out of your animal spirit and become yourself once more. Thank your animal spirit for the gift of the journey you have had together today. Sit as you were before, breathing deeply with your eyes closed. In your mind, reach out to your soul group, the group of souls that you are intrinsically part of, people, ancestors, beings, animals. Whoever it is, call to them and ask them to join you and to bring with them an insight as to why you have chosen to walk the earth at this time. Open your eyes and join your soul group sitting around the circle. You see familiar faces from your previous journeys. Talk with your soul group a while and make a mental note of the teachings they bring...

Now it is time to return. Thank your soul group for their insights and for joining you today. Give thanks to the circle for the time you have spent there.

Walk through the fields and back towards the oak tree until you reach the door.

Open the door to the staircase spiralling down and smell the rich soil once more.

Once again, you travel down to the doorway you entered by (not down to your cave). It is the end of the night, as you open the door and go out you hear the drums of the solstice party, you see folk dancing around the circle. You join in the dance, laughing, spiralling around the tree. In one moment, you all stop and look to the east. The Sun rises glowing, flaming light across the sky. The shortest night is over... Stand looking at the Sun while it rises...

Slowly become aware of the place in which your body lies or sits and allow your spirit self to step into your body and become one again. Gently allow the circle to slip away, and bring yourself back to consciousness.

Drink some water, eat some chocolate, record your journey and get some fresh air.

SOLSTICE CEREMONY

Have some music playing for this ceremony and as many lit candles as you can.

In the centre of the space, at your feet, place the Sunwheel.

Put the altar in the north

I walk the circle three times, imagining a boundary of pure energy around me.

"A time that is not a time, in a place that is not a place"

At the north point of the circle, I invite the elements of earth to join me.
At the east point of the circle, I invite the elements of air to join me.
At the south point of the circle, I invite the elements of fire to join me.
At the west point of the circle, I invite the elements of water to join me.

Within the centre, I invite spirit to join me.

Silently I invite my ancestors and guides to be with me.

Raise energy through doing the Tree of Life visualisation (page 15).
Say clearly and loudly:

I am strong.
I am powerful.
I can do, be and have, anything I want.
I can (sew/draw/...name some of your talents).
I can create and enjoy the life I dream of.
I will succeed.

Now say, "I let go the past and focus only on the now, because it is the actions that I take today that creates my future tomorrow. Today is a fresh start. Today I will make an impact. Today I am one step closer to my dreams. I am grateful for today!"

Release the energy of power you have created and send some of it into the Universe and (if you made one) send some of it down to the Sunwheel you have created. Full of energy, take up your Sunwheel and hold it above your head. OR raise your arms to the Sun. Saying,

"I am grateful for the Sun! I am grateful for the air. I am grateful for the earth. I am grateful for the water. I am grateful for all that I have, for all that I have learnt and all that I will become!"

Release the energy built up inside you.
Reverse the Tree of Life visualization and become yourselves once more.
Give thanks and share cakes and wine.
Thank the elements, guides and ancestors for joining you and walk the circle round in the opposite direction at the start.

Now it's time to celebrate summer solstice!

King of the Sky, the summer sun burns bright,

At the height of its power, the height of its might.
Every molecule bursting with life giving power,
Giving all that it can until the very last hour.

Revellers meet in henge and in town,
The party starts as the Sun goes down.
A celebration of life, of power and transition,
Gathering each year in this centuries old tradition.

It's the longest day, the shortest night
A last burst of power before the summer takes flight.
The merry-making ends with the coming of the dawn,
We stand energised witnessing the winter sun be born.

The Wheel turns...

CHAPTER 11

Lammas – The First Harvest, Sacrifice and Rebirth

At Lammas, the land is bountiful. The corn and wheat are golden waiting for us in the fields, ready to be cut down to transition. The apples are beginning to ripen in the trees. The first harvest is beginning. In our modern world, it's often easy to forget the trials and tribulations and hard work our ancestors had to endure to survive. For us, if we need bread, we simply drive over to the local grocery store and buy a few bags of pre-packaged bread. If we run out, it's no big deal, we just go and get more. For our ancestors, the harvesting and processing of grain was crucial. If crops were left in the fields too long, or the bread not baked in time, families could starve. Taking care of one's crops meant the difference between life and death.

By celebrating Lammas as the first harvest, we honour the land and reconnect with the process of sustaining life. At the same time, we give thanks for the abundance we have in our lives, and are grateful for the food on our tables. Lammas is a time of harvest, sacrifice, transformation, of rebirth and new beginnings. On the land, as the first crops are gathered, so too is it time for us to gather our first harvests, to reap the fruits of our seeds sown at Ostara. To begin to store the things that will give us sustenance throughout the dark winter months ahead and to sacrifice what we do not need and offer it back to the earth.

Lammas is not only a time of celebrating our strengths, and evaluating our progress, it is also a time of sacrifice and rebirth. The corn sacrifices its life and transforms, or is reborn, as the bread we eat, the beer we drink.

Lammas energy can be bittersweet. Although we can glory in the fruits of our labour and enjoy the warmth of the Sun, Lammas is the first point in the Wheel where we can feel the life energy ebbing away, the first hint of the darker times and hibernation to come. Imbolc was the first time of life being visible in the land and, equally, Lammas is the point where we begin to see life ebbing away. It begins the preparation, the gathering of that which will sustain us until life returns to the land in spring. For me, Lammas truly marks the last day of summer. From here on the land will slowly withdraw its energy until it begins its winter slumber.

HISTORY OF LAMMAS

Lammas is the last of the Celtic fire festivals during the Wheel. You may have noticed that the fire festivals mark the transition points in life's cycle. The awakening of new life at Imbolc, the conception at Beltane, the sacrifice made for life to continue at Lammas, and death at Samhain. For me, these fire festivals echo and embody the natural journey of life, be it plant, human or animal. The life cycle is something we all share, another great equaliser and mirror.

Lammas, also called Lughnasadh, is one of the Celtic festivals which we know was celebrated across the Bristish Isles. The combination of the name Lugh, and nasadh meaning 'game or assembly', suggests that Lughnasadh began as a funeral feast for the god Lugh celebrated with sporting competitions, honouring the tradition Lugh began of holding games to commemorate his mother Tailtiu named the Tailteann Games[137], later called the Lammas games. The games and assembly were the two most important components for the Celtic celebrations as well as rituals for continued fertility. Wales and England also had similar festivals at a similar time known as Gwyl Awst and Lammas[138].

Lunghnasdha was held across Ireland, Scotland and the Isle of Man, at the midway point between the summer solstice and the autumn equinox. On the opening day of the festival, the community gathered in a high place. There were pageants and dramatic performances depicting local versions of Lugh's story. They would feast on the first of the harvest's corn reaped from the field, made hastily into small cakes, as well as bilberries, and in some places a sacrificial bull[139]. Lastly the young people of the community would focus on some form of fertility magic, such as the Welsh game 'Rhibo' where a boy and girl were tossed in the linked arms of six people[140].

There would be great assemblies of the community and trading fairs, and, of course, the Tailteann games, which lasted for two weeks[141]. There the best warriors and athletes would gather for the games, which included competitions like long jump, high jump, running, hurling, spear throwing, archery, wrestling, boxing, swimming and chariot and horse racing[142]. In Teltown, County Meath, the site of the ancient games, there is even evidence of artificial lakes dating from the time[143]. The Tailteann games at Teltown have been revived periodically

---

137 Alexi Kondratiev Celtic Rituals An authentic guide to ancient Celtic Spirituality pg 178– 188
138 ibid.
139 Seamus MacGabhann Landmarks of the people: Meath and Cavan places prominent in Lughnasa mythology and folklore. Pg 11.
140 ibid.
141 Geoffrey Keating. Foras feasa ar Eirinn ... The history of Ireland, tr. and annotated by J. O'Mahony. pg. 301
142 Navan & District Historical Society "Teltown" www.navanhistory.ie http://www.navanhistory.ie/index.php?page=teltown
143 Howard Goldbaum, "TELTOWN (TAILTEANN) Kells, Co. Meath"

throughout history, the last time in 1964[144]. Legend has it that St Patrick actually visited the Tailteann games where he cursed the river Sele's waters to darken[145].

Although Lammas is a Celtic fire festival, there was a strong emphasis placed on water in the ritual celebrations. The Celtic equal and opposites. At Beltane, the cattle were driven through the fire for purification. At Lammas, the horses of the community were purified by being driven through water. In a ritualised mock race, men rode naked across the river, forcing the horses to swim[146].

Historically, Lammas has a strong connection to sacrifice. Known in British folklore as John Barleycorn, the "sacrificial king" is cut down in the field to provide us with bread and beer. Sacrifices at Lammas were made to thank the gods for the first harvest and to guarantee an abundant harvest. In many cultures, there was a theme of a dying and resurrecting king within their mythology. The Corn God embodied this concept. In the past in some parts of the world, Lammas was a time of physical sacrifice. In some cultures this was purely symbolic. In others, the sacrifice was an actual king or mock 'king' offered as a human sacrifice[147].

There are many accounts of sacrificial kings, both actual and mythological. So much so that the lines between fact and fiction are often blurred. Such is the case in the martyrdom or sacrificial offering of King Oswald, who offered his life for his people and then his body parts were buried in different parts of the land[148]. Or in the mystery surrounding the death of King William II (Rufus the Red, or William Rufus) on Lammas in the year 1100. King William II actively rejected the relatively new Christian beliefs. His death in a 'hunting accident' in the New Forest is believed by some historians to have been a case of the traditional Lammas sacrifice being disguised for the sake of the Christian priests. Although, other historians believe that it was a plot by the church to remove the troublesome king. Either could be right. The interesting and slightly suspicious fact is that Walter Tyrrel, who shot the fatal arrow, returned to his own country unpursued or reprimanded after the 'accident' and lived there without any repercussions[149].

---

wwwvoicesfromthedawn.com
144 ibid.
145 Navan & District Historical Society "Teltown" www.navanhistory.ie http://www.navanhistory.ie/index.php?page=teltown
146 Alexi Kondratiev Celtic Rituals An authentic guide to ancient Celtic Spirituality pg 184
147 Anne Franklin Paul Mason Lammas: Celebrating Fruits of the First Harvest pg 70
148 David Rollason Northumbria, 500–1100: Creation and Destruction of a Kingdom Pp 198–199
149 James Plumtree "Stories of the Death of Kings: Retelling the Demise and Burial of William I, William II and Henry I*" pg 17

GROWING WITH THE SEASON

Your First Harvest

As you have been walking with the Wheel, you have planted seeds, worked on projects, dreams and goals. Some of these will have already manifested and bloomed in your life. These are your first harvest. For some of us, it's making a livelihood; for others, it's growing a family; it's a successful career, or it could be working through a personal struggle, such as increasing your self-confidence. Sometimes our first harvest will be obvious, sometimes it will surprise us. It may be that your first harvest is something you have not planned but have learnt throughout the Wheel.

Discovering What is Your First Harvest?

Discovering your first harvest gives you the opportunity to evaluate and celebrate your progress on the journey of manifestation. Look at your vision boards and step by step plans you made at Imbolc and Ostara. Answer the following questions:

- What have you completed?
- Do you need to cross off steps you have fulfilled? If so, do it. Crossing off things you have done is a really satisfying way of recognising your achievements)
- Which goals/projects have you not worked upon, have not succeeded or no longer feel right for you at this time?
- Which projects and goals do you no longer wish to work upon?
- Which of the goals/projects you have worked upon have succeeded?
- What do you have left to manifest of this year's goals and dreams?
- Have you unexpectedly harvested something?

Write a list in your notebooks for each of your goals that you can harvest here and now. Start your list with the sentence

My first harvest is ....

Read your answers aloud. As you do this, you will get a sense of which of your achievements you feel most passionate about and excite you the most. This is your first harvest, the fruition of your labour and dedication. It may be that the negative voice creeps in and tries to tell you that this is not a fantastic achievement or not enough. Use the power of NO and remind yourself that any achievement is something to be proud of and to be celebrated.

Do not concern yourself with what you haven't done or what you haven't completed. Lammas is the first harvest. There is plenty of time to finish that which needs finishing and to work upon that which needs it.

Sacrifice

In our modern lives, our sacrifices are not so brutal as in the days of the sacrificed kings. The vegetables in the garden give of themselves to feed us (and for that I am eternally grateful). However, in order to grow and reap this harvest, the gardeners give sweat and tears, and inevitably leave a blood sacrifice to the hordes of mosquitoes, insects and prickly weeds. There is no way around it; nature feeds on itself, we simply cannot expect a harvest without sacrifice.

Usually, when we have to make it consciously, sacrifice is something we resist. It is a difficult, unpopular theme to come to terms with in our modern mindset. Older, more mature and connected cultures than ours actually understood sacrifice, or the ability to make an offering, better than we do today. The simplest way I have found to understand sacrifice or offering is that sometimes, in order to have something that you love, you have to give up something else that you love.

When you read about the sacrifices of ancient people, whether those sacrifices were a bull calf or bundle of grain, they always gave their best. A calf free of blemish, a sheaf of full ears with no grains missing. Lifeforms with genetic futures in them, that could have been held onto and hoarded, eaten, or bred, were offered. They also sacrificed the most beautifully made weapons or jewellery. Culturally they understood that, in order to make a sacrifice, you had to give up something you really wanted or needed.

These ancient people offered sacrifices in faith that the harvest or hunt would be better. They restricted the gratification and comfort in their present selves in service of their future selves, and also of the people that would come after them. They didn't hedge their sacrifices. Sacrifice was an absolute leap of faith, giving up the apparent and valuable, for something yet to arrive. Sacrifice is losing something beloved and known in a gamble with the unknown. It is giving something up to a cause larger than yourself, without being quite sure what, if anything, you will get back in return. In sacrifice, there are no guarantees. There is no real sacrifice if you know the result.

Throughout this Wheel you will have made sacrifices consciously or unconsciously. In your journal reflect upon this Wheel's journey. Ask yourself:

- What sacrifices have you made?

- What is the result of these sacrifices (if apparent)?

Now look at your harvest, firstly begin to cross off the projects and dreams you have not worked upon so far, that you simply don't feel motivated for. This is part of your sacrifice. Some plants need to have help to remove leaves or deadheads to help them grow further, and this is our deadheading. Of course, keep this idea in the back of your mind. It maybe that the time is not right in your life for these things and they may be suitable for another point in your life. After all, not every seed can grow into a mustard plant. By sacrificing some of your dreams, you are accepting realistically the time you have to work with manifesting your goals at Samhain.

Making a Conscious Sacrifice

Making a conscious sacrifice refocuses our commitment after the summer. Look at your harvest and choose one to three dreams, goals or projects that you feel passionate about and as yet are incomplete. In your journal, answer the following questions:

- What will you have to, or are willing to, sacrifice to manifest this into a reality in your life?
- How will this impact your life?
- How will you make this sacrifice?
- When will you make this sacrifice?

Choosing a sacrifice might seem a strange notion but by doing this consciously you are reinforcing the work of self-power at summer solstice by taking responsibility for your life instead of reacting. Remember too that resentment is a block to your progress. If you have to sacrifice something unwillingly, you could resent it and block your own growth. So, by giving something up freely you are prepared and accepting when a sacrifice comes.

Moving Forwards with Manifesting Your Goals

It is easy to have dreams, think up projects and set goals, it is harder to complete them. At first we have a surge of fresh new energy and then when change comes too slowly or is too scary we can settle into old patterns, get distracted and beat ourselves up because we are not keeping the agreements we set for ourselves.

So, we stagnate in a negative pattern and we begin to send out negative vibrations into the world. The exact opposite of what we want. However, it is a natural part of the growth process. If you look at a plant or even a child, growth comes in spurts or periods. One moment they fit the same clothes for months and then nothing will fit. At Lammas, we need to initiate a period of growth. To rededicate and focus on completing the work we started at Imbolc.

It is time to commit to action. Look back at your journaling as answer to one simple question:

- What do you need to do by Samhain to have completed the three dreams you have kept, or to go to the level you feel is a success on this Wheel?

When you have clarity in your answers to these questions, as at Ostara, make a step by step guide to achieving your goals (or edit the existing one if it is still applicable and realistic). Put dates by the times you intend to start and complete these actions.

A word of caution – don't put yourself under undue pressure here. Yes, you have things to do and a time limit. You have to accept that there is enough time. I know it is easy to say and not easy to do. Accepting that there is enough time is a challenge (believe me this one took me awhile). It's about changing the dialogue in your mind. If you tell yourself you don't have enough time, you won't have enough time. In a way, you are right, none of us has unlimited time, we all of us only have 24 hours in a day, 7 days a week. Worrying about not having enough time takes away your time. You have to simply trust all the time, you need to do what you choose to do and get going.

So, to accept, change your inner dialogue. Every time the stress bunny pops up into your head, screaming that you don't have enough time, repeat this mantra in your head and eventually the stress bunny will disappear down the rabbit hole for good:

I have all the time I need to do what I choose to do.

Or

I have the time I have.

GET SUPPORT FROM YOUR COMMUNITY

Harvest time is always a time of people pulling together, a community helping each other. As I watch the tractors in the fields around me, they work night and day to get the harvest in. I get very little sleep due to the noise! I can see that working alone to bring the harvest in would be back breaking, exhausting hard work. You simply cannot bring in a harvest alone without breaking yourself. In older days, a whole community, men, women, elderly and children would come together to bring in the harvest in time. Kids used to get a week off school to help with the potato harvests called 'Prattie gathering holidays' in Scotland[150]. Even today, families come together to bring in the harvest.

It is surprising how many of us find it hard these days to ask for help as we did in the past. In nature, trees in a forest share their resources with each other. It is natural to ask for help and support and sometimes it is essential for your motivation. Lammas is a time to reach out to your community for help and support in your manifestation process.

You need to find a person to help you manifest your goals before Samhain. This person is your accountability partner. It should be someone who is motivated in their own life, will be willing to give you some time every week to help you with your progress and, IMPORTANTLY, someone who will not let you make excuses. There is no point asking someone who will respond with comments such as "poor you, well just don't do anything this week." Not beneficial. Your accountability partner is your support team (on a side note here I don't recommend using a partner as your accountability partner, it can create more problems than it solves). If you put it out in the Universe that you want positive help and support, the right help will come. And it can go both ways. You can also give back to them by asking if they would like you to be an accountability partner for them.

---

150 Maghera Heritage Centre "Potatoes: Maghera Roots" www.maghera-heritage.org

How to Set up an Accountability Partnership

Give your partner a copy of your mini goals (and get a copy of theirs, if you are going to be their accountability partner).

Now make an agreement around how your accountability relationship will work. For example, it could be that once a week you are going to be contacted by your partner by text, on the telephone, or via social media to check in.

Make sure your accountability partner knows that their job is to see how it's going with you and motivate you in fulfilling your goals if you are having challenges. Make them aware that this is not about being an agony aunt. Of course, be understanding but their job is to help you back on track to the independence of doing the work you need to do to create your goals, projects or dreams.

Ask your accountability partner to make notes of your conversations and send them to you, so you both can keep track of your progress. I find it helpful to make an agreement for an action each week with my goals, and then have my accountability partner send me a message with those agreements written down so I can keep focused.

Good Tips as an Accountability Partner:

It is important to remember boundaries and to set them in your accountability partnership. Remember to:

- Listen first, talk after.
- Set a time limit to your partner's talk time
- If you are being an accountability partner for each other, only deal with one person's situation per text/fb/call (doing both together gets confusing)
- Guide people to find their own solutions, offering your suggestions as a last resort
- Praise small steps
- Remind them of their success experiences

Other great questions an accountability partner can ask you are:

- What are you doing to enjoy life?
- What are the stress factors coming into your life right now?
- What is getting way too much air time in your thoughts right now?
- How can you help you?
- What is working for you right now?

- What is the most important thing you need to do to achieve your goal right now?
- When will you do that?
- How are you going to reward yourself when X is done?

Remember to celebrate!

One of the most challenging things when working on goals is knowing when you are succeeding. An accountability partner is a great help here. Not only do they have an outsider's perspective and therefore can point out your progress. But as you explain to them where you are at, your awareness of your own triumphs becomes apparent.

One of the most important things an accountability partner can ask you is, "How are you going to celebrate your achievements this week?" Creating the life you want is not always about working. You have to enjoy the journey, or what is the point? I once had an accountability partner who introduced the idea of paying a fine when we didn't meet our target, needless to say this did not work out well. I felt riddled with guilt constantly. So, we made the agreement to celebrate our achievements. Positive attracts positive. It was much more motivational and fun too! So, ask your accountability partner to help you get motivated by celebrating!

Keep it real

With my accountability partner, I asked for her support to help me finish writing the first draft of this book by a specific time. When I moved house, I got out of my daily writing practise. So, I set a goal that I would write for one hour at the same time for five days in a week. My accountability partner brilliantly asked me if this was realistic for that week. It was great to get a chance to reflect on my decision and knowing the phone call was coming motivated me to hold myself on target. My end goal was not only to have it written, and it was also to treat myself to a fancy dinner and a bottle of champagne when I was done. Something I only ever do for special occasions.

TRANSFORMATION AT LAMMAS

Another theme at Lammas is the idea of transformation, as the corn and wheat becomes the bread and beer. Transformation is a constant in life. Around us the world evolves, transitioning from birth to death and constantly growing in between. Each and every Wheel we walk, we also transform actively and passively. If you have been following the book during this Wheel you have not only worked towards your goals, you have also worked upon yourself. You have experienced self-love, you have explored your own power. In a sense, you have been reborn. You are in the process of making the transformation to a stronger conscious and connected you.

What have you learnt about you during this Wheel's transformation?
On a piece of paper, draw you or something representing you in the centre.

- Around the picture write positive statements about you starting with the phrase I was ...

- Around the picture write positive statements about you starting with the phrase I am ...

- Around the picture write positive statements about you starting with the phrase I can ...

These can be things you knew at the beginning of the Wheel but also (and preferably) the things you have discovered. If you are stuck, look back through your notes.

Keep this picture in your new notebook for the next Wheel and, when it is next Lammas, compare it with the new one. It is amazing how often we can keep learning more and more positive facts about ourselves as we transform and grow.

Rebirth

Like transformation, the theme of rebirth is constantly present at Lammas. The seed becomes the wheat. The wheat is cut down and turned into beer. If you have followed the steps in this chapter, you now know where you have succeeded so far, the work you still have to do and the sacrifices you will have to make. Plus, you can see how far you have come in this Wheel's journey, how strong you can be when you consciously take charge of your life.

This work will have given you a clear image of where and who you want to be within your life at Samhain. It maybe that you are already that person, or partly that person. In which case, you just need to make this person shine forth.

A full rebirthing takes a lot of time, preferably undisturbed privacy and a lot of experienced support. It is not a process to undertake lightly and certainly not a process I would recommend pursuing alone. However, to give you the motivation to continue your personal transformation during this Wheel, a visualisation of rebirthing of your own self-image will achieve the energy you need to take you forward and focus you. This visualisation can be repeated when you need it.

"Begin to breathe deeply. In and out. In and out. Deep into your lungs. Use your stomach to push all the air out of your body. Continue to breathe deeply.

In your mind's eye, surround yourself in a bubble where you sit. Nothing can harm you in this bubble. It is elastic and can move wherever you move. Nothing can be there apart from you, the elements and your guides.

In your mind's eye, see yourself stand up. Your right hand is clenched, holding something. Below your bare feet is earth. You reach down and with your left hand you dig a hole in the earth. From your right hand you drop a seed into the hole and cover it up. You look up at the Sun and close your eyes as the soft rain falls. You join with your real body breathing slowly.

As you sit there breathing deeply, you see in front of you a small shoot begin to push through the earth. The shoot grows taller and thicker in front of you and as it unfurls you can see that inside the stem, unfolding, is you. Not the you that you are now, but the you that you will become. Shining bright, growing in front of you, until at last the future you steps out. Your new body is glowing, radiating love, happiness and abundance. Strong on its feet, connected to the earth and reaching for its dreams. Once more you stand up and face this shining you. For a moment you gaze into her eyes and then in one movement she enters you, joins with you. You become one. At this moment your body begins to glow and shine, you feel rooted in the earth, your heart stretching to the sky and your spirit wild, free and confident.

Be there glow experience. Do nothing more than feel.

Now allow that light to dim down a little, don't let it go completely out. Take a few deep breaths. Allow your spirit self to settle into you once more. Be one. Feel yourself breathing slowly, feel yourself as one complete being. Breathe deeply. In and out. In and out. Deep into your lungs. Use your stomach to push all the air out of your body. When you feel ready, begin to stretch your arms and legs and, when ready, open your eyes "

Make sure you drink a lot of water after this visualisation. It can also be helpful to record in your notebook how you felt during this visualization.

Gratitude

When you have an attitude of gratitude the Universe keeps giving you more to be thankful for. But it is easy to forget what we are grateful for in our busy lives.

The tradition of giving thanks for the first harvest goes back deep within human DNA. There is not a more apt and fitting time to be thankful for your life.

Being grateful does not always have to be about the big things. In fact, often if you focus on being grateful for the big things e.g. a new promotion, a holiday in the sun; you can set your expectations too high and it has the opposite effect, kick starting a downward spiral. Not that you can't be grateful for these things, it's just easier to start simply.

After all, when asked what are they grateful for, children often answer with pure simple gratitude. They are grateful for their families, their toys, their food (often ice cream), and once I heard my personal favourite, the colour blue!

So, when being grateful, keep it simple. You can be grateful for your breath, for your morning cup of tea or the smile on your daughter's face when she blows bubbles in her milkshake. The beauty of being grateful is that there is (generally) no way of being wrong. So start with the simple things and see how, by enjoying these gifts consciously, the sweeter life becomes.

On a separate sheet of paper, write a list of the things you are grateful for within your life right now, right at this minute.

Start each point with, I am so happy and grateful for …

The gratitude list doesn't need to be a long one – over time event you can keep adding to it. Make it a daily practise or even introduce it as a daily family dinner tradition. Daily gratitude makes you feel so positive, so blessed with abundance. It is a practise I cannot recommend enough. Whether life is easy or difficult, gratitude will always lift your energy levels and revitalise you.

LAMMAS TRADITIONS

Clooties

Similarily to Imbolc, at Lammas, people would visit holy wells, bringing small offerings, usually coins or strips of cloth called 'clooties', and leave them at the well after walking around it in a 'sunwise' (following the same path as the Sun) direction in an effort to gain health and wealth from the gods[151].

Lammas Bread

The Anglo-Saxon word "hlaf-mass" or "loaf-mas" is thought to be the origin of the word "Lammas." In the Anglo-Saxon Chronicles, it was called the "Feast of Fruits"[152]. According to a book of Angl Saxon Charms on Lammas Day it was advised that the villagers bring a loaf of bread made from the first wheat of the new harvest. The loaf was blessed and then the sacred bread would be broken into four pieces. Each piece was placed in the corner of the grain storage barn or silo to protect the rest of the harvest stored there[153]. In some places, English tenants were obligated to present freshly harvested wheat to their landlords on Lammas Day[154].

In early Ireland, it was believed to be a bad idea to harvest your grain before Lammas, possibly because this meant that the previous year's harvest had run out early, this was a serious failing in agricultural communities. On August 1st, the first sheaves of grain were cut by the farmer and his wife made the first loaves of bread of the season. Lammas bread was often made into shapes including wheat, figures of the 'corn god', corn dollies and others[155].

Craft Festivals

In the medieval ages Lammas-tide was the traditional time of year for craft festivals. Medieval guilds would create displays of their wares, decorating their shops and themselves in elaborate bright colours and ribbons. The held parades and performed ceremonial plays and dances[156].

---

151 Murray Pittock Celtic Identity and the British Image Pg 62
152 Ronald Hutton The Stations of the Sun: A History of the Ritual Year in Britain Pg 330
153 ibid.
154 Rev. T. F. Thiselton-Dyer, M.A British popular customs, present and past; Pg pg 359
155 Scholastica Joycors "Lammas Day – Festival of the Wheat" Pg 13
156 Michele Morgan Simple Wicca Pg 58

The First Cut of the Harvest

In Scotland, there was a special ritual for the first cut of the harvest made on Lammas Day. The custom was called the "Beannachadh Buana." The PEOPLE dressed in their best and went to the fields. The head of the family would lay his hat on the ground and, facing the Sun, cut the first handful of corn. He would then WAVE the corn three times around his head sun-wise and raise it as the 'Iollach Buana' – the reaping salutation. The family would then recite the reaping blessing thanking for 'corn and bread, food and flocks, wool and clothing, health and strength, and peace and plenty.'[157]

John Barleycorn

The Ballad of John Barleycorn is the traditional British folk song telling the tale of the sacrificial King John Barleycorn. A character who represents the crop of barley harvested. The tale tells of the character John Barleycorn who grows, is harvested and endures all kinds of indignities to make the drinks which can be made from the barley harvest, beer and whiskey. The symbolic understanding of the cycle of life celebrated at Lammas.

Some historians relate John Barleycorn to the Anglo-Saxon mythical figure Beowa associated with Barley and agriculture[158]. There are many different versions of the song. There still exists a 15th century version from Scotland called, 'Quhy Sowld Nocht Allane Honourit Be' which metaphorically describes the process of harvesting, malting and brewing beer[159]. The most famous version was written by Robert Burns in 1782. Here is a modern version of the tale sung by the Fairport Convention:

There were three men come out of the west their fortunes for to try, and these three men made a solemn vow John Barleycorn should die. They ploughed, they sowed, they harrowed him in, throw'd clods all on his head, and these three men made a solemn vow John Barleycorn was dead.

They let him lie for a very long time till the rain from heaven did fall, and little Sir John he throw'd up his head and he so amazed them all. They let him lie till the long midsummer, till he looked all pale and wan, Then little Sir John grow'd a long, long beard and so became a man.

They hired the men with the scythe so sharp to cut him down at the knee, They rolled him and tied him around by the waist, served him most barbarously. They hired the men with sharp pitchforks and they pierced him to the heart. But the loader he served him far worse than that for he bound him to the cart. They wheeled him around and around of the field till they came upon a barn, and these three men made a solemn mow of poor John Barleycorn.

They hired the men with the crab tree sticks and they beat him skin from bone. But the miller he served him far worse than that for he ground him between two

---

157 Alexander Carmichael .Carmina Gadelica Hymns and Incantations ... pg 248
158 Kathleen Herbet. The Lost Gods of England pg 16 – 18
159 George Bannatyne The Bannatyne Manuscript, volume 2 of 4, p. 306–308,

stones. There's little Sir John in the nut-brown bowl and brandy in the cask, and little Sir John in the nut-brown bowl proved the stronger man at last.

For the huntsman he can't hunt the fox nor so loudly blow his horn, and the tinker he can't mend his kettles nor his pots without a little drop of John Barleycorn[160].

Lammas Fairs

The Lammas games tradition was replaced, or taken over by existing trading fairs. These were sometimes called 'Hiring Fairs', also known as 'Mop Fairs', created by Edward III in an attempt to regulate the labour market with the 'Statute of Labourers' in 1351 due to the national shortage of labour following the Black Death plague. The fairs were to match workers with employers for the coming harvest[161]. However, the fairs soon turned into major feasts in their own right with all the other trappings of a fair. Some of these fairs still exist today, For example, Ballycastle in Northern Ireland celebrates the Oul' Lammas Fair, chartered in 1606[162].

The Green Corn Festival

The "Green Corn Festival" is the first harvest festival of Lammas and is celebrated by Native America tribes such as the Creek, Cherokee, Seminole, Yuchi, and Iroquois Indians. It is held on the Full Moon after the first corn crop is ready to harvest and is a time of giving thanks.

The ceremony lasts for several days. During the first few days of the ceremony, known as Busk, people fast and cleanse themselves and their homes. They drink the "Black Drink" to induce vomiting. This clears the internal system so that the first taste of food that enters into the body after the cleansing is that of the first corn harvest. The foods prepared are all traditionally related to the corn from the first harvest, such as roasted corn, corn tortillas, corn soup and cornbread[163].

CONNECTING TO THE SEASON

Grounding Walk

Very often, the period from solstice to Lammas is a time where we get out of rhythm with our normal routine. As much as it is a breath of relief in order to collect our harvest and prepare for winter, the daily rhythm of our lives is what will help us get there. I recommend taking a grounding walk at Lammas. A slow silent walk where you can contemplate the work the you have to do to prepare

---

160 Fairport Convention "John Barleycorn" # 7 Tippler's Tale Kobalt Music Publishing Ltd.1978 Vinyl
161 William Blackwood."The QuarterlyJournal of Agriculture" ser1. v1 pg 655
162 Sean O'Halloran, Margaret Bel The Ould Lammas Fair Pg 11
163 Christian Roy Traditional festivals: a multicultural encyclopedia.pp. 35–37

for the winter, the actions you will take. Doing a Tree of Life will help you ground and centre on this walk.

As always, take time to contemplate your growth and nature's growth since the summer solstice. You can also reflect on your growth throughout the four Celtic cross quarter festivals, Samhain, Imbolc, Beltane and Lammas. When looking at this, you may see some interesting insights into how you work and grow as a person, as well as how you connect to the world via the seasonal year and its relevance for you today.

Record your reflections in your journal.

Make a Lammas Loaf

As well as celebrating this year's harvest from the fields, you also have your own first harvests to celebrate from the work of your goals. Combining the tradition of making a harvest loaf with celebrating your achievements is a lovely way to celebrate Lammas.

As you make your bread, knead the dough and think about this harvest you are grateful for, remember to thank yourself and the support you have had in growing this into your life. I like to take my Lammas loaf to a special place in nature and offer it as thanks for the help and support I have received in creating my harvest.

Ingredients

- 2 cups strong white bread flour or white spelt flour
- ½ teaspoon salt
- ½ teaspoon quick yeast
- 1 teaspoon sugar
- 1 / 1 ½ cups of water
- 1 egg

How to make:

- In a large bowl, mix together the flour, salt, quick yeast and sugar
- Carefully measure the water and roughly mix it into the flour
- Knead well until the dough feels smooth and pliable
- Divide the dough into three pieces
- Take one third of the dough and roll out into a rectangle (the size of your largest baking tray)
- Cut out the shape of a large mushroom and place this on an oiled baking tray. Brush the mushroom all over with water

- Cut the second piece of dough into 30 pieces and roll each out thinly
- Lay these onto the stalk of your mushroom shaped dough to make the stalks of the wheat sheaf
- Cut the last piece of dough in 3 and make 20 small sausage shapes from each piece
- Working from the outer edges, press the end of each one onto the top of the mushroom to form the ears of wheat
- Using scissors make several snips in each wheat ear to create the impression of grain
- Use dough scraps from the first piece of dough to plait a twist to lay across the stalks of the wheat sheaf
- Beat the egg and brush it all over the dough
- Bake in a pre-heated oven at 170 for 25 minutes
- To keep the sheaf as a decoration bake, lower the temperature to 100 and bake for a further 5 hours. (When quite cold you can brush the dough with varnish)

Collect seeds

Harvest time is also also a time to start collecting seeds for the next year ready to plant at Ostara. This can be a fun activity for the whole family just make sure you have paper bags ready.

Some plants develop seeds within pods, others hide their seeds inside fruits or berries, and still others hold their seeds directly inside the dying flower heads. In all cases, any seeds produced will develop close to where the flowers originally appeared.

Once seeds have finished growing, they will generally change colour (from whitish or green to tan, brown, or black) and begin to dry out. Pods will start splitting open, berries or fruits will shrink and wrinkle, or flower heads will begin to fall apart, dropping the seeds within. When this happens it is the time to harvest!

Go to a Fair or Farmers Market

The tradition of fairs in August continues today. If you are lucky enough to live in Ireland, there are many Lammas fairs still held. However, many countries have community events, fairs, school sports days or farmers markets. These are the perfect places to not only celebrate with harvest energy, but also to connect to the community.

Hold Your own Lammas Games and Feast

When I lived in Avebury, we revived the tradition of the Lammas games and feast. We held the games during the afternoon and had a community bring-a-dish picnic. This is easy to do with friends and family and is a fun way to celebrate the harvest and each other.

LAMMAS CRAFTS

Corn Dollies

In many societies, the cutting of the final sheaf of grain was a cause for celebration and a great ritual. In some places in Britain, it was a competition to see who could cut the last sheath by throwing scythes at it! When the last sheath was cut down, it was often made into a corn dolly. In Scotland, the corn dolly was made into a corn maiden (after a good harvest) or a cailleach, hag or cone (after a bad harvest). She could be dressed with ribbons, and sometimes had clothes.

This last sheaf would live in the home, often above the fireplace or hearth of the home, until the next harvest. Or it might be placed in the branches of a tree or mixed with the seed for the next year's sowing[164].

Making the corn dolly is an ancient tradition that has passed down the generations to today. The first corn dolly known to exist comes from the 18th Dynasty of Egyptians (1570–1370 BC)[165]. There are many superstitions around the last sheaf and the corn dolly worldwide, regarding pregnancies and marriages. In some parts of Europe and Mexico, the tradition was to weave the last sheaf into a large pregnant corn mother, it was believed that the person who bound the last sheaf would be pregnant in the next year[166].

Corn dollies can be simple or as complicated as you like. Personally, I often have two left hands when it comes to crafting, so I use the simplest method.

This is an easy way to make a corn dolly, and a great project for younger children. If you can plait a braid, you can make this.

You'll need:

- 3 pieces of wheat (pre-soaked it they are not very supple)
- A clothes peg
- Twine or ribbon

---

164 Sir James Frazer The Golden Bough. Pp.403–445
165 Anne Franklin Paul Mason Lammas: Celebrating Fruits of the First Harvest pg 86
166 ibid.

How to make:

- Take three pieces of wheat and cross them
- Then plait your wheat in the same way you would plait hair, bending the wheat stems gently over each other to make your braid
- Keep plaiting along your wheat, leaving a section of each stem at the end so you will be able to tie your corn dolly
- Use a clothes peg to hold your plait in place while you gather your materials to fasten it
- Tie the end of the plait to neck of the wheat heads
- Hang the corn dollie above the oven until the next year's harvest

Lammas Journey

Now it's time to return to your sacred grove. The purpose of this journey is to connect with the harvest energy and gain new insight into the time from now until Samhain. In this journey, you could ask for advice on how to move forward in your life or how is it you need to transform?

Remember, if you meet someone or something you are unsure of, simply ask it three times:

"Are you here in love and light?" If it is not, it will go away. Now it is time to take your Lammas journey..... Remember, be clear as to why you are journeying...

Breathe deeply and slowly, sitting or lying in a comfortable position. Make sure you're warm enough and have a glass of water close by. As you breathe, feel your surroundings slip away, whilst you cocoon yourself in a safe protective circle.

In your mind, begin to see yourself standing high on a hill. The fields around you are golden with the ripe corn rippling in the gentle breeze. The Sun shines high above, in the clear blue sky. It is a time of bountiful stillness and the land is ripe.

As you walk further up you become aware that, high up on the hill, a lone tree stands an ancient oak. The leaves are easy to see now small, fresh and new, opening. The oak stands strong as you walk in a circle around the tree.

At the bottom of the oak almost hidden in the trunk you can see a wooden door, half covered with ivy. Slowly, you walk towards the door. It opens with a creak and you can make out dimly lit stairs spiralling up into the tree and spiralling down. Tentatively you begin to make your way up the stairs. To each side of you is soil and roots. You can smell the musty damp of the rich fertile and damp earth around you.

Further and further up you travel until, in the middle of the tree, you find a door of gnarled and aged wood, the stairs continue upwards but this is not your

LAMMAS – THE FIRST HARVEST, SACRIFICE AND REBIRTH

journey today. Slowly you open this door. As it opens, a bright white spring light fills the space around you and you step out into a wide open field and on the horizon you can see a knoll of trees. You walk towards the trees breathing in the fresh warm air, enjoying the birdsong. This world is similar to our own yet somehow more alive, more vivid. more beautiful shimmering.

At the entrance to the woods you pause, you can feel the steady pulse of the forest. At the entrance to the woods you can see apples beginning to grow in the trees, rosehips blooming in the bushes. You walk through the woods to your grove.

As you enter into your grove, you can see in the centre a golden figure. He seems to partly be made of corn, partly of sunshine. Greet him, do not be afraid, he is there to help you find the answers you need.

He turns and beckons you to follow him. Trust him. He walks you wordlessly through the woods and out into the open golden fields. Ask him what is it you must do from now on to Samhain. He will take you on a journey. Follow him and listen well. I will call you when it is time to return...

Now it is time to return to your grove, bid your guide farewell and take a moment to lay in your grove look up at the Sun shining between the leaves. Contemplate what you have learnt, what you have seen...

It is time to return. When the time is right for you, take one last look at your grove. Walk through the woods and back towards the oak tree until you reach the door. Open the door to the staircase spiralling up and down and smell the rich soil once more. Once again, you travel down to the doorway you entered by (not down to your cave).

You open the door. As you walk away from the tree and you look up to the sky, you can see the Sun is lower in the sky and, as you look across the fields, you can see the cut down corn and wheat formed in sheaves standing proud in the fields. The harvest has begun!

Slowly become aware of the place in which your body lies or sits and allow your spirit self to step into your body and become one again. Gently allow the circle to slip away and bring yourself back to consciousness.

Drink some water, eat some chocolate, record your journey and get some fresh air.

Ceremony

Put the altar in the North

I walk the circle three times, imagining a boundary of pure energy around me.

"A time that is not a time, in a place that is not a place."

At the north point of the circle, I invite the elements of earth to join me.
At the east point of the circle, I invite the elements of air to join me.
At the south point of the circle, I invite the elements of fire to join me.
At the west point of the circle I invite the elements of water to join me.

Within the centre, I invite spirit to join me.
Silently, I invite my ancestors and guides to be with me.
It is the time of the first harvest.
Life, growth, death and rebirth,
all have come full circle.
Moons ago, I planted seeds,
and through the summer watched them grow.
I have tended the fields in our lives,
and now I am blessed with abundance.
The harvest has arrived!

I take my bread and say:

For this harvest I have sacrificed... For this I am proud of myself.
I am thankful for my harvest.

If you are doing the circle with others, then share the bread and pass it around. As you pass it on each person says:

May you reap the blessings of the harvest.

Pass the cup around the circle and each person makes a short prayer of gratitude.

Thank the elements, guides and ancestors for joining you and walk the circle in the opposite direction from the start.

Now it's time to celebrate Lammas!

> *The Corn King is cut down on the land,*
> *We toast his sacrifice with ale in our hand,*
> *And eat the bread from the harvest made,*
> *The harvest turned to food and drink,*
> *Now is the time to learn and think,*
> *Of what we can do to grow even stronger,*
> *As the summer recedes and the nights grow longer.*
> *We share our rewards and thank the earth,*
> *That brings our fruitful abundance to birth.*
>
> *The Wheel turns ...*

CHAPTER 12

Mabon and the Autumn Equinox – Entering the Dark

The land at autumn equinox, also called Mabon, is beautiful. In her dying days, nature brings out her deepest colours, the golden light and ripens her berries. Willian Cullen Bryant said, "Autumn... the year's last, loveliest smile." For me, this is such a true statement. I don't think I know anyone who doesn't feel the joy of swooshing through the autumn leaves as they walk in the parks or woods, no matter how old or young. Autumn equinox is a time of slowing down. The plants and trees give birth in their final release of life. Sending out the last of the seeds that will hide under the earth, waiting until spring to burst into life. For us it is a bittersweet time, enjoying the beauty, full of gratitude and at the same time saying see you later to the warmth of the summer and life. As the animals prepare for hibernation, we also prepare for the winter months. This is the time of collecting the berries and nuts, preserving them, making jams and jellies. A time of preserving the sweetness. Storing it to see us through the darker months ahead. A time where we collect the seeds ready to plant in the new Wheel, the next spring.

At autumn equinox, we collect and take stock of the second of the three harvests of the Wheel. As with Lammas, this is also a time of giving thanks and recognising our strengths, taking pride in our achievements. As with Ostara (the spring equinox) this is also a time of balance, where night and day are equal and where we take the opposite transition from the spring equinox. At autumn equinox we transition from our light to our dark...

HISTORY OF MABON

Autumn equinox celebrations are nothing new, they date back for millennia. The Greeks, British, Japanese and Scandinavians have all had their own traditions for celebrating the end of the harvest and/or the equinox. There are some prehistoric sites that are aligned to the equinox sunrises and sunsets. Some of these sites include Sliabh na Callige in Loughcrew Ireland, Hovenweep Castle on the Utah

– Colorado border[167] and Mnajdra, a megalithic temple complex found on the southern coast of the Mediterranean island of Malta[168].

Autumn equinox today is also called Mabon[169] which is a fairly new term used in many earth-based religions to recognize the autumnal equinox and to honour the Earth for her bounteous harvest named as recently as the 1970s in the book Creating Circles and Ceremonies[170]. Mabon was a Welsh hunter god, the Child of Modron, mentioned in one of Wales' oldest tales, Culwch and Olwen and in the book of Taliesin[171]. For modern day Druids, it is the celebration of Alban Elfed, which means 'The Light of the Water', a time of balance between light and dark[172]. Apart from the name, compared to the spring equinox we know relatively little about how the autumn equinox was celebrated by the Celts, although there is evidence that communities had ceremonies and celebration at the end of the harvest at this time[173].

The Anglo-Saxons referred to September as Halegmonath or Holy Month[174]. There are also references in the Scandinavian Sagas to Haustblót[175], or the autumn sacrifice, which took place after the harvest season during í móti vetri, 'onset of winter. The Vikings held four sacrificial blots in a year at the solar festivals including autumn equinox[176]. The word blot basically means 'worship' or 'sacrifice' and at a blot a sacrifice was made to the gods and the spirits of the land. The sacrifice often took the form of a sacramental meal or feast.

Within Greek mythology, the autumn equinox marks the return of the goddess Persephone to the darkness of the underworld, there she is reunited with her husband Hades and the world becomes barren as her mother Demeter goes into mourning[177]

At both the equinoxes, some Japanese Buddhists celebrate Higan, called Aki no Higan, in autumn, introduced by Emperor Shomu in the 8th century to give peasants more opportunity to devote time to their spiritual practices[178]. Higan means "from the other shore of the Sanzu River." In Buddhist tradition, crossing the mythical Sanzu River meant passing into the afterlife. During Higan, Japanese Buddhists will return to their hometowns to pay respects to their ancestors[179].

---

167 Danu Forest The Magical Year pg 193
168 Anthony Bonanno Malta an Archaeological Paradise Pg 23
169 Edain McCoy.The Sabbats a New Approach to Living the Old Ways pg 185
170 Oberon Zell-Ravenheart & Morning Glory Creating circles & ceremonies: rituals for all seasons & reasons. Pg. 227
171 Kristoffer Hughes The Book of Celtic Magic: Transformative Teachings from the Cauldron of Awen. Part 2 Chapter 8
172 Danu Forest The Magical Year pg 191
173 Alexi Kondratiev. A Celtic Rituals. An authentic guide to Celtic Spirituality pg 191
174 William A. Chaney. The Cult of Kingship in Anglo-Saxon England: The Transition from Paganism to Christianity Pp. 60–61
175 Douglas Robert Dutton An Encapsulation of Óðinn: Religious belief and ritual practice among the Viking Age elite with particular focus upon the practice of ritual hanging 500–1050 AD 2015 pg 94
176 Nationalmuseet "The Viking blót sacrifices" www.en.natmus.dk.
177 Dean Miller The Seasons: Natural Rites and Traditions Man, Myth and MAgic Pg. 29
178 Wagashikoechin "O-Higan – Equinox" www.wagashirezepte.de
179 ibid.

As Christianity began to overtake the older religions, Mabon began to be celebrated as Michaelmas, or the Feast of Michael and All Angels, on the 29th of September. The day is associated with the beginning of autumn and the shortening of days; in England, it is one of the "quarter days", the Christian festivals that are close to the solstices and equinoxes. In Britain on Michaelmas Day the family would eat goose fattened on the stubble of the field, leading to goose fairs which became a traditional activity at this time of year[180].

GROWING WITH THE SEASON

Pre-equinox Turmoil

As you are now more connected to the rhythm of the year and nature around you, you may have noticed that, as with before the spring equinox pre-Mabon there will often be a lot of chaos within your life.

Many people experience chaos, both positive and negative, or a period of instability in their lives or mental capacity before the solar festivals of the equinoxes and solstices. Showing that, no matter how sophisticated we have become, we are ultimately part of nature. Every year without fail there is some kind of crisis in my life at these times. It is a bit like the storm before the calm. The hard part of growth before the transition.

The only advice I can give you here is roll with it. Trust that this period is necessary and will end. Look at the lessons this chaos is teaching you, write about it and, in the mean-time, be good and kind to yourself.

The Second Harvest

At Mabon we collect and take stock of the second of the three harvests of the Wheel. It is a festival both of abundance, gratitude and letting go. This is the ultimate time of giving thanks for the support, strength and sweetness that has sustained us throughout this Wheel, and will sustain us throughout winter. It is a time for gratitude, for looking at the harvest you have gathered within this Wheel, accepting it and being grateful both to the Universe and to yourself. A time of completing projects and tying loose ends.

Reflecting on Your Harvest

Autumn is the perfect time for reflecting as we prepare to enter the dreaming state of hibernation. Reflecting on our efforts makes us appreciate them more and have a clear insight into what is healthy for us within our lives. You can use the following questions to help you reflect on your harvest and your goal manifestation process of this wheel.

---

180 Ben Johnson "Michaelmas" www.historic-uk.com https://www.historic-uk.com/CultureUK/Michaelmas/

1. What new things have happened in the last year that you are happy with and want to keep in your life? This can include people or other changes.
2. What is currently present in your life that you are fairly happy with, but you wish would work better or flow more abundantly?
3. What have you been working on that has not yet manifested (shown up) for you?
4. What do you feel proud of yourself for learning or doing in this Wheel?
5. What is it that has inspired and supported you throughout this Wheel?
6. What have you discovered about yourself?

GRATITUDE FOR YOUR BOUNTY AND ABUNDANCE

Gratitude for your bounty is at the heart of the Equinox. Gratitude can also be a way of celebrating your achievements. A simple way to do this is to ask yourself:

- What are you grateful for here and now?
- What is the harvest of this Wheel?
- What makes your life abundant?

Now write a gratitude/ harvest list. This can be for both small and big things. Include the things you harvested from your efforts throughout this Wheel. Another lovely way to celebrate your bounty is to write yourself a thank you letter for the hard work you have done for yourself during this Wheel.

Put the list or letter in your sacred space and whenever the autumn blues begin to take hold of you, look at this list. It will help you to see not only your power to achieve but also remind you of the wondrous things that make your life beautiful. A way of reminding ourselves how truly blessed we are to be alive and to have the gift of creating our own realities.

RELEASING OUR SEEDS

Looking at our harvest at equinox can be both a joyful and sad process. We have the chance to be proud of our accomplishments and to recognise them. However, we are also faced with the regrets of unfinished projects or goals unmet. We have to accept the consequences of our actions and recognise there is no way of turning back and changing what has passed. Acceptance makes us stronger. We begin to realise that we cannot be perfect and that it is ok to be imperfect. In fact, it's natural.

Although Mabon may seem like a barren time at first glance, it is actually mother nature's most bountiful time. I see Mabon to be a festival of abundance despite the energy of letting go. Remember, at equinox the land is not only letting go of leaves, it is also releasing seeds. These seeds will bring the harvest of the future. It is time for you to let go of some dreams, to release them and see when and if you will plant them again.

Here at equinox, that which we really cannot act upon or manifest before Samhain has to be left behind ready to pick up at another time. We have to accept the consequences of our actions and recognise there is no way of turning back and changing what has passed. Acceptance makes us stronger.

This second harvest gives us the opportunity to see which projects are almost complete and to know where we will focus our energy for this last moon until Samhain. Some projects, goals and seeds need one last boost to complete the vision we had, some will be slightly altered from our vision but have led to new and exciting paths. Do not focus on the dead leaves and shrivelling branches of dreams, take the last gasp of energy within the world around you to complete what needs completing.

It is time to ask yourself, what will you let go of before Samhain? What will be the seeds you store for the New Year?

Choose one of your projects to let go of. In your notebook write:

I choose to let go of my dream /goal of .... from now until Samhain. I trust the universe to guide me to manifest this in my life if it is necessary for me. By letting go of ....now, I give space and energy to the process of manifesting .... I trust the Universe to guide me to manifest this in my life.

It is a good idea to evaluate your progress with your accountability partner. As the winter is drawing closer and this Wheel is coming to a close, we need to now focus on our most important goals to manifest. Choose the two that you can make the final push to complete by Samhain.

PRESERVING THE SWEETNESS

I like to call the autumn equinox the sweet harvest, as the berries are the sweetness of the year's work which we will preserve to lift our spirits in the winter. Just as our Imbolc candles contained our spring inspiration for the work, the sweetness sustains us in the dark.

Being Sweet to our Bodies – Preserving our Strength

At autumn equinox we need to preserve strength and sweetness fort the darker times. We have a whole winter to get through. And although these days it is easier than ever before, biologically we still need our strength to do it. One of the ways of helping ourselves to do this is to preserve our mental and physical health. Modern life doesn't support these needs. If you look at the media and advertising focus today, they remind us to get ready for summer. However, it is really winter where we need our physical and mental health. The coming winter will also give us much needed downtime. Downtime is part of the growing period. We need to re-energise to be able to grow in spring.

Here are a few easy ways I have found to be sweet to my body in autumn and prepare for the winter to come.

Vitamin D

As we enter the dark, it is often a time where depression and lack of motivation can take hold of us. A good way to combat this is with Vitamin D. Vitamin D acts on the areas of your brain that are linked to depression, but exactly how vitamin D works in your brain isn't yet fully understood. However, I know for me this works. Remember we are all biologically different, so always consult a medical practitioner before you begin to take a new supplement, especially if pregnant.

Sunlight

As the nights and mornings begin to get darker, the lack of sunlight has a profound effect on our mindset. Sunlight is also essential for good health in the darker days. Whenever there is a burst of autumn sun seize this opportunity. Get outside. Take a walk in the woods, cycle, take your lunch break outside or simply enjoy a cup of tea in the garden. However you get it, sunlight will motivate you and energise you. If you are fortunate, as I am, and have access to a light box in my local sauna, this also will help give you a boost in the dark months.

Preserve your physical health

A strong body helps a strong mind. We know that exercise creates endorphins, and endorphins basically make you happy. Endorphins trigger positive feelings in the body, similar to those released with morphine. However, unlike with morphine, the activation of these receptors by the body's endorphins does not lead to addiction or dependence. Endorphins diminish the perception of pain and can act as sedatives.

Exercise is also a potential reducer of stress. Listen to your body and see how you feel and follow you own needs. I am no exercise expert and often find it difficult to motivate myself. However, I have found that doing exercise, even once a week; has a positive impact on my physical and mental health during autumn and winter.

Eat healthy

I find at this time of year my body craves more fat and ginger. When you begin to listen to your body you may find that at different points during the Wheel your body craves different foods, usually following the seasonal growth of vegetables. For example, I cannot stop craving spinach around Imbolc or peas in the summer. Enjoy your food, make eating a good meal with friends and family a habit at this time of the year. After all, nothing is more depressing than sitting alone eating a microwave meal. I love potluck dinner nights where everyone takes something along. It's a great way to try new foods and share different family traditions.

Changing your sleep patterns

Doing this at the equinox can also be beneficial. Going to bed earlier and waking up with the light follows a natural rhythm that humans have been following for thousands of years. In our modern life, light does not play the same role as it did in the days before electricity. However, no harm will come to you if you re-attune your body's rhythm to the cycle of the Sun.

Remember me time

There will be days where you feel like curling up on the sofa with a duvet and hot chocolate. Allow yourself to do this without feeling any guilt. Sometimes the daily chores can just wait. In the outside world many creatures are beginning to hibernate, and it is ok for us to want to mirror this. Obviously, it's not the best thing for us to do every day. It is ok to sometimes give in to our hibernating needs. In Denmark we have a word "hygge", unfortunately it cannot be directly translated, it means something like being cosy, snuggly and in good company. Autumn is a time for being hyggelig and being cosy in ourselves.

A TIME TO REBALANCE

The equinoxes are a time of balance, a moment of equal day and night, where the world is in perfect unity. Day and night reflect each other and at this time we have the biological need to balance within ourselves, reflecting the balance with the world around us. There are many practical ways to rebalance yourself. It is important to balance yourself both internally and externally.

Rebalancing Your Chakras

One of the best ways to balance yourself internally is to rebalance your chakras. When working with the chakras, each one has a different colour and a different interpretation. Some say that you cannot balance the chakras without visualising the colours. However, I was taught to work with the chakras using first a white light to represent each one. It worked for me, especially as trying to remember the colour sequence took energy from the balancing I was trying to achieve. Now I use both, whatever fits my mood for that day. Here is my chakra meditation:

Sit in a comfortable position, preferably connecting with the floor.

Begin to breathe slowly and with purpose, in through your nose and out through your mouth.

Now, from the base of your spine, in a deosil direction (with the movement of the Sun) visualise a root connecting and growing downwards to the earth.

Once connected and grounded within the earth, feel energy rising up your roots and into you first base chakra.

Allow the light to slowly start to spiral and spin within your chakra. The light cleans away any dark cobwebs within your chakra. As it spins faster and faster, feel cleansed and energised here in your base chakra.

Repeat this process for all of your chakras, remembering not to stop the previous chakras spinning.

Once you reach your crown chakra, you are in perfect balance. Now you can choose to allow the energy to burst out of your crown chakra and return like golden rain to the earth, or to begin closing your chakras.

To close your chakras, you begin with slowing down the spinning, sending the energy in a widdershins direction (the opposite movement to the Sun). When the spinning has stopped, find a way to imagine your chakra closing, some people use the image of a flower closing for the night.

Once closed, repeat the process with all of the other chakras until you reach your base chakra.

Once this is closed, return the energy to the earth and slowly visualise the root you planted returning to you from the earth.

Many people feel light headed after this process, eat something and for the rest of the day drink **a lot** of water.

Balancing internally is important. Another way to balance or to meditate and visualise yourself is to use the Tree of Life meditation, both within nature and at home. However, it is equally important to balance externally. As within nature, there is an inner chemical process, where the nutrients from the earth, water and sun transform into the external process of growth. Wherever possible, to connect with nature we have to mimic nature. Yoga or Thai chi are two well-known ways to balance mentally and physically. You will find the way that works for you.

Sunlight and Shadow – Moving from the Light to the Dark

The message of both of the equinoxes can be summarized in the Taoist teaching of sunlight and shadow.

Go within.

Focus your senses. Face the challenge.
Balance sunlight and shadow.
Blend with the path.
This is the way of the Tao.
TAO. 56[181]

As we looked at in the spring equinox, there is a place in the world for both our dark and light sides. There is a place in us where the two meet and intertwine. Neither is better than the other, neither is less important. They both make up our whole unique and perfectly imperfect self.

---

181 Diane Dreher Women's Tao wisdom: ten ways to personal power and peace Pg 133

MABON AND THE AUTUMN EQUINOX – ENTERING THE DARK

Accepting our Light

As much as the equinoxes are about balance, they are also about transition from dark to light at spring equinox and from light to dark here at autumn equinox.

In psychology today there is a lot of focus on working to get to know our shadow selves. However, working with our light self is equally important, and sometimes a little harder than working with our shadow. It can be challenging to see our light but, believe me, it is seen by others and that is the starting point of embracing our inner light. Autumn equinox is a significant time for deep reflection on encouraging and nurturing your own inner light.

This often-ignored area of your life can have a dramatic impact on your health and well-being. The good news is that, when it's acknowledged, the positive health impacts can be exponential. Once you connect to this light, you can then cultivate it, take it out and share it for all the world around to see. You just need to give yourself permission to shine.

We are all born to shine. Not just some of us, but every single one of us, in our own unique way. As Marianne Williamson so wisely said in her book A Return to Love: Reflections on the Principles of A Course in Miracles:

"Our greatest fear is not that we are inadequate,
but that we are powerful beyond measure.
It is our light, not our darkness, that frightens us."

There are many different ways you can work with accepting and honouring your inner light. Whichever way you choose to deepen the connection to your inner light, as you nurture and grow it, you will begin to understand that this source of inner light is always there supporting and guiding you to find a greater sense of harmony and effortlessness, even during those darkest of days.

Access my inner light meditation

Here is a simple mediation practice you can do to access your inner light.

Find a quiet space where you know you won't be disturbed.

Sit comfortably with a nice tall spine, eyes closed and your hands resting in your lap, palms open.

Begin by taking several long, deep, full breaths (down into your belly).

Visualise a beautiful light at your heart space and begin to visualise that light within your heart (keeping your focus and attention on this light).

When the mind wanders, simply return it to this beautiful light at your heart.

Silently repeat the mantra, "my inner light shines" as you focus on the light at your heart space.

Stay here in this space of your heart for a few minutes, repeating the mantra silently and focusing on the light in and around you.

When you are ready to move out of meditation, sit quietly taking a few moments breathing with ease before moving out into the rest of your day.

Allowing your smile to shine

Another simple way to access your inner light is by looking in the mirror and smiling back at yourself. I mean really smiling – full-heartedly smiling (think of your biggest smile and multiply it). See your eyes light up in the mirror; this joy, bliss. Love is your inner light beaming back at you. It may sound strange reading it here now, but go and practice it and you'll be amazed at the shift in your emotional state.

Asking for feedback

Other people can see you light better than you can. Ask five people you know, that love you and care about you, to give you three words that describe you to them. Explain to them that they must only give positive and sincere feedback. Collect these words around a picture of yourself and ask yourself if you can see the truth in these words.

Creativity

Creativity, has been called the antithesis of our shadows. I also think it honours our light. Painting, writing, building, creative expression of any kind will help you to embrace your soul and accept it. In your creativity you allow yourself to flow out of you, giving space to your all your potential instead of repression. Creativity is the perfect activity to give space for your shadow and your light to emerge and support you to feel more balance within yourself.

A small ceremony you can do to honour your light and dark self through your creativity is to be creative. Then place your creative pieces in your sacred space and repeat the following affirmation out loud:

"I honour the place of dark within me. I honour the place of light within me. I honour and accept myself with all of my strengths and my flaws. I honour and accept myself as I am."

Travelling from the Light to the Dark

As spring equinox (or Ostara) is the time of year where we make the transition from the dark to the light, autumn equinox is the time where we transition from the light to the dark. From the work at Ostara, you have an understanding of your shadow. You are (hopefully) more comfortable and accepting of this side of you. Now it is time to get to know your light, to acknowledge yourself and to be proud of your achievements.

Taking Pride in your achievements

Being proud of yourself can have negative connotations. For example, someone who has too much pride in themself could be called egotistical. However, I

MABON AND THE AUTUMN EQUINOX – ENTERING THE DARK

disagree. We often look outside of ourselves when searching for recognition, praise and approval of our actions. If we do this then we are not accepting and honouring ourselves. We expect the world to accept and honour us and therefore will always be seeking approval instead of approving ourselves.

In the past Wheel, you have come to know yourself better, succeeded in following your dreams and made steps to develop as a person and reconnect with the natural world. You have dedicated yourself to living consciously, mindfully and being responsible for your path in life. This is a beautiful thing. You may have even surprised yourself along the way, actually I hope you have!

It's time for you to acknowledge this journey. A great way to do this is to make a list of all that you are proud of yourself for this Wheel. Start each point on the list with the words

I am proud of myself for......................

Be proud of your struggles as well of your triumphs. After all, these make up the journey, and the journey is the important part, not the destination.

Put this list in your sacred space and keep it there as long as you wish it to be there. Remember you'll be making a new list next year.

Reward your successes

Whilst working with your accountability partners, hopefully they have been reminding you to reward yourself for all of your successes this year. But you also need to give yourself permission to celebrate without anyone else reminding you to do it. It's time to decide how are you going to reward you for the work you have done this Wheel.

Here and now, in your notebooks write:

I am going to .... as a reward to myself for my work, dedication and growth during this Wheel of the Year.

Make sure you do this before Samhain. No matter how busy your life, taking time to celebrate you and to celebrate your life is one of the most important things in life, and the most often and easily forgotten.

CELEBRATING AND TRADITIONS

Crying the Neck

Autumn equinox was the time where the corn and wheat harvest were both finally finished. This depended from year to year on the weather conditions. The ending of the harvest in Devon and Cornwall was accompanied by a custom called Crying the Neck. The man who cut the last sheath would hold it aloft and shout:

"I 'ave 'un! I 'ave 'un! I 'ave 'un!"
The rest would then shout:
"What 'ave 'ee? What 'ave 'ee? What 'ave 'ee?"
and the reply would be:
"A neck! A neck! A neck!"

Everyone then joined in shouting and cheering for the man who had cut the neck. The man with the neck would then run down to the farm house where a girl would be waiting with a bucket of water. If the farmer managed to get into the house without being detected he was allowed to kiss her. If not, she would pour the water over him[182]! The last sheath was sometimes made into a corn dolly.

Go a-nutting

The 21st of September is traditionally the day to go-a-nutting and gather nuts. It was believed that Sunday was a bad day to gather nuts, because you might meet the devil doing the same thing. The 21st of September was called the Devil's Nutting Day even if it was a Sunday, because on this day, the devil had been out gathering nuts when he ran into the Virgin Mary in the forest. Whereupon he got scared, dropped his bag of nuts and fled[183]!

Traditionally the young people of the village were sent out to go-a-nutting. At Eton, it was a tradition to give the students a play day to go out and collect nuts to give as presents to the teachers. Before being allowed to go-a-nutting the students had to write verses on the fruitfulness of autumn[184].

Harvest Festivals

There are many existing harvest festivals traditionally celebrated by different religions at autumn equinox. Christians hold a Harvest Festival the Sunday nearest to the Harvest Moon, the full moon closest to autumn equinox. The tradition began in 1843 when Robert Hawker created a special thanksgiving service at his church at Morwenstow in Cornwall[185]. Today in many parts of Britain, churches and schools participate by holding a harvest supper celebration. Part of the celebrations include gathering and distributing to parts of the community in need.

In the Jewish calendar, Sukkot, also called the Festival of Gathering, is celebrated near the harvest moon. Sukkot is a seven day festival during which plants known as the four species are gathered,

blessed and waved in the six directions, east, south, west, north, up and down, to symbolise that God is everywhere[186].

---

182 FSir James Frazer The Golden Bough. Pg 445
183 J. Harvey Bloom Folk Lore, Old Customs and Superstitions in Shakespeare Land Pg 126
184 Rev. T. F. Thiselton-Dyer, M.A British popular customs, present and past; Pg 73
185 C.E. Byles The life and letters of R.S. Hawker (sometime Vicar of Morwenstowe) Pg 171
186 Tracey R Rich "Sukkot " www.jewfaq.org

Wines and Cider

Mabon falls at the time of the grape harvest. The German Oktoberfest celebrations were once festivals for the wine harvest, particularly in Bavaria. Drunken orgies were prominently celebrated in both Germanic lands and Rome at this time of year. Berry and even heather wines were made at this time of year as well as cider[187].

CONNECTING WITH THE SEASON

Go for a Walk

Mabon is definitely a time for appreciating nature's bounty, so get out and see what is happening out there! Take an attitude of gratitude with you on your Mabon walk and look for all the things to appreciate now, about the coming winter and also the last six months. From Ostara, you have walked in the light half of the year. Ask yourself, how have you changed? How has nature changed? Has your journey mirrored nature's? Importantly ask yourself what can I be grateful for in this journey?

Record your reflections in your journal.

Foraging for Nature's Bounty

This time of year is traditionally very food focused. Autumn's bounty is a generous one and mankind has taken advantage of that for centuries. Collecting berries and fruit is a fantastic autumn equinox tradition and a great way to connect with nature at this time of year. Some folklore says that autumn equinox marks the end of the blackberry season. In Scandinavia and other parts of the world it is common to see people heading into the woods to collect mushrooms at this time of year. Get your wellies on and get out into nature and see what you can find to eat (although remember to check if the food you have found is ok for human consumption. Our ancestors knew more about that then we tend to today).

Sharing Your Abundance

Just as with the American holiday of Thanksgiving, there are many beautiful ways to celebrate abundance in your life. One of the most beautiful is to pay it forward and to share your abundance with others at Mabon. Here are a few of the ways I like to share my abundance at Mabon

---

[187] Edain McCoy .The Sabbats a New Approach to Living the Old Ways pg 189

Donate to a harvest festival or homeless shelter:
Many churches and homeless organisations do harvest donation drives in the autumn. A great way to spread your abundance further is to empty your cupboards of food, clothes and other things you might not use and give these things to people who can use them.

Make an autumn mandala:
The forest is a rainbow in autumn. Take a walk in the forest and make a beautiful mandala from the autumn leaves and berries. As you make your mandala, reflect on the abundance in your life and allow your mandala to express your gratitude. Leave it in the woods for other people to enjoy whilst they are walking.

Feed the birds and wild animals:
As the months become colder, our friends in nature will find it harder to find food. Leaving food out for them is a way of sharing our abundance (make sure to leave out the right and healthy food for them, there are many organisations you can find online with good guidelines).

Preparation for the Coming Winter

In the past autumn equinox would have been the turning point of the year where our ancestors knew they would spend more time indoors and there would be less light. This was a time to prepare the longhouse for the long winter to come. Here's a few ideas you could try:

Autumn cleaning
So, as with Ostara, it is a therapeutic exercise to cleanse and clean you and your home at Mabon. Get your winter woollies out of storage and prepare for the coming cold.

Clean up and cull your digital files
How often do you take time to clean up your files or delete those millions of selfies that you didn't share on social media? Make Mabon the time to clean up digitally (and possibly backup your files to keep what you want to keep). You will feel so much lighter afterwards.

Cleansing yourself and your home with smudging
Smudging is a physical way of getting rid of the energetic cobwebs and cleansing yourself and your home.

Personal smudging: Use an incense stick or a bundle of white sage. Hold it at least 5cm from your physical body. Start at your feet and, moving the incense in a circular motion, begin to waft away the energetic cobwebs. Imagine the dead leaves or cobwebs detaching from you and disappearing into the ether, becoming nothing. Move it around every part of your body and include the area above your head and the bottom of your feet. The cleansing will leave you feeling refreshed and revitalised.

Cleansing your home: In a similar way, you can use incense to cleanse your home. Move through each room wafting with incense and remember the corners too. Afterwards, if the weather permits it, open all the windows and allow fresh air into your home.

MABON CRAFTS

Bramble Jelly

Take a long autumn walk, pick a pound or two of berries and make this simple jelly which can be enjoyed spread thickly on some delicious, freshly baked bread (which after Lammas you are a dab hand at making!). It's really easy and quick to make and seems to set as if by magic (thanks to the pectin in the fruit), so you don't need to be a jam-making expert to make it!

Ingredients and Utensils:

- 2 cups ripe blackberries
- 3/4 cup of water
- 2 cups granulated sugar
- juice of 1 lemon
- 350ml preserving jar (sterilised)
- large nylon sieve and a piece of gauze roughly 12 inches square

How to make:

- Wash the blackberries thoroughly and place in a heavy-based saucepan
- Add water, cover and stew very gently for about 20 minutes
- Mash the blackberries every now and then to reduce them to a pulp, get as much juice out of them as possible
- Add the sugar and lemon juice to the pan and, keeping the heat very low allow the sugar to dissolve completely. It should take about 10 minutes
- Now turn the heat up to full and boil the mixture rapidly for 8 minutes, stirring frequently to stop the jelly from sticking
- Meanwhile, warm a large bowl
- Line the sieve with the gauze, place it over the bowl and pour the blackberry mixture into the lined sieve

- Using a wooden spoon, push all the liquid through into the bowl as quickly as you can, squeezing the remaining pulp to get as much juice out as possible. If the jelly starts to set before you've finished, just put it back into the pan and gently reheat it
- Now pour the jelly into the jars, cover with a waxed disc and tie down
- When it's set, eat and enjoy!

Loose Autumn Equinox Incense

Another way to preserve your harvest is to make incense from dried flowers and resins.

You'll need:

- 2 parts sandalwood
- 2 parts pine
- 1 part rosemary
- 1 part cinnamon
- 1 part dried apple
- 1 part dried oak leaf

How to make:

- Add your ingredients to your mixing bowl, one at a time
- Measure carefully and, if the leaves or blossoms need to be crushed, use your mortar and pestle to do so
- As you blend the herbs together, say out loud the things which you are proud of yourself for and grateful for this autumn equinox
- Store your incense in a tightly sealed jar
- Use within three months
- To use your incense burn it on a charcoal brick

JOURNEY WITH YOUR LIGHT SELF

Now it's time to return to your sacred grove. The purpose of this journey is to connect with your light self.

Remember, if you meet someone or something you are unsure of, simply ask it three times, "Are you here in love and light?" If it is not, it will go away.

Now it is time to take your autumn equinox journey..... Remember be clear as to why you are journeying...

Breathe deeply and slowly, sitting or lying in a comfortable position. Make sure you're warm enough and have a glass of water close by. As you breathe, feel your surroundings slip away, as you cocoon yourself in a safe protective circle.

In your mind, begin to see yourself standing high on a hill. The fields around you are filled with the stubble of the cut down corn. The trees are beginning to change colour. The world around you is colder, the sky slightly grey. The Wheel is turning to autumn.

As you walk further up, you become aware that, high up on the hill, a lone tree stands. An ancient oak. The leaves of the oak are part golden part green. Around your feet there are leaves already fallen from the branches. The oak stands strong, the leaves crunch under your feet as you walk in a circle around the tree.

At the bottom of the oak, almost hidden in the trunk, you can see a familiar wooden door, half covered with ivy. Slowly you walk towards the door. It opens with a creak and you can make out dimly lit stairs spiralling up into the tree and spiralling down. Tentatively, you begin to make your way up the stairs. To each side of you is soil and roots. You can smell the musty damp of the rich, fertile earth around you.

Further and further up you travel until, in the middle of the tree, you find a door made from gnarled and aged wood. The stairs continue upwards, but this is not your journey today. Slowly you open the door. As it opens, a bright white light fills the space around you and you step out into a wide-open field. On the horizon you can see a knoll of trees. You walk towards the trees, breathing deeply the fresh air. This world is similar to our own yet somehow more alive, more vivid, more beautiful, shimmering.

At the entrance to the woods you pause, you can feel the steady pulse of the forest. You can see blackberries, plums and apples growing wild and ripe, ready to be picked. Your grove is empty but different. Now your grove is painted in bronzes, yellows, reds and browns, the colours of the leaves painting the ground in the sunlight. Here the autumn has arrived. You sit for a while and connect with the energy of your grove.

You stand and decide to take a walk through one of the paths leading off your grove. As the trees part, you come to a beautiful waterfall, the water clear and fresh, the light dances upon the ripples. You kneel by the water's edge and peer into the cool liquid below. You can see your reflection in the water. As you watch, the reflection begins to glow. Radiant golden light. Your reflection begins to move on its own. Moving up through the water until in front of you sits a beautiful shimmering version of you. This is your light self. Greet him/ her, and ask him/her, "please reveal to me what it is I don't see in my own light." Sit together for a while and talk. Enjoy the lessons he/she has to teach...

Now it is time to return to your grove, bid your light-self a farewell. Return to your grove. The ground is covered with more leaves and the air is chillier than before, the Sun lower in the sky. Take a moment to sit in your grove, look up at the Sun shining between the leaves. Contemplate what you have learnt, what you have seen...

It is time to return. When the time is right for you. take one last look at your grove.

Walk through the woods and back towards the oak tree until you reach the door. Open the door to the staircase spiralling up and down and smell the rich soil once more.

Once again you travel down to the doorway you entered by (not down to your cave). Walk away from the tree. As you look up to the sky, you can see the Sun is setting in a glory of oranges and reds, it is almost as if the sky is on fire. The trees around you are now in their full autumn colours, blazing in the light of the sunset. Behind you, the Moon is already in the sky. Look up to the setting sun and feel its dying warmth. See the silver moon and feel its power. Stand balanced between sun and moon. Feel it until the moment the sun disappears. Thank the world for this beautiful gift of life. The Wheel has turned once more.....

Slowly become aware of the place in which your body lies or sits and allow your spirit self to step into your body and become one again. Gently allow the circle to slip away and bring yourself back to consciousness.

Drink some water, eat some chocolate, record your journey and get some fresh air.

CEREMONY

Put the altar in the north
I walk the circle three times imagining a boundary of pure energy around me
"A time that is not a time, in a place that is not a place"

> *At the north point of the circle, I invite the elements of earth to join me.*
> *At the east point of the circle, I invite the elements of air to join me.*
> *At the south point of the circle, I invite the elements of fire to join me.*
> *At the west point of the circle, I invite the elements of water to join me.*
> *Within the centre, I invite spirit to join me.*
> *Silently, I invite my ancestors and guides to be with me.*
>
> *Leaves fall, and the days grow cold,*
> *Fruits ripen and seeds are stored.*
> *Equal day and equal night,*
> *The winds of winter take flight*[188].

---

188 Inspired by Cunningham S. Wicca: A Guide for the Solitary Practitioner Pp. 140–141

MABON AND THE AUTUMN EQUINOX – ENTERING THE DARK

To prepare for the gift of winter, I cleanse my body and soul by smudging myself with white sage to blow away the cobwebs and make ready for the new.

Gratitude Toasts – If alone, I give thanks for my bounty, or I pass the cup around the circle and each time say the following sentences in order:
I thank myself for the effort and energy I have put into my journey.
I thank those who have supported and loved me on this journey.
I thank the earth and sky for their strength and guidance on this journey.
I have sown and reaped the fruits of my actions, good and bad.
Grant me the courage to plant seeds of joy and love in the coming year.
I/We give thanks for the gift of my/our lives.
Thank the elements, guides and ancestors for joining you and walk the circle round in the opposite direction at the start.

Now it's time to celebrate Mabon!

Leaves fall; the wind plays,
Lengthen night and shorten day.
Sweetness preserved for the dark,
Time to hibernate and wait for the lark.

Harvest so bountiful,
My work complete and plentiful.
Autumn, nature's last smile,
It's time for me to rest for a while.

The Wheel turns…

CHAPTER 13

Samhain – The Ending and the Beginning

The Wheel has turned full circle and we are once again at Samhain, the ending and the beginning of our journey. The nights are longer, the days are colder. As the trees let go of the leaves, the autumn berries, fallen to the ground, shrivel and nourish the earth. We can feel in our bones that winter is nearly here. Maybe you can feel this Samhain, more than last, the subtle shifts in nature's energy (and within yourself). As you work more and more with the Wheel you may feel the veils between the worlds beginning to shift, becoming thinner. As both begin to end one Wheel and start the journey once more.

As you can remember from the first chapter, the themes of Samhain are death and rebirth. A time where our ancestors are close. A time to honour those that walked before us, remember the gifts they brought us. A moment to remember and reconnect with our roots. It is also a time of transformation and letting go. This Samhain you can return to Chapter One and repeat the processes you enjoyed the most or, if you didn't try them all, then try something new. Remember, you don't have to try everything, just what feels right to you.

However, Samhain also holds within it other lessons. In this final chapter I will present you with the two final teachings of Samhain. The lesson of knowing what sustains us, with the completion of this Wheel's manifestation process, and the teaching of understanding the pattern of life's growth and our own evolution.

In my opinion, there is often a little too much focus on the death aspect of Samhain. People sometimes forget that, as much as Samhain is an ending, it is also a beginning. Come rain, sun, wind or snow, Samhain morning is always a fresh new start.

At the same time Samhain highlights our growth, it also highlights the story of human survival. At Samhain, our ancestors began the process of preserving the proteins that would nourish them through the winter. Meat formed the crucial lean-season food for the Neanderthal people during winters when plants were seasonally buried under deep snow. At Samhain, the beasts were slaughtered leaving only the creatures that would survive alive to live through the winter. Then the meats were salted and smoked to preserve the goodness[189]. This work

---

[189] Florence Marian McNeill The Silver Bough, Vol. 3. pp. 11–46

was about ensuring sustenance and survival. Today we still need to have intense nourishment of both our body and soul during the winter time, and that comes from the work we have done throughout the Wheel.

SAMHAIN AND THE SPIRAL OF GROWTH

The Wheel is not just a wheel. It is also a spiral. Just as growth is not a straight line, it is a consistent evolving spiral. Each Wheel is the circle part of the spiral, one cycle of the growth journey. Each rotation spirals into the next cycle, and the next and the next. Samhain is the point on the spiral which is the strongest point of transition in this journey of growth and life. It is that, in my opinion, which makes it the strongest and most powerful of the points of the year. In my mind, it is why, here and now, the veils are at their thinnest, as both this world and the spirit world transition once more.

Mathematicians and scientists both recognise the spiral of growth, the logarithmic spiral which often appears in nature. Jacob Bernoulli, a prominent mathematician in the mid -1600s, named it Spira Mirabilis. Bernoulli was fascinated by one of its unique mathematical properties: the size of the spiral increases but its shape is unaltered with each successive curve, a property known as self-similarity[190]. The Spira Mirabilis has evolved in nature, appearing in shells and sunflower heads.

The spiral of growth relates to the Fibonacci sequence. The Fibonacci sequence is a numerical pattern which can be used to describe the growth pattern in an amazing variety of phenomena, Seed heads, branches, pine cones, bananas, apples, animal reproduction and even the human body follow this sequence[191]. Scientists have pondered why this sequence is so often repeated in nature. One school of thought suggests that the ratio possibly exists because that particular growth pattern evolved as the most effective.

These mathematical patterns relate to a rhythm of growth, similar to the rhythm of the seasons. How each of us understands and relates to the spiral of growth is as unique as we ourselves are. Like the plants in nature, we all grow and bloom at own pace. As you deepen your journeying with the Wheel, through each one you will gain a deeper understanding of your own growth spiral. Your own rhythm of the seasons of your life.

As I always say, there is no wrong or right in nature, it just is. There is no right or wrong rhythm of life. From here on in, with nature as your guide, it is time to find out what your own rhythm is, to connect with your own spiral of growth. Find what is right for you as you continue your journey with the Wheel. It takes many Wheels to find this rhythm. By connecting you own personal development and manifestation process with the seasons, reflecting nature's journey in your life path, you begin to notice patterns, correlations. Maybe this is the emotional journey that links with the solar festivals of the solstices and the equinoxes,

---

190 Jacob Bernoulli, Lineae cycloidales, evolutae, ant-evolutae ... Spira mirabilis. pp. 138–139.
191 Can Akdeniz The Fibonacci Sequence Chp 9.

your energetical rhythm connecting with the Celtic fire festivals. It is through repeating these actions each Wheel and observing your journey that you will begin to feel your rhythm.

THE STORY OF YOUR WHEEL

A powerful way to connect with your personal rhythm and observe your spiral of growth is to find the story of your wheel. Traditionally, the Wheel of the Year's story is told by legends surrounding the pagan goddesses and gods. A story where both the goddess and god represent the archetypes of the stage of life. Child, young lover, mother / father, the wiseman, the crone and death. The story differs from culture to culture, with different legends, names and tales. Today you will often see the Wheel shown as an image reflecting the seasonal changes or traditional crafts.

As you have walked this Wheel, you have taken a walk, connected with the land's energy, made observations about your own growth journey and that of nature. You have a deeper understanding of the Celtic and Nordic beliefs surrounding the festivals that mark the turning of the seasons, and you have learnt tools and techniques to tune in and connect with each of these. You have also taken a journey each time within the lower, middle and upper worlds of your spirit world tree. In between each chapter you have worked with the energy of the seasons, with your own personal growth and goals. These elements are all parts of your story of this past Wheel.

At Samhain, it is a good point to look back and acknowledge the journey you have taken. By doing this each Wheel, you will get an understanding of your own growth rhythm as you begin to notice commonly occurring themes at the same point each Wheel. Similarly, you will begin to notice shifts and changes as your own life shifts and changes through the different stages of the earth walk journey. To remember this journey, it helps to record it so that you can continue to look back to enrich your understanding, live a conscious life and enjoy your journey.

As we saw at Yule, stories as a celebrative and learning tool have always been part of human culture since man first walked the Earth. Before the written word, we created images on the walls of caves and on stones to tell our story. So, you can use both of these creative ways to honour each Wheel's journey. I do this activity every Wheel. I find it helps me to keep walking with the Wheel and keep constantly developing as an individual as a conscious commitment.

Draw the Wheel divided into eight parts and write the names of the festivals by each section

Brainstorm what you remember from this Wheel's journey for each of the festivals. Include anything you remember including life events

Now look through your notes from this Wheel and add to your brainstorm anything you remember as significant for you. It could be your observations, your journeys, your realisations, the goals you have achieved, the craftings we made or memories from the workshops

From these notes, create your story for this wheel. Imagine yourself telling the story to someone

THE LAST HARVEST – SUSTENANCE FOR THE DARK TIMES

At Samhain, we celebrate the last of the three harvest festivals. Samhain was a time to take stock of the herds and food supplies. Cattle were brought down to the winter pastures after six months in the higher summer pastures in a procedure called transhumance which is still practiced today[192]. Samhain was also the traditional time of slaughtering livestock[193]. It is thought that some of the rituals associated with the slaughter have been transferred to other winter holidays with the rise of Christianity. For example, on St. Martin's Day (11 November) in Ireland, an animal—usually a rooster, goose or sheep—would be slaughtered and some of its blood sprinkled on the threshold of the house. It was offered to Saint Martin, who may have taken the place of a god or gods and it was then eaten as part of a feast. This custom was common in parts of Ireland until the 19th century[194].

Our ancestors of course needed ways of preserving food. Heavily smoked and salted foods were relied upon to carry people over the lean times of late winter and into spring. The hands-on work of Samhain was very much about survival in the dark to come. All food was made ready to sustain the people throughout the harsh journey through winter.

Since Imbolc, you have been working on your goals and manifesting your dreams. As the last step in your manifestation process of this Wheel at Samhain, we celebrate the very last of your harvests. Just as our ancestors selected which cattle would die and become the winter protein, so too will you make choices that will be your sustenance during the winter months.

Choose Your Sustenance

Look back at your vision board. One of your goals will be the one that you repeatedly turned to throughout the Wheel. It is the goal you have the most passion for, the one that brings the most joy and happiness into your life. It maybe that this goal is complete or incomplete. However, it is the one that resonates with you the most, and most importantly, the goal that gives you the most energy. As we turn to the winter, this work will be your sustenance. It will be this that keeps the hearth fire burning in your soul in the dark of winter.

In your notebook, make a note of which goal you will keep as your focus until Imbolc. Commit to at least three and no more than six actions you will take

---

192 Finola Finlay. Robert Harris. "Booleying" www.roaringwaterjournal.com
193 Kristin Olsen Shamrock Petals and Leprechaun Gold Lulu.com, 2011 pg 73
194 Irish Archaeology "Animal 'Sacrifice' and Blood Letting, Saint Martin's Feast in Ireland" wwwirisharchaeology.ie

throughout the winter to return to this source of energy. So for example, if one of your goals was to be more creative in your life, then maybe choose three creative projects to complete over the winter.

You could put a list of your actions somewhere you will see it often, to remind you to sustain your energy during the winter. If you liked working with your accountability partner, you could arrange to keep up with the contact to support you to give yourself an energy boost in the winter.

For the rest of your goals, it is time to slow down or to stop working on them entirely. Winter energy is all about hibernation. What we physically need at this time is to conserve our energy, and energy boosters to get us through the dark. Winter is a time to accept that we cannot complete everything all at once. Allow yourself to indulge in down time after Samhain. You both need and deserve it.

Take Pride in Your Work

In some countries, our ancestors placed their professional tools on the hearthstone. Sometimes this was a matter of family pride, since professions were handed down through generations. You have been working hard this Wheel and it is EXTREMELY important to be proud of yourself.

Just as at Mabon, I think it is relevant to be extremely proud of yourself at Samhain. After all, you have been working and growing throughout the whole Wheel. Choose the things you are most proud of and write in your notebook the sentence:

I am proud of myself for..................in this my (year date) journey.

Fill in the blanks with the things you are proudest of from your journey. If you like, you can put something to celebrate your achievements on your altar.

CELEBRATE YOUR ACHIEVEMENTS WITH OTHERS!

At Mabon, you chose a way you will celebrate your achievement alone. However, Samhain is another community festival. Often the last chance to see each other before the spring. Celebrating our achievements is so much more enjoyable with other people, and it is perfectly acceptable to make a fuss of your achievements, this has been a whole year's work!

Telling someone else what you have achieved and sharing that celebration with them makes it more real. Remember, life is full of the little moments and memories that are beautiful. Achieving and working on goals throughout a whole year is not one of the little moments. It's big. It's one of those big landmark moments that make life beautiful. So, find a friend and make a day or an evening celebration of your hard work and your accomplishments.

CONNECTING WITH THE SEASON

Once you have walked a full Wheel at Samhain it is so important to go out for your walk and take time to reflect upon your journey from the year's beginning, from Samhain to now. Take a walk out in the autumn daylight. Notice how the world around you has changed. Ask yourself:

- What last signs of autumn do you see?
- What signs of winter are around you?
- How has your life and the world around you changed in this last Wheel?
- Is nature displaying the same things as this time last year, or do you see something new?
- If you do see something new, how does this reflect with where you are now at the ending and beginning of the Wheel?

Take some time to connect with the earth, to balance and grow. If you find it a challenge to connect to the earth or still your mind, a Tree of Life meditation can help you to reconnect and find peace.

At Samhain, we reflect not only on the journey from the equinox, but the journey of the whole wheel. In doing this, we honour the journey of our growth by working with understanding the rhythm of our own growth. Being aware of this rhythm gives you the strength and the flexibility to survive and flourish with whatever life throws at you.

Crafting Your Wheel

A special and powerful way to honour and remember your journey is by creating a picture of it. You can do this by drawing, painting, or by collaging pictures from collected from magazines, or digitally if you prefer. You can also use words such as self-love for Beltane.

Hang your Wheel of the Year above your sacred space until Yule, and then store this and your story somewhere safe until next Samhain. When you have made a new story and picture, you can compare them and start to look for your rhythm. You may choose not to do this every year. Personally, I do this every five years, the time gap makes it easier for me to see the changes in my rhythm.

Journeying in the Future

Throughout this Wheel, we have journeyed through the World Tree. In the dark half of the year, we journeyed in the cave, but in the light half of the year we journeyed in our grove, and once at summer solstice we travelled in our highest plane. From here on, it is up to you how you journey and decide what is the purpose for your journeys. I like to use the following themes in my seasonal journeys but sometimes my totems have another idea about what we are going to do, so I let them lead me. They generally know best.

Samhain: In my cave I invite my ancestors.
Yule: In my cave I reconnect with my inner child.
Imbolc: In my grove I search for inspiration.
Ostara: From my grove I take a journey to visit my shadow self.
Beltane: In my grove I celebrate Beltane and allow my spirit guides to reveal whatever it is I need to know.
Litha: In my upper world I connect with the source of my power.
Mabon: From my grove I take a journey to visit my light self.

When journeying alone, it is important to remember the guidelines in the journeying and visualisation chapter, and don't forget to have chocolate on hand for grounding!

CEREMONIES THROUGH THE WHEELS TO COME

As with journeying, it is up to you how you make ceremony and decide what is the purpose for your ceremonies. The ceremonies included in each chapter are based on my experiences and preferences. However, you will come to find your own way. Some people like to do a big ritual, some prefer to meditate in nature to celebrate, others prefer to gather with friends and feast. It is up to you. You can return to the guidelines for creating your own ceremony to get you started. Try different things and have fun experimenting until you find what works for you.

There is a lot of inspiration for creating ceremony online and in books. I personally love the book Earth Wisdom by Glennie Kindred, which covers both traditions and inspiration for ceremony celebrating the Wheel of the Year.

Ceremony can also be family traditions. Remember, celebrating the turning of the Wheel can become as much of a family tradition as modern day Christmas, with less commercialism (wheel of the Year by Teresa Moorey and Jane Brideson is a great book if you have children and would like to include them in the celebrations). In my path we tend to not include people in the ceremonies until they are over 18 however each family has their own way, which is as it should be.

Enjoy celebrating Samhain it's the ending of your Wheel and the beginning of a new one.

> *The Samhain fires have burned to ash,*
> *The doorway closes to the past.*
> *In the east the rising sun,*
> *Heralds a new Wheel has begun.*

SAMHAIN – THE ENDING AND THE BEGINNING

It's time to rest the plough and rest our bones,
There are no more seeds to be sown.
It's time to still the mind and still the soul,
Hibernate from the winter's cold.

Through storms and snow we will survive,
Sharing the hearth with our tribe.
Through the darkness of the winter nights,
Dreaming of this Wheel's delights

The Wheel turns ….

CHAPTER 14

Walking the Wheel of the Year from Now on

It has been an honour and a pleasure to share this Wheel with you all. However, the Wheel turns and we must all journey on our own earth walk. Yet, this doesn't mean we will not meet again as this book is always on your shelf as a reminder for the Wheels to come. For me, one of the most important things about my journey in life and strengthening my connection with nature is celebrating the festivals with my community. Celebrating the different points of the Wheel with friends and family is a beautiful way of connecting with the Wheel and taking time as a community to celebrate our lives.

You are also welcome to join my online community, Walkers of the Wheel Tribe, to connect with people across the world. Here you will find a like-minded group of people who have the same respect for nature and understanding of its cycle as you. We all sometimes need to touch base with our tribe, and you are a very welcome part of this online circle. It is a great place to make new friends and forge strong connections

Of course, you can also come to Re:root Wheel of the Year workshops and gatherings in Denmark. In the Re:Root Walkers of the Wheel Tribe you will find information about these events. These are open events for families. It is my hope that, as our tribe grows, we will be able to hold them frequently throughout the coming Wheel's. You are also more than welcome to create your own non-profit Wheel of the Year gatherings and invite the tribe. If you contact me directly, I will share them in the group.

For me, walking with the Wheel is a powerful, humbling, inspiring and joyful experience. Each Wheel my roots of connection grow stronger and my life is in a natural flowing pattern.

I know from the last 22 years of my life that the more you work with the Wheel, the more connected, balanced and powerful you will become. Because, blood, skin and bone, you know this path and connection as surely as your body knows how to breathe. You have within you the potential to do, be or have anything you want. Connecting with the Wheel allows you to not only re:root within yourself, it also allows you to re:root your life and make the most of your journey

From here on in, you lead your journey. You take with you what you want to use and leave the rest behind for another time. Walking the Wheel enriches life the more we do it. However, the way in which you choose to do that is entirely up to you. As I have always said and will always say

"Nature is not cruel. Nature is not kind. Nature just is."

The right way for you is your way.

When you need it, nature is there to guide you. Whether in the roots of the trees, the crevices in the stone, the foam on the wave or the scent in the wind. You are a part of nature. Nature is your wisest teacher and you are nature's guardian. As she supports us, so we take care of her. So we can grow together dancing to the rhythm of life, the heartbeat of the Earth.....

Thank you for the gift of this journey together.

My love and blessings to you.

Recommended Reading

Here is a selection of my favourite books that you might find interesting to enrich your experience of walking with the Wheel of the Year.

SEASONAL SPIRITUALITY

Blake, Deborah; Connor Kerri; Marquis, Melanie; Neal, Carl. F; Pesznecker, Susan; Rajchel, Diana. *Series: Llewellyn's Sabbat Essentials* St Paul: Lewellyn Worldwide 2001

Forest, Danu, *The Magical Year Seasonal Celebrations to Honour Nature's Ever Turning Wheel*. London: Watkins Publishing 2016

Hoff, Benjamin; and Ernest H. Shepard. *The Tao of Pooh*. New York: Penguin Books 1983.

Kindred, Glennie *The Earth's Cycle of Celebration* G. Kindred 1994

Kindred, Glennie, Garner Lu *Creating Ceremony* G. Kindred 1994

Kindred, Glennie *Elements of Change* G. Kindred 1994

Kindred, Glennie *Earth Wisdom* London: Hay House 2005

McCoy, Edain. *The Sabbats a New Approach to Living the Old Ways* St Paul: Llewellyn Publications 1999

Moorey, T, Brideson, J. *Wheel of the Year Myth and Magic Through the Seasons* London: Hodder and Stoughton Educational 1997

Paxson, Diana L. Essential Asatru: *Walking the Path of Norse Paganism* New York: Citadel 2006

Redfield, James *The Celestine Prophecy* London: Bantam Books (Transworld Publishers a division of the Random House Group) 1994

PERSONAL DEVELOPMENT AND SELF HELP

Carnegie, Dale. *How toWwin Friends and influence People*. New York: Simon and Schuster. 1964

Rubin, Gretchen Craft. *The Happiness Project: Or, Why I Spent a Year Trying to Sing in the Morning, Clean My Closets, Fight Right, Read Aristotle, and Generally Have More Fun*. New York, N.Y.: Harper, 2011.

Holden, Robert, Ph.D.; Hay, Louise *Life Loves You 7 Spiritual Practices to Heal Your Life* London: Hay House Inc.; Reprint edition 2016

Elrod, Hal. *The Miracle Morning:The Not-so-obvious Secret Guaranteed to Transform Your Life Before 8AM* Place of publication not identified : Hal, Elrod International, Inc., 2014

Schwartz, David J. *The Magic of Thinking Big: Fireside Edition*. New York: Simon & Schuster, 1987

Siegel, R.D. *The Mindfulness Solution: Everyday Practices for Everyday Problems*. New York: The Guilford Press. 2010

HISTORICAL

Herbet, Kathleen *The Lost Gods of England* Ely: Anglo-Saxon Books 1994

Kondratiev, Alexi *A Celtic Ritual. An Authentic Guide to Celtic Spirituality* Scotland: Collins Press 1998

Lindow, John *Norse Mythology: A Guide to Gods, Heroes, Rituals, and Beliefs* Oxford, New York: Oxford University Press, 2001

Pollingto,n Stephen *The Elder Gods: The Otherworld of Early England* Ely: Anglo-Saxon Books, 2011

Stewart, R.J *Celtic Gods Celtic Goddesses* London: Cassell Illustrated 1990

Wallis, Faith (Trans.) *Bede: The Reckoning of Time*. Liverpool: Liverpool University Press 1999

Bibliography

Akdeniz, C. *The Fibonacci Sequence* Introbooks 2019

Armo, F. "La Charniere De Mai: Beltaine, Fete Celtique ou Fete Irlandaise?" Ollodagos: actes de la Société Belge d'Études Celtique: 28 (2013)

Atlantic Religion "The Days of Kronos and Saturn" www.atlanticreligion.com 24th August 2019 https://atlanticreligion.com/tag/kronia/

Bannatyne, G. *The Bannatyne Manuscript, Volume 2 of 4*, Glasgow: Printed for the Hunterian Club Edition, 1896

Berman, Marc G. Jonides John, Kaplan Stephen *The Cognitive Benefits of Interacting With Nature Sage Journals Psychological Science* Volume: 19 issue: 12, (2018)

Bernoulli, J. (1692). *Lineae cycloidales, evolutae, ant-evolutae ... Spira Mirabilis.* English translation in: F. N. David, Games, Gods, and Gambling (New York: Hafner, 1962)

Blackwoo,. W "The Quarterly Journal of Agriculture" ser.1 v.1. Edinburgh: William Blackwood 1863 (digitalised in 16 Dec 2008 by The University of Michigan)

Bladey C. *Folklore Accounts- III May Games* www.cbladey.com 23rd August 2019 http://cbladey.com/mayjack/mayobserve.html#III._MAY_GAMES

Blarmires, Steve. *The Little Book of the Great Enchantment.* Cheltenham: Skylight Press 2008

Bloomberg, N *Passover Haggadah Basics for Christians* Glenside: Chaim. 2015

Bonanno, A. *Malta an Archaeological Paradise* Valetta: M.J. Publications 2003

Bounford, Julie E. *The Curious History of Mazes: 4,000 Years of Fascinating Twists and Turns* New York: Welfleet Press 2018

Bradshaw Foundation *Stonehenge the Age of Megalithaas – When was Stonehenge Built?* www.bradshawfoundation.com 24th August 2019 http://www.bradshawfoundation.com/stonehenge/stonehenge.php

Briggs, K. *An Encyclopedia of Fairies.* New York: Pantheon Books. 1976

Byles, C.E. *The life and letters of R.S. Hawker (sometime Vicar of Morwenstowe)* London: John Lane 1905

Carmichael, A. *Carmina Gadelica Hymns and Incantations with Illustrative Notes On Words, Rites, and Customs, Dying and Obsolete: Orally Collected in the Highlands and Islands of Scotland and Translated into English by Alexander Carmichael.* Volume 1 London: Oliver and Boyd 1940

BIBLIOGRAPHY

Carter, R. *Ancient History Vol I Ancient Eygyptians* New York: R. Carter 1844

Chaney, W.A. *The Cult of Kingship in Anglo-Saxon England: The Transition from Paganism to Christianity 10970* Oxford: Oxford University Press 1970

Charles, L; Harper Jr.; John Templeton S*piritual Information: 100 Perspectives on Science and Religion* West Conshocken PA: Templeton Foundation Press, 2005

Chinese Sage *Ancestor Veneration in China* 23 Oct 2017 https://www.chinasage.info/index. www.chinasage.info/ancestors.htm

Cooper, J *The History of the Yule Log* www.whychristmas.com 28th January 2019
 https://www.whychristmas.com/customs/yulelog.shtml

Costa M. "Christmas Recipe: 17th century gingerbread biscuit" www.londonmumsmagazine.com December 23rd 2016 https://londonmumsmagazine.com/mums-tips/feeding-the-family/recipes-feeding-the-family/christmas-recipe-17th-century-gingerbread-biscuit/

Crippen, T. G. *Christmas and Christmas Lore* Detroit Gale Research Co. 1971

Cunningham, S. *Wicca: A Guide for the Solitary Practitioner* St Paul: Llewellyn Publications 1997

Czech Gallery *Czech Easter (Velikonoce)* http://www.czechgallery.com August 30th 2019 http://www.czechgallery.com/czecheaster/czech_easter.html

Daisy Carrington "Summer Solstice: Traditions Around the World" www.edition.cnn.com 24th August 2019 https://edition.cnn.com/travel/article/summer-solstice-world-traditions/index.html

Draco, M. *Pagan Portals – Have a Cool Yule: How-To Survive (and Enjoy) the Mid-Winter Festival* Alresford: Moon Books 2017

Dreher, D. *Women's Tao Wisdom: Ten Ways to Personal Power and Peace* London: Thorsons 1998

Dues, Greg *Catholic Customs and Tradition: Advent and Christmas* New London: Twenty-Third Publications, 2008

Dutton, D.R. *An Encapsulation of Óðinn: Religious belief and ritual practice among the Viking Age elite with particular focus upon the practice of ritual hanging 500 -1050 AD* PhD. Diss. University of Aberdeen 2015 file:///home/chronos/u-b71b59c49110e6181f7717b6c73a5a76e3b9c427/MyFiles/Downloads/An_Encapsulation_of_Odinn_Religious_Beli.pdf

Fairport Convention *John Barleycorn* Track 7, Tippler's Tale Kobalt Music Publishing Ltd.1978 Viny

Finola, Finlay; Robert Harris. *Booleying* www.roaringwaterjournal.com 26th August 2019 https://roaringwaterjournal.com/tag/booleying/

Foing, B. *If We Had No Moon Astrobiology Magazine* www.astrobio.net Oct 30th 2010 https://www.astrobio.net/retrospections/if-we-had-no-moon/

Forest, D. *The Magical Year Seasonal Celebrations to Honour Nature's Ever Turning Wheel* London: Watkins Publishing 2016

Franklin, A; Mason, P. *Lammas: Celebrating Fruits of the First Harvest* St Paul: Lewellyn Worldwide 2001

Frazer, J. G . *The Golden Bough*. (original 1922 Macmillan &Co. Pg 630) London: The Chancellor Press 1994

Freeman, M. *February the Festival of Imbolc* www.chalicecentre.net 20th August 2019 www.chalicecentre.net/february-celtic-year.html

Gailhabaud, Jules *L'Architecture Du 5me Au 17me Siècle Et Les Arts Qui En Dépendent: La Sculpture, La Peinture Murale, La Peinture Sans Verre, La Mosaïque, La Ferronnerie, Etc, Volume 4*. Ghent University Gide, 1659 (Digitalised 2 Sep 2009)

Galván, J. A. *They Do What? A Cultural Encyclopedia of Extraordinary and Exotic Customs from Around the World*. Oxford: ABC-CLIO. 2014

Gani, Aisha *Go Back to Halloween's Roots and Carve a Turnip, Charity Suggests* https://www.theguardian.com 23rd October 2018 https://www.theguardian.com/lifeandstyle/2015/oct/26/go-back-to-halloweens-roots-and-carve-a-turnip-charity-suggests

Goldbaum,*H.TELTOWN(TAILTEANN)Kells*,Co.Meathwwwvoicesfromthedawn.com 24th August 2019 https://voicesfromthedawn.com/teltown/

Graves, R. *The White Goddess; A Historical Grammar of Poetic Myth*. New York: Octagon Books 1978

Harvey Bloom, J. *Folk Lore, Old Customs and Superstitions in Shakespeare Land* Vancouver: Read Books Ltd 2017

Hawkins, GS. *Stonehenge Decoded* Great Britain. Souvenir Press (Published in Paper back by Fontana Books 1970) 1996

Herbet, K. *The Lost Gods of England* Ely: Anglo-Saxon Books 1994

Historie Online *Juletræets Historie* www.historie-online.dk December 1st 2017 http://www.historie-online.dk/temaer-9/arstidens-skikke-14–14–14/jul-32–32/juletraeets-historie

History.com Editors *Day of the Dead (Día de los Muertos)* A&E Television Networks 23 August 2019 https://www.history.com/topics/halloween/day-of-the-dead

Hone, W. *The Table Book or, Daily recreation and information concerning remarkable men, manners, times, seasons, solemnities, merry-makings, antiquities and novelties, forming a complete history of the year.1827* London: Hunt and Clarke 1827

Hull, A. G. EFC The Collected Works of CG Jung Complete Digital Edition Practice of Psychotherapy Vol 16 Princeton: Princeton University Press 1970

Hutton, R. *The Stations of the Sun: A History of the Ritual Year in Britain* Oxford: Oxford University Press 1996

IDEA *Other Ancient Calendars* www.webexhibits.org August 21st 2019 http://www.webexhibits.org/calendars/calendar-ancient.html

Ireland Fun Facts *Irish Christmas Facts – Traditions of the Celtic Holiday Season* www.ireland-fun-facts.com 28th August 2019 https://www.ireland-fun-facts.com/irish-christmas-facts.html

Irish Archaeology *Animal 'Sacrifice' and Blood Letting, Saint Martin's Feast in Ireland* wwwirisharchaeology.ie 26th August 2019 http://irisharchaeology.

ie/2016/11/animal-sacrifice-and-blood-letting-saint-martins-feast-in-ireland/

Jackson.J *Black Elk: The Life of an American Visionary* New York: Farrar, Straus and Giroux 2016

James, E. O. *The Influence of Folklore on the History of Religion.* Numen 9, no. 1 (1962): 1–16. doi:10.2307/3269410.

Johnson B. *Michaelmas* www.historic-uk.com 26th August 2019 https://www.historic-uk.com/CultureUK/Michaelmas/

Jolly. K.L. *Popular Religion in Late Saxon England: Elf Charms in Context* North Carolina: University of North Carolina Press, 1996

Joycors, S. *Lammas Day – Festival of the Wheat* The Yeoman Newsletter of the Barony of Bright Hills August 2018 Volume 32, Issue 8

Kaldera, R. *Seasonal Holidays and Blóts* http://www.northernpaganism.org 26th August 2019 http://www.northernpaganism.org/resources/prayers-rituals/seasonal-holidays-and-blóts.htm

Keating, G. *Foras feasa ar Eirinn ... The History of Ireland, tr. and annotated by J. O'Mahony.* Emeryille CA: Andesite Press 2017

Kennedy, P. *St Brigid and the Harps* www.libraryireland.com 20th August 2019 https://www.libraryireland.com/LegendaryFictionsIrishCelts/V-13–1.php

Kevin Knight *Christmas* www.newadvent.org 19th Febuary 2019 http://www.newadvent.org/cathen/03724b.htm

Kondratiev, Alexi A. *Celtic Ritual: An Authentic Guide to Celtic Spirituality* Scotland: Collins Press 1998

Kristoffer Hughes, *The Book of Celtic Magic: Transformative Teachings from the Cauldron of Awen* St Paul: Llewellyn Publications 2014.

Krup,p E. C. *Echoes of the Ancient Skies: The Astronomy of Lost Civilizations Dover Books on AStronomy* Massachusetts: Courier Coperations 2003

Kvilhaug Maria Labyrinths and Ritual in Scandinavia http://freya.theladyofthelabyrinth.com 28th Oct 2016 http://freya.theladyofthelabyrinth.com/?page_id=356

Lambert T. *A Brief History of Holidays* www.localhistories.org 24th AUgust 2019 http://www.localhistories.org/holidays.html

Lexico Dictionary s.v. *Sensuality* www.lexico.com 12th November 2018 https://www.lexico.com/en/definition/sensuality

Liao, M. *Summer solstice Marks Shorter Days and Yin's Rising* www.theepochtimes.com
September 20th 2018 https://www.theepochtimes.com/summer-solstice-marks-shorter-days-and-yins-rising_2554510.html

Lindow, J. *Handbook of Norse Mythology.* Santa Barbara CA: ABC-CLIO, 2001

MacGabhann, S. *Landmarks of the people: Meath and Cavan places prominent in Lughnasa Mythology and Folklore."*Riocht na Midhe, XI 2001

MacLeod S.P. *Celtic Cosmology and the Otherworld: Mythic Origins, Sovereignty and Liminality* North Carolina: McFarland & Company 2018

Madam Sif *Øllebrød – en lang historie* www.madamsif.dk/ 25th August http://madamsif.dk/2017/02/27/oellebroed-en-lang-historie/

Maghera Heritage Centre *Potatoes: Maghera Roots* www.maghera-heritage. org 24th August 2019 https://www.maghera-heritage.org.uk/2017/07/15/potatoes-maghera-roots/

Magnússon, Haukur *The Christmas Cat.* Grapevine. Fröken Ltd. Retrieved 12th December 2013.https://grapevine.is/icelandic-culture/art/2008/12/10/the-christmas-cat/

Manson, M. *7 Strange Questions That Help You Find Your Life Purpose* www.markmanson.net June 23rd 2019 https://markmanson.net/life-purpose

Markale, Jean. *The Pagan Mysteries of Halloween: Celebrating the Dark Half of the Year.* Vermont: Inner Traditions International 2000

Massingham, Hart R. *Making Gingerbread Houses: Storey Country Wisdom Bulletin* (A-154)

McCo,y Edain. *The Sabbats: A New Approach to Living the Old Ways* St Paul: Llewellyn Publications 1999

McNeill, F. Marian (1961, 1990) *The Silver Bough, Vol. 3.* Glasgow: William MacLellan,

McNeill, F. Marian *The Silver Bough, Vol. 3.* Glasgow: William MacLellan, 1968 pp.

Miles, C. A. *Christmas Customs and Traditions, Their History and Significance* New York: Dover Publications 2011

Miller, D. *The Seasons: Natural Rites and Traditions Man, Myth and Magic* New York Cavendish Square Publishing, LLC, 2014

Montague, Whitsel *Springs and Wells in Celtic Spirituality* www.store.isisbooks.com 20th August 2019 https://store.isisbooks.com/Springs_and_Wells_s/402.htm

Moorey, T, Brideson, J. *Wheel of the Year Myth and Magic Through the Seasons* London: Hodder and Stoughton Educational 1997

Morgan, M. *Simple Wicca* York Beach ME: Conari Press 2000

Morriso, Dorethy. *Yule: A Celebration of Light and Warmth (Holiday Series)* Woodbury: Lewellyn Publications 2000

Nationalmuseet *The Viking Blót Sacrifices* www.en.natmus.dk. 25th August 2019 https://en.natmus.dk/historical-knowledge/denmark/prehistoric-period-until-1050–ad/the-viking-age/religion-magic-death-and-rituals/the-viking-blot-sacrifices/

Navan & District Historical Society *Teltown* www.navanhistory.ie 24th August 2019 http://www.navanhistory.ie/index.php?page=teltown

Newal, V.l. *An Egg at Easter: A Folklore Study*, Bloomington: Indiana University Press, 1971

O'Halloran, S; Bel, M. *The Ould Lammas Fair* County Atrim : Clachan Publishing 2013 Pg 11

Olsen, K. *Shamrock Petals and Leprechaun Gold* Lulu.com, 2011

Parker, Robert. *On Greek Religion.* Ithaca, New York: Cornell University Press. 2011

BIBLIOGRAPHY

Paxson, D.L. *Taking Up the Runes: A Complete Guide To Using Runes In Spells, Rituals* ... San Francisco: Red Wheel/Weiser LLC. 2005

Perry, L.P. (Dr) *Mistletoe Myths and Medicines* www.uvm.edu 29th December 2018 http://www.uvm.edu/pss/ppp/articles/mistlmyths.html

Pine, R. *The Heart Sutra: The Womb of the Buddhas* USA: Shoemaker & Hoard 2004

Pittock, M. *Celtic Identity and the British Image* Manchester: Manchester University Press 1999

Pliny the Elder. *Natural History. Book XVI, Chapter 95.* (English Translation Karl von Tubeuf) : *"Monographie der Mistel" [Monograph of the Mistletoe,* Munich Berlin : Oldenbourg Verlag, 1923

Plumtree, J. *Stories of the Death of Kings: Retelling the Demise and Burial of William I, William II and Henry I"* Southern African Journal of Medieval and Renaissance Studies 21 2012

Pratchett, T. *Witches Abroad: (Discworld Novel 12)*, Manhattan: Random House 2010

Rabin, D. Forget C. *The Dictionary of Beer and Brewing* London. Fitzroy Dearborn Publishers 1998

Real Iran *Iranians Welcome Nowruz with Spring-Cleaning* www.realiran.org August 21st http://realiran.org/iranians-welcome-nowruz-spring-cleaning/

Ridgway, C. *The Tradition of Kissing Under the Mistletoe* www.tudorsociety.com Jan 11th 2018 https://www.tudorsociety.com/tradition-kissing-mistletoe/

Rimondini M (Editor) *Communication in Cognitive Behavioral Therapy* New York: Springer 2011

Rollason, D. *Northumbria, 500–1100: Creation and Destruction of a Kingdom* Cambridge: Cambridge University Press,2003

Rood J. *The Festival Year A Survey of the Annual Festival Cycle and Its Relation to the Heathen Lunisolar Calendar* Háskóli Íslands: University of Iceland 2013 Pg 25

Ross, S *What You Might Not Know About May Day* www.infoplease.com 23rd August 2019 https://www.infoplease.com/calendar-holidays/major-holidays/may-day

Roy, Christian. *Traditional festivals: a multicultural encyclopedia*.Santa Barbara, CA: ABC-CLIO. 2005

Russell, P. *Sanas Chormaic. In Celtic Culture. An Encyclopedia*, ed. J.T. Koch Oxford: ABC- CLIO 2006

Saffy Curiosities, *Grotesqueries, Follies & Strange Customs No 7 Customs Associated with Eggs and Eastertide* www.web.archive.org August 30th 2019 https://web.archive.org/web/20080304191655/http://www.petticoated.com/curious28.htm

Scott, B. *But Do You Recall? 25 Days of Christmas Carols and the Stories Behind Them* Anderson: Brian Scott 2015

Secunda, Floria Zonara.*Saturnalia Practices of Nova Romans* www.novaroma.org January 16th 2019 http://www.novaroma.org/religio_romana/saturnalia.htm

Sermon R. *Wassail! The Origins of a Drinking Toast* 3rd Stone (46)

Shetland News *Doctors can now prescribe 'nature' as a therapy* www.shetnews.co.uk 23 August 2019 https://www.shetnews.co.uk/2018/10/05/doctors-can-now-prescribe-nature-as-a-therapy/

Shirley TwoFeathers *The Charming of the Plough* www.shirleytwofeathers.com August 18th 2019 https://shirleytwofeathers.com/The_Blog/pagancalendar/the-charming-of-the-plough/

Shoemaker, A.L; Yoder D. *Christmas in Pennsylvania 50th Anniversary Edition* Mechanicsburg: StackPoole Books 2009

Siegel, R.D. *The Mindfulness Solution: Everyday Practices for Everyday Problems.* New York: The Guilford Press. 2010

Slade, P. *Seasonal Magic Diary of a Village Witch* Somerset: Capall Bann Publishing Ltd 2001

Smith, A. *The History of Mulled Wine* www.vivino.com 23 December 2016 https://www.vivino.com/wine-news/the-history-of-mulled-wine

Snorri, Sturluson *Saga of Olaf Herladson*, Heimskringla Part II – translated by Lembek K. Stavnem, R. Snoris Edda På dansk Latvia: Gyldendal 2012

Soldiser *Yule Celebrations in Ancient Scandinavia* www.soldiser.com Dec 21st 2018. https://soldiser.com/blogs/news/yule-celebrations-in-ancient-scandinavia#_ftnhttps://soldiser.com/blogs/news/yule-celebrations-in-ancient-scandinavia#_ftnref1ref1

Šprajc, I; Sánchez, N; Pedro, F. *El Sol en Chichén Itzá y Dzibilchaltún: la supuesta importancia de los equinoccios en Mesoamérica.* Arqueología Mexicana. XXV (149)

Stewart, RJ. *Celtic Gods Celtic Goddesses* London: Cassell Illustrated 1990

Stone, Áine. *Wheel of the Year* https://thecelticjourney.wordpress.com 16th May 2019 https://thecelticjourney.wordpress.com/the-celts/wheel-of-the-year/

Stow, J. *The Annales, or a Generall Chronicle of England...*, London, 1615, SCT 01578.

Taylor, C. *Treasures for the Christmas Tree: 101 Festive Ornaments to Make & Enjoy* New York: Stirling Publishing Company

TED X Talks *How to stop screwing yourself over | Mel Robbins | TEDxSF* Jun 12, 2011 https://www.youtube.com/watch?v=Lp7E973zozc&t=17s 21:39

The Guardian *New year resolution? Don't wait until New Year's Eve* www.theguardian.com 14th January 2019 https://www.theguardian.com/science/2007/dec/28/sciencenews.research

Thistleton-Dyer, T.F. B*ritish Popular Customs, Present and Past;* London, G. Bell and sons 1876

Thorley, Anthony' Gunn, Celia. M *Sacred Sites: An Overview* 2007, 2008, The Gaia Foundation

Tracey R Rich *Sukkot* www.jewfaq.org 26th August 2019 http://www.jewfaq.org/holiday5.htm

Travel China Guide *A Full List – 21 Customs of Chinese New Year* www.travelchinaguide.com August 21st 2019 https://www.travelchinaguide.com/essential/holidays/new-year/customs.htm

Ven. K. Sri Dhammananda Maha Thera *The Moon and Religious Observances* www.budsas.org March 28th 2019 https://www.budsas.org/ebud/whatbudbeliev/217.htm

Ven. Thich Nguyen, Tang *Buddhist View on Death and Rebirth* www.urbandarhma.org 19th Febuary 2019 https://www.urbandharma.org/udharma5/viewdeath.html

Videnskab.dk *Historien om gækkebrevet: Startede som små valentinskort* www.videnskab.dk August 29th 2019 https://videnskab.dk/kultur-samfund/historien-om-gaekkebrevet-startede-som-smaa-valentinskort

Visit Sweden *Midsommer i Sverige* www.visitsweden.dk 23rd August 2019 https://visitsweden.dk/midsommer-i-sverige/

Wagashikoechin *O-Higan – Equinox* www.wagashirezepte.de 25th August 2019 https://wagashirezepte.de/en/o-higan-equinox/

Wallis, F. (Trans.) *Bede: The Reckoning of Time*. Liverpool: Liverpool University Press 1999

Walsh, J.J. *Were They Wise Men Or Kings?: The Book of Christmas Questions* Louisville: Westminster John Nox Press 2001

Wasai LLC *Chinese New Year Taboos Top 10 Things To Avoid During The Spring Festival* www.chinesenewyear.net August 22nd 2019 https://chinesenewyear.net/taboos/

Weber, C. *Brigid: History, Mystery, and Magick of the Celtic Goddess* San Francisco: Red Wheel/Weiser LLC. 2015

West, M.L. *Indo-European Poetry and Myth* New York: Oxford University Press Inc 2007

Wishart, D.J. *Sun Dance* www.plainshumanities.unl.edu August 24th 2019 http://plainshumanities.unl.edu/encyclopedia/doc/egp.rel.046

Wyrd Designs *The Holy Tides: Charming of the Plough / Disting / Solmonaþ* www.wyrddesigns.wordpress.com August 15th 2019 https://wyrddesigns.wordpress.com/2019/02/03/the-holy-tides-charming-of-the-plough-disting-solmonath/

Zell-Ravenheart, O. *Creating Circles & Ceremonies: Rituals for all Seasons & Reasons*. Franklin Lakes, NJ: New Page Books. 2006.

Zettler, R.L; Horne, L. Hansen D.P; Pittman, H. *Treasures from the Royal Tombs of Ur* Philadelphia: University of Pennsylvania Museum 1998

(Various Authors) *History of Witchcraft Internet Book of Shadows* www.sacred-texts.com 24th August 2019 https://www.sacred-texts.com/bos/bos188.htm